"This book is essential to design math learning spaces where all children are seen, heard, and thrive. Detailed classroom vignettes showcase six structures for rich mathematical discussions that center diverse mathematical ideas, active listening, and collective contributions. Children's mathematical brilliance is affirmed, shared and grown—isn't that what we all want? Thank you for bringing us this gift."

Julia M. Aguirre, *Professor, Faculty Director of Teacher Certification Programs, University of Washington, Co-author of* Cultivating Mathematical Hearts

"What a gift! *Intentional Talk and Listening* offers both a vision and practical guidance on how to plan for and facilitate rich mathematics discussions that treat children with the academic and social care and respect they deserve. Alongside the many educators and children featured in the book, Elham Kazemi and Allison Hintz make what can feel 'out of reach' possible!"

Kara Jackson, *Professor of Mathematics Education, University of Washington, Co-author of* Systems for Instructional Improvement

"This book is a must read for any educator wanting to further their understanding of the power of classroom mathematical conversations. The descriptions of the different targeted discussion structures, all grounded in vivid classroom examples, emphasize the importance of valuing students' ideas, and provide specific resources to implement them. As a reader, one can feel the authors' deep respect for all the teachers and children portrayed in this book."

Marta Civil, *Professor and Roy F. Graesser Chair, The University of Arizona, Co-author of* Access and Equity

"Building and maintaining equitable and humanizing mathematics classrooms where every voice matters and where everyone is heard requires ongoing intentional work. In this important and well-written book, Elham Kazemi and Allison Hintz provide compelling examples and practical strategies to help teachers and students become powerful speakers and listeners."

Danny Bernard Martin, *University of Illinois Chicago, Co-author of* The Impact of Identity on K-8 Mathematics

"Kazemi and Hintz recognize that students' willingness to share their thinking is a gift to teachers, classmates, and themselves. Based in this deep insight, their book presents vignettes in which teachers elicit students' mathematical ideas and orchestrate discussions that bring the class into significant mathematics content. Templates, structures, and commentary on the vignettes provide guidance on how to plan and lead such discussions. This is an important resource for all educators who aim to develop elementary students into mathematical reasoners."

Deborah Schifter, *Consultant, Teacher Educator, Co-author of* Interweaving Equitable Participation and Deep Mathematics

"Elham Kazemi and Allison Hintz's *Intentional Talk and Listening* help mathematics classroom discussions come alive for readers! Through excerpts from classrooms, we get windows into how conversations about mathematics can be culturally responsive to students' lives, and we learn more about how to support students to listen intently to one another. The ideas in this book are actionable and powerful, which make the book a 'must read' for all mathematics teachers."

Amanda Jansen, *Professor, University of Delaware,*
Author of Rough Draft Math

"'What if we thought about children's willingness to share their ideas and experiences with their peers and teachers as gifts?' In this powerful second edition, Elham Kazemi and Allison Hintz illuminate how listening to children's thinking is not only a source of deep learning, but also a profound source of joy. With new vignettes and fresh insights that honor students' voices and the rich knowledge they carry from their lives and communities, this book offers practical guidance for leading purposeful, inclusive math discussions that foster understanding, connection, and delight in mathematical thinking."

Cathery Yeh, *Associate Professor of Curriculum and Instruction, Core Faculty in the Center for Asian American Studies, The University of Texas at Austin,*
Co-author of Reimagining the Mathematics Classroom

"Kazemi and Hintz's book supports teachers to honor children as sense-makers and to elicit and build on students' mathematical ideas. The authors provide extensive, detailed classroom examples that illustrate how teachers can craft targeted classroom discussions that provide openings for each student to participate. This book is an important resource for teachers who, alone or with peers, want to reflect on, plan, and implement discussions in which students are serious and joyful as they delve into rigorous mathematics."

Susan Jo Russell, *Consultant, Teacher Educator, Co-author of*
Interweaving Equitable Participation and Deep Mathematics

"Productive and collaborative discussions are an essential component of math learning communities that foster the development of positive math identities and a strong sense of agency for each and every student. Such discussions invite all students to express their ideas, to revise and build on them, to have others respectfully listen to and engage with their ideas, and to be seen as mathematical thinkers who make meaningful contributions to classroom conversations. *Intentional Talk and Listening* presents images of what dynamic math discussions look and sound like, and it offers structures and pathways that support the facilitation of such discussions. In this edition, Kazemi and Hintz affirm, expand, and deepen our understanding of what it means to place children's mathematical thinking at the center of the work so that students and teachers can learn with and from one another."

Karen Economopoulos, *Director, Investigations Center for Curriculum and Professional Development, TERC,*
Co-author of Investigations in Number, Data, and Space

INTENTIONAL TALK AND LISTENING

Second Edition

INTENTIONAL TALK AND LISTENING

HOW TO STRUCTURE AND LEAD PRODUCTIVE MATHEMATICAL DISCUSSIONS

ELHAM KAZEMI & ALLISON HINTZ

Foreword by Megan Franke

NEW YORK AND LONDON

A Stenhouse Book

Designed cover image: © Elham Kazemi

Second edition published 2026
by Routledge
605 Third Avenue, New York, NY 10158

and by Routledge
4 Park Square, Milton Park, Abingdon, Oxon, OX14 4RN

Routledge is an imprint of the Taylor & Francis Group, an informa business

© 2026 Elham Kazemi and Allison Hintz

The right of Elham Kazemi and Allison Hintz to be identified as authors of this work has been asserted in accordance with sections 77 and 78 of the Copyright, Designs and Patents Act 1988.

All rights reserved. Except for the pages in the appendix, which may be photocopied for classroom use, no part of this publication may be reprinted or reproduced or utilised in any form or by any electronic, mechanical, or other means, now known or hereafter invented, including photocopy and recording, or in any information storage and retrieval system, without permission in writing from the publisher.

Trademark notice: Product or corporate names may be trademarks or registered trademarks and are used only for identification and explanation without intent to infringe.

First edition published by Stenhouse Publishers 2014

Credit: Chapter 2, *'Ohana Means Family* book cover and interior spread. Text copyright © 2020 by Ilima Loomis. Illustrations copyright © 2020 by Kenard Pak. Image used by permission of Holiday House Publishing, Inc. All Rights Reserved.

Library of Congress Cataloging-in-Publication Data
Names: Kazemi, Elham, 1970- author | Hintz, Allison, 1962- author
Title: Intentional talk and listening : how to structure and lead productive mathematical discussions / Elham Kazemi and Allison Hintz.
Description: Second edition. | New York, NY : Routledge, 2026. | First edition published by Stenhouse Publishers 2014. | Includes bibliographical references and index.
Identifiers: LCCN 2025019357 (print) | LCCN 2025019358 (ebook) |
ISBN 9781625316448 paperback | ISBN 9781032681344 ebook
Subjects: LCSH: Forums (Discussion and debate) | Mathematics--Study and teaching (Elementary) | Problem solving--Study and teaching (Elementary)
Classification: LCC QA20.F67 K39 2026 (print) | LCC QA20.F67 (ebook) |
DDC 372.7--dc23/eng/20250421
LC record available at https://lccn.loc.gov/2025019357
LC ebook record available at https://lccn.loc.gov/2025019358

ISBN: 978-1-625-31644-8 (pbk)
ISBN: 978-1-032-68134-4 (ebk)

DOI: 10.4324/9781032681344

Typeset in Minion Pro
by KnowledgeWorks Global Ltd.

For Grace, Neeku, Roshann, and William

Second Edition

INTENTIONAL TALK AND LISTENING

HOW TO STRUCTURE AND LEAD PRODUCTIVE MATHEMATICAL DISCUSSIONS

ELHAM KAZEMI & ALLISON HINTZ
Foreword by Megan Franke

Routledge
Taylor & Francis Group
NEW YORK AND LONDON

A Stenhouse Book

Designed cover image: © Elham Kazemi

Second edition published 2026
by Routledge
605 Third Avenue, New York, NY 10158

and by Routledge
4 Park Square, Milton Park, Abingdon, Oxon, OX14 4RN

Routledge is an imprint of the Taylor & Francis Group, an informa business

© 2026 Elham Kazemi and Allison Hintz

The right of Elham Kazemi and Allison Hintz to be identified as authors of this work has been asserted in accordance with sections 77 and 78 of the Copyright, Designs and Patents Act 1988.

All rights reserved. Except for the pages in the appendix, which may be photocopied for classroom use, no part of this publication may be reprinted or reproduced or utilised in any form or by any electronic, mechanical, or other means, now known or hereafter invented, including photocopy and recording, or in any information storage and retrieval system, without permission in writing from the publisher.

Trademark notice: Product or corporate names may be trademarks or registered trademarks and are used only for identification and explanation without intent to infringe.

First edition published by Stenhouse Publishers 2014

Credit: Chapter 2, *'Ohana Means Family* book cover and interior spread. Text copyright © 2020 by Ilima Loomis. Illustrations copyright © 2020 by Kenard Pak. Image used by permission of Holiday House Publishing, Inc. All Rights Reserved.

Library of Congress Cataloging-in-Publication Data
Names: Kazemi, Elham, 1970- author | Hintz, Allison, 1962- author
Title: Intentional talk and listening : how to structure and lead productive mathematical discussions / Elham Kazemi and Allison Hintz.
Description: Second edition. | New York, NY : Routledge, 2026. | First edition published by Stenhouse Publishers 2014. | Includes bibliographical references and index.
Identifiers: LCCN 2025019357 (print) | LCCN 2025019358 (ebook) |
ISBN 9781625316448 paperback | ISBN 9781032681344 ebook
Subjects: LCSH: Forums (Discussion and debate) | Mathematics--Study and teaching (Elementary) | Problem solving--Study and teaching (Elementary)
Classification: LCC QA20.F67 K39 2026 (print) | LCC QA20.F67 (ebook) |
DDC 372.7--dc23/eng/20250421
LC record available at https://lccn.loc.gov/2025019357
LC ebook record available at https://lccn.loc.gov/2025019358

ISBN: 978-1-625-31644-8 (pbk)
ISBN: 978-1-032-68134-4 (ebk)

DOI: 10.4324/9781032681344

Typeset in Minion Pro
by KnowledgeWorks Global Ltd.

CONTENTS

Foreword by Megan Franke — xi
Acknowledgments — xiii

CHAPTER 1 INTRODUCTION — 1

CHAPTER 2 OPEN STRATEGY SHARING — 23

CHAPTER 3 TARGETED DISCUSSION: COMPARE AND CONNECT — 59

CHAPTER 4 TARGETED DISCUSSION: WHY? LET'S JUSTIFY — 81

CHAPTER 5 TARGETED DISCUSSION: WHAT'S STRATEGIC AND WHY? — 111

CHAPTER 6 TARGETED DISCUSSION: DEFINE AND CLARIFY — 133

CHAPTER 7 TARGETED DISCUSSION: TROUBLESHOOT AND REVISE — 161

CHAPTER 8 CONCLUSION: REFLECTING AND LEARNING — 179

Appendices A–H — 193
References — 211
Index — 215

FOREWORD

By Megan Franke

In this new edition of *Intentional Talk and Listening*, Elham Kazemi and Allison Hintz explore the relationship between talking and listening, highlighting how collective engagement in classroom conversations can enable students to learn mathematics and see themselves as valued members of the mathematics community. They take you inside of classrooms to detail how valuing the brilliance of students in listening and talking can support participation for each of our students in mathematical conversations.

Everything we know about student learning and classroom practice tells us that classroom conversations are crucial to mathematics learning. We know that students who explain the details of their mathematical ideas, engage with the details of others' mathematical ideas, and have others engage with their own mathematical ideas achieve mathematically. We also know that engaging in mathematical conversations in productive ways can help students see themselves as smart and competent in mathematics. We have seen that students who take part in mathematical conversations also learn to listen to others, ask insightful and respectful questions, and reflect on their own understandings. For these reasons and more, we must make the most of and continually improve our classroom mathematics discussions.

We know that orchestrating classroom discussions can be challenging. Elham and Allison build on existing classroom discussion work as well as the teachings of those inside and outside of education to help us consider the collective, varied forms of participation, listening and learning together in ways that leverage the strengths in our diversity. We hear from both Vivian Paley and Robin Wall Kimmerer. They draw on the teachings of these authors to reimagine and detail what it looks and feels like to navigate the moment-to-moment interactions within mathematics classroom discussions. They tease out the different types of mathematical conversations that can occur. They share ways to design and carry out strategy sharing conversations as well as a range of more targeted talk. The principles and tools provided for each kind of discussion will guide you toward meeting your mathematical goals as well as the needs of each and every one of your students.

Whether you are a teacher new to mathematics conversations or have been enjoying them with your students for a long time, *Intentional Talk and Listening* will offer you ways of thinking about and enacting conversations. Elham and Allison provide vignettes, a set of principles to guide your decision making, and a collection of tools to help you navigate this complex work. This combination will help you develop your vision of what is possible, know how to improve what you are doing now, and continue to learn and improve your practice. You will want to read it more than once; you will want to mark pages, copy the tools, and revisit the student and teacher interactions often. This book is a partner in your ongoing design and support of student participation in mathematics conversations.

Intentional Talk and Listening will help you create a classroom where all of your students are engaged in mathematical discussions in ways that help them learn and see themselves as mathematicians.

ACKNOWLEDGMENTS

The first edition of *Intentional Talk* was in the making for more than ten years, and we owe many thanks to Toby Gordon, our amazing editor at Stenhouse, for sparking the idea of a book on classroom discussions and for helping it come to fruition. Her encouragement and guidance helped us see this work to the finish line. Our first edition was helped by the ideas of two anonymous reviewers, who took great care in giving us feedback to strengthen our drafts. For this second edition, *Intentional Talk and Listening*, Kassia Omohundro Wedekind and Tracy Zager helped us get the ideas off the ground. As our editor, Kassia gave us thoughtful feedback, attending to detail and helping us make important decisions about what to include, with a keen eye for the joy of young mathematicians.

We give special thanks to the staff and students at three elementary schools that inspired many of the vignettes in the book. First, teachers, coaches, and students at Lakeridge and Sartori Elementary Schools in Renton, Washington, fill these pages with their brilliant ideas. It has been a life-changing experience working with you. Thank you for opening your classrooms and being willing to take risks, try new ideas, and teach us so much about cultivating rich classroom communities that nurture children's minds as well as their humanity. Second, Mahlo nui loa to the teachers, students, instructional leaders, and families at Kamaliʻi Elementary School in Kihei on the Hawaiian Island of Maui. Your community has embraced our learning together with open hearts. We are inspired by each of you and the ways you taught us about place-based mathematical joy and sensemaking. A special thank you to Kacie Seitz who gives so generously from her heart and spirit to bring joy to mathematics.

We are grateful to the photographers who helped us capture the beautiful images of teachers and students used throughout the book: Matt Hagen, Becky and Ken Trask; and to Lynsey Gibbons and Kendra Lomax for helping us organize images for the first edition.

We have learned so much from the scholarship and practice of many others in the field of mathematics and teacher education. It is difficult to convey how much we are indebted to the team of scholars and teachers that have contributed to the development of Cognitively Guided Instruction (CGI): researchers Tom Carpenter, Elizabeth Fennema, Megan Franke, Linda Levi, Susan Empson, Randy Philipp, and Vicki Jacobs; and the CGI teachers from Madison, Wisconsin, especially Annie Keith and Mazie Jenkins. We believe that children's mathematical thinking is at the heart of inspired teaching. Megan Franke, thank you for everything. We stand in awe of you. The principles that have guided our work derive from our collaboration with Megan and other members of the *Learning in, from, and for Teaching Practice* (LTP) group: Magdalene Lampert, Hala Ghousseini, Heather Beasley, Kate Crowe, Adrian Cunard, and Angela Turrou. We are grateful for the way the LTP group challenged us to bring to life the important work teachers do when leading mathematical discussions.

The ideas about listening integrated into this second edition would not be possible without the dedicated and detailed research of Drs. Andrea English and Kersti Tyson. Andrea, a philosopher, and Kersti, a learning scientist, are cherished research partners and inspiring scholar mothers. For over a decade, we have studied teacher and student listening with school community partners in Scotland, New Mexico, and Washington state. Andrea and Kersti, thank you for your humanity and deep care for children to be heard, understood, and treasured as joyful mathematicians.

Our knowledge about teaching and discourse have been greatly informed by the inspirational work of many other scholars and their teaching and research teams: Deborah Ball, Virginia Bastable, Jo Boaler, Courtney Cazden, Suzanne Chapin, Paul Cobb, Maarten Dolk, Cathy Fosnot, Karen Fuson, Kim Hufferd-Ackles, Cathy Humphries, Magdalene Lampert, Kay McClain, Sarah Michaels, Catherine O'Connor, Mike Rose, Susan Jo Russell, Deborah Schifter, Peg Smith, Mary Kay Stein, Terry Wood, and Erna Yackel.

This second edition benefited from a growing body of examples of ambitious, culturally responsive and inclusive teaching in mathematics including the work of Julia Aguirre and Maria Zavala, Kathryn Chval, Marta Civil, Bobbie and Jodie Hunter, Danny Martin, Karen Mayfield-Ingram, the EQSTEM project, Kara Jackson, Rachel Lambert, and Cathery Yeh.

We have benefited from collaboration with our colleagues in the Mathematics Education Project (MEP) and Mathematics Education Research Group (MERG) at the University of Washington and the Expanding the Community of Mathematics Learners (ECML) project, where we, Allison and Elham, met. So many of our ideas about designing professional learning experiences and working with teachers have emerged from the energetic and thoughtful ideas of our colleagues: Julia Aguirre, Ruth Balf, Filiberto Barajas-López, Sunshine Campbell, Adrian Cunard, Christopher Fraley, Lisa Jilk, Megan Kelley-Petersen, Anita Lenges, Becca Lewis, Katie Lewis, Teresa Lind, Kendra Lomax, Laura Mah, Leslie Nielsen, Katy Pence, Ryan Reilly, Rosemary Sheffield, Gini Stimpson, and Bryan Street. These are just a few of the hundreds of teachers and teacher educators who have dedicated themselves to improving their practice, digging deeply into content together, and transforming the mathematical learning experiences of children.

Our families have been a source of love, strength, patience, and laughter. Abolghassem and Nahid, thank you for your many sacrifices, love, and wisdom. Mark, Roshann, and Neeku, you are always and forever a source of joy and light and adventure. Becky and Ken, or "Mimi and Papa," thank you for your ever-present loving support that has grown with us throughout the years. Shawn, Grace, and William, *I love us*!

CHAPTER 1

INTRODUCTION

Leading mathematical discussions can be both invigorating and challenging. Over many decades of being mathematics teachers and learners, we have found so much joy in listening to children's thinking, observing and taking in what it feels like to be in mathematics classrooms where their teacher regularly asks, "Tell me how you figured that out." We begin this second edition of *Intentional Talk and Listening* by connecting to ideas from a book about the interweaving of Western science and Indigenous knowledge systems. Robin Wall Kimmerer writes in *Braiding Sweetgrass*, "Gifts from the earth or from each other establish a particular relationship, an obligation of sorts to give, to receive, and to reciprocate" (2013, 25). What if we thought about children's willingness to share their ideas and experiences with their peers and teachers as gifts? Kimmerer invites us to be "open-eyed and present" when receiving gifts (2013, 24). If children are willing to freely share their ideas with us, then we enter into a particular kind of ongoing relationship with them, and one that we would hope is worthy of the gifts they give us. Children would expect us to attend to their ideas, to appreciate them, to help them listen and take in each other's ideas. The ongoing relationship created among learners in a classroom would reflect respect and curiosity. We would need to be judicious in our use of instructional materials and our engagement with learning standards to continually reciprocate children's ideas and experiences, to follow their lead, to encourage them to keep asking questions, to keep seeking.

Kimmerer writes that "all flourishing is mutual" (2013, 15). In this second edition, we hope to expand our conversations about mathematics by appreciating the reciprocities that are necessary for mutual flourishing in the classroom, particularly the reciprocity between talking and listening and between bringing ourselves to mathematics and vice versa.

We know leading discussions that support mathematicians to flourish requires intentional planning and facilitating. There's lots to worry about in doing good work as a teacher in facilitating discussions that focus on students' sense making and their sense of belonging in and to mathematics. We've also come to learn that not all mathematical discussions have the same purpose or should be led in the same way. In this book, we describe how considering your goals for math talk and listening can help you better design discussions to meet those goals and teach children to participate meaningfully.

Our work with classroom discussions is guided by four principles:

1. Teachers must communicate through their interactions that all children are sense makers and that their lived experiences and ideas are valued.
2. Discussions can have different mathematical and social goals, and different types of purposes require planning and leading discussions differently.
3. Students need to be supported in knowing how to share and listen to ideas.
4. Teachers need to orient students to one another and the mathematical ideas so that every member of the class is involved in achieving the mathematical and social goals.

These principles are at the heart of creating classrooms where children can participate equitably. Sarah Michaels, Mary Catherine O'Connor, and Megan

Williams Hall write about classroom communities that live by these principles as engaging in "accountable talk," or "talk that seriously responds to and further develops what others in the group have said" (2010, 1). We build on this work to consider how careful listening and contemplation is necessary for building strong learning communities. The challenge, of course, lies in putting these principles into action, which is what we hope to help you do.

In this second edition, we build on the focus of classroom talk featured in the first edition to layer in an explicit focus on classroom listening and further explore how talking and listening are related to each other. In the years since we wrote the first edition, in collaboration with Kersti Tyson and Andrea English, Allison has learned a lot more about listening as a form of active classroom participation and the reciprocity between teacher listening and student listening. Throughout this second edition, we will discover how discussions will be stronger and more equitable as students learn how, and are supported, to engage in sense making as talkers and listeners.

In order to support both sides of discussion—talking *and* listening—we pay close attention to how the teachers in the classroom vignettes in this book support students to listen to each other and themselves, what to listen for, and how to work with what they have heard. We put forth the idea that listening is not just about being quiet, it is an active form of participation as children make sense of classmates' and their own evolving thinking.

In this second edition, we also expand our focus on talk to carefully consider what we talk about in classroom discussions. Thanks to ongoing work in mathematics education, we have learned a lot about how to engage in mathematical practices such as modeling and argumentation that help children explore what it means to do mathematical work and how to use mathematics to make sense of their world, to be stewards of their communities, and take action toward more just futures. We have many more resources in mathematics education about what culturally responsive and equitable instruction looks like and how to build on children's mathematics, community, and cultural funds of knowledge. Our commitment to support student sense making and nurture positive mathematical identities has opened up collaborations with teachers to plan and facilitate discussions that draw on and build upon the rich cultural and linguistic resources that students bring to the classroom and through which they learn about each other.

The classroom vignettes in this book reflect insights we have gained into leading mathematical discussions while working closely with teachers who are committed to respecting and engaging with children's ideas. These vignettes take place in racially, culturally, and linguistically diverse classrooms. We hope the everyday brilliance of the teachers and children in these pages will help us all strive toward creating classrooms that disrupt longstanding assumptions about who can and cannot excel in mathematics (Aguirre, Mayfield-Ingram, and Martin 2024; Lambert 2024; Zavala and Aguirre 2024). Responding to Rochelle

Gutiérrez's view that mathematics teachers help shape students' developing identities Maria Zavala and Julia Aguirre (2014) explain that,

> *This means that whether we know it or not, we shape how children experience mathematics, feel about mathematics, and see themselves as mathematics learners and doers. Holding oneself accountable is a way to move toward disrupting our broken system. It requires teachers to understand their role as identity workers and to be genuine learners with children and families about mathematics, student thinking, culture, language, and other aspects of responsive pedagogy.* (14–15)

We'll now say a bit more about what we mean by each principle for classroom discussions, give you a glimpse into the ways particular mathematical goals can help you run a discussion, and then outline what lies ahead in the rest of this book.

Principle 1: Teachers Must Communicate Through Their Interactions That All Students Are Sense Makers and That Their Thinking and Experiences Are Valued

In a strong classroom community, each child has to feel like they are contributing meaningfully. Children's ideas and experiences have to matter to both the teacher and to each other. This doesn't mean that everyone has to participate in the same way. But at a minimum we want everyone to be able to say, "I feel alive in this space because I know my teachers know me, and they got me." Creating communities where children process their experience together means that children feel okay about taking risks and putting their ideas out there. For some children, taking these leaps and feeling the trust in the room takes time. Discussions open up the possibilities that students will share their partial and incorrect understandings. How we respond to errors and partially developed ideas sends important messages about taking risks. It is not easy for students to express their ideas if there is a high burden to be correct and understand everything the first time around.

We need to remember that there's always logic behind why students think the way they do. When we listen to what a child understands and what they are coming to understand, we listen beyond right answers. We also need to publicly recognize students' ideas, making sure we don't single out just a few students as mathematically "smart." There are many ways to be smart in mathematics, and often children's lived experiences help shape their many smartnesses, which include making connections across ideas, representing problems, working with models, figuring out faulty solutions, finding patterns, making conjectures, persisting with challenging problems, working through errors, and searching for strategic solutions (Featherstone et al. 2011). Being smart in mathematics is not just about speed and accuracy. Vivian Paley writes that being curious about children's ideas signals to them that they are respected: "What are these ideas that I have that are *so* interesting to the teacher? I must be somebody with good ideas" (1986, 127). We want all students in the class to regard themselves as mathematical thinkers and to see themselves as people who bring important knowledge and understandings to our discussions and who grow their ideas as a result of working with others.

Principle 2: Discussions Can Have Different Mathematical and Social Goals, and Different Types of Purposes Require Planning and Leading Discussions Differently

Your purposes, both mathematical and social, act as your compass as you navigate classroom discussions. Your intentions help you decide what to listen for, which ideas to pursue, and which ideas to highlight, and how to build a community of listeners and speakers who are learning together. In *5 Practices for Orchestrating Productive Mathematics Discussions* (2011), Margaret Smith and Mary Kay Stein describe the importance of teachers clearly identifying the intended purpose of a discussion as they plan it out. The mathematical ideas at the heart of a lesson will help you distinguish between different types of classroom discussions you can have with your students. Sometimes your aim is to have students share as many different ideas as possible in the discussion so they see a range of possibilities. We call this *Open Strategy Sharing*, because we're working on building students' repertoire of strategies. The class generates lots of ideas, and the discussion likely moves across a number of mathematical practices as well as mathematical concepts, procedures, representations, and explanations (see Figure 1.1). Students listen for and contribute different ways to solve the same problem. Within all

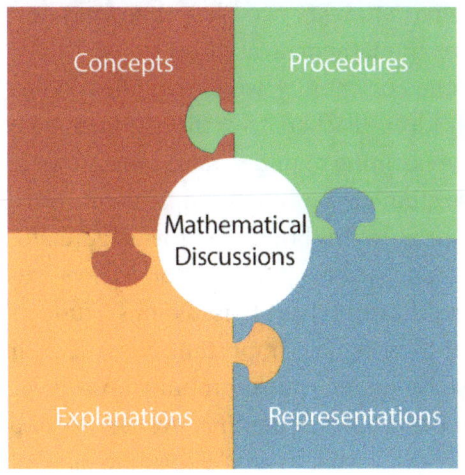

Figure 1.1 The terrain in mathematical discussions

mathematical discussions, you're always attending to how your classroom community is developing.

At other times you might want to focus the discussion on a particular idea. We call this "targeted discussion." Through targeted sharing the discussion zooms in on a particular idea. This more focused sharing involves specific goals, like defining and using key terms or concepts correctly, revising an incorrect strategy, or making sense of a particular representation. Students listen and contribute their thoughts in order to make sense of new ideas. The table below lists the targeted discussion structures that will be the focus of Chapters 3 through 7.

Targeted Discussion Structure	Goal
Compare and Connect	To compare similarities and differences among strategies
Why? Let's Justify	To generate justifications for why a particular mathematical strategy works
What's Strategic and Why?	To explore and evaluate strategic solutions in particular situations
Define and Clarify	To define and discuss appropriate ways to use mathematical models, tools, vocabulary, or notation
Troubleshoot and Revise	To reason through which strategy produces a correct solution or figure out where a strategy went awry

Principle 3: Students Need To Be Supported In Knowing What and How To Share and Listen To Ideas

To make classroom discussions come alive, students need help knowing how to participate as speakers and as listeners. In mathematical discussions, we also work on social goals that benefit how the community works together. When students have the chance to express their ideas, teachers have more information about what students *do* understand and are coming to understand, what they are grappling with, and where they might be stumbling or confused. Students learn through classroom discussions *what* to share. In this book, we provide guidance for how to structure each type of discussion. We also pay attention to how students learn to contribute meaningfully in different types of discussions. Students learn what to share as we prompt them to articulate important parts of their explanations and affirm that their everyday, family, and community knowledge bases are welcome and helpful to mathematical understanding. We can use and offer sentence starters that cue students to know what to say: "Explain to us what you meant by ___," "What would you do if the number was ___?" and "How is your way the same and different from ___?" "Where do you see this idea at home or in our community?"

Listening is an active form of sense making that requires explicit support. When we ask children to listen, we are not asking them to be quiet, we are asking students to make mathematical sense of what they are hearing. We can help students learn what to listen for so they can understand others and their own thinking and contribute to the conversation: "Listen for how she broke apart the numbers," "Think about whether you are understanding how she used the number line to show her thinking and what questions you might have," "How does ___'s example from her life help us think about this problem?"

Similarly, students learn *how* to share through our explicit support. Reinforcing norms supports students in knowing how to share. For example, you might need to reinforce where to place oneself ("Stand here so we can see your work"); how loudly to speak ("Speak loudly so everyone can hear your idea"); and what tools to use ("Use the drawing in your journal to help"). We want to help children be successful in meaningful mathematical learning at the same time as we tap into and draw on the resources they bring to the classroom (Aguirre, Mayfield-Ingram, and Martin 2024). We help students learn how to listen by modeling listening ourselves ("I hear you saying"), how to consider and build on what they heard ("What do you hear ___ telling us?" "What does ___'s thinking make you wonder?"), and how to listen to themselves ("Are you considering revising your thinking?"). The way a teacher listens has a direct influence on how children listen. Or, as our colleague Kersti Tyson says, "Children listen the way they are heard." As teachers, we shape the listening culture in our learning communities. Listening as mathematical sense makers is complex and inspiring work for students and teachers.

Principle 4: Teachers Need to Orient Students to One Another and the Mathematical Ideas

One of the challenges of leading discussions is bringing the whole class into the discussion. Most classrooms have several students who are eager to share and will always raise their hands and volunteer their thoughts. If we always call on these students, it's easy for others to remain passive or become anxious about how to enter the discussion. But that's not the only problem; if students have their hands raised just to get in their two cents, you'll end up with a bunch of ideas that don't build on each other or go anywhere. Teachers have to use strategies that help students learn *how* to listen to and consider each other's ideas and the mathematics. We call this orienting students to one another and the mathematics. Teachers can draw attention to the meaningful contributions that all students make and can encourage students to take risks by "assigning competence," or identifying and naming students' specific contributions (Featherstone et al. 2011). The vignettes in this book will demonstrate many different ways that teachers advance the mathematical agenda of a discussion by strategically highlighting a student's insight or contribution, especially when a student might not be feeling confident about their standing with the rest of the class.

So how do these principles come together in teacher-led discussions? These principles come to life alongside our decisions about how to invite students to experience mathematics as a subject worth studying. As we revised this book for the second edition, we drew on scholars and teachers who have creatively designed tasks so students can connect with and expand how they see themselves in the world of mathematics. We frequently say that reading opens up worlds for students, and we want the same to be true of mathematics. Let's consider two examples, *Open Strategy Sharing* and two types of targeted discussions, to see these principles in action.

Open Strategy Sharing: The Case of Mental Math

You might already have some experience leading discussions that fall into our *Open Strategy Sharing* category. Discussing mental math strategies is a good example of *Open Strategy Sharing*. It is a routine practice in elementary mathematics classrooms and is designed to build children's ability to flexibly, efficiently, and accurately learn arithmetic strategies. As a routine, it also allows students to engage in structural thinking, to use the properties of operations and the structure of numbers to make decisions about how to break apart numbers. The teacher starts by posing a computational problem, such as $5 + 2$, $12 - 7$, 21×4, or $96 \div 6$, and invites children to share the different ways they figured out the answer.

In our example, Ms. Lind picks a multiplication problem for her fourth graders to solve as a warm-up to her main lesson. She decides on 25×18 because she thinks students might leverage the idea that four groups of 25 make 100. Because 18 is close to 20, she imagines that some students might try to round and adjust the final answer. There are many good listening and discussion opportunities that can emerge. She's expecting to have the students spend about ten minutes sharing a few different ways of solving the problem. After writing 25×18 on the board, she steps to the side and provides time for her students to solve this problem mentally. As she sees that children have arrived at their solutions, she whispers to them to write their strategies in their math journals (she hopes this will help students remember the steps of their strategies). Jotting

Chapter 1 Introduction

down their thinking also allows students to document their own ideas so that when they listen to their peers, they can make sense of classmates' ideas while also holding on to their own ideas.

The jottings also allow Ms. Lind to notice the ways that students have approached the problem. When it looks like everyone has at least one solution, she asks the students to call out together what they got for the product. She records their ideas on the board to help make sure she doesn't put any one child on the spot to be correct or incorrect and to give herself the chance to see if there are multiple ideas in the room. She hears two different answers, 498 and 450. Students in this classroom are used to hearing a couple different answers. They trust that by hearing and examining their strategies, they will be able to determine if one of them is correct. With all the ideas out, she begins by calling on a child who she could see has used a strategy that's fairly common in the class. Ms. Lind also knows that asking Faduma to use her notebook will help her feel more comfortable sharing.

Ms. Lind: Okay, Faduma, tell us about what you wrote as you figured out this solution. I want everyone else to think about whether you are understanding what Faduma did and if you used a similar or different strategy.

Ms. Lind's opening words help students know what to share and invite listeners into the discussion. She tries to help them know what to listen for by asking them to listen for two things: what questions they might have for Faduma to be able to understand what she did and to think about how their own strategy might be similar or different from hers.

Faduma: Since I can multiply numbers by 10, I broke up the 18 to a 10 and an 8. I multiplied 25 times 10 and 25 times 8. I got 250 plus 200, which is 450.

Ms. Lind: Thank you.

As Ms. Lind records Faduma's solution on the board, she notices that many students signal that they used the same strategy with the sign for "me too," inspired by the sign from American Sign Language. Children make the sign with one hand near their chest (or even close to their head), folding over their three middle fingers and rocking their hand back and forth (Parrish 2010; see Figure 1.2). Children are making it visible that they listened to and understood Faduma's strategy and think their strategy is similar.

Figure 1.2 Students show the sign for "me too"

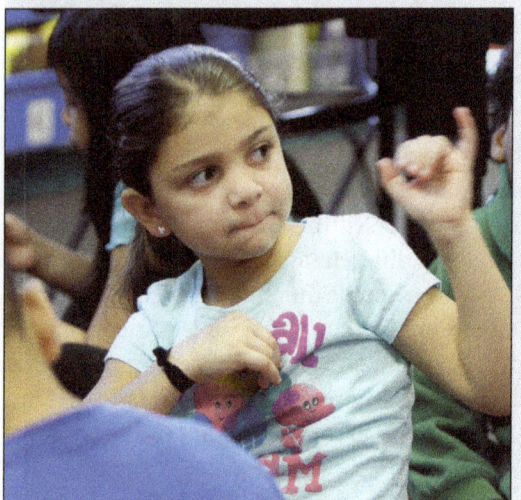 

Ms. Lind: I've written on the board what I heard Faduma say. And many of you are showing me that you did the same thing. Who can add on to help us explain why we would split the 18 the way Faduma did?

This question reinforces Ms. Lind's cue for listeners to see if they understand Faduma's ideas, which she gave at the beginning of the discussion. The question now invites listeners to think within Faduma's strategy to consider why she split the number 18 into a 10 and an 8. Listeners can draw on Ms. Lind's recording as well as their memory of Faduma's verbal description of her strategy to begin to explain why the number 18 was partitioned as it was.

Jordan: Well, it's like Faduma said, multiplying by 10 can be easier to do. So since one way of thinking about 25 times 18 is that you have 25 18 times, you can first do 25 10 times and then you have 8 more 25s.

Students signal agreement with Jordan. And Ms. Lind adds some words to what she has recorded to help make this explanation visible in the class display (see Figure 1.3).

Figure 1.3 Faduma's strategy

$25 \times 18 = 450$ (this means 25 18 times)

$25 \times 10 = 250$ (this means 25 10 times)
$25 \times 8 = 200$ (this means 25 8 times)

Ms. Lind: Does anyone have any questions for Faduma?

Chapter 1 Introduction

Marcus: I do. I did it a different way and I got a different answer. Eighteen is close to 20 so I did 20 times 25 to get 500, but then I subtracted 2 to get to 498. I don't get why our answers are different.

Ms. Lind records Marcus's strategy on the board (Figure 1.4) to display for others what he is saying. She already begins to wonder whether she should pursue his question now or wait for another discussion.

Figure 1.4 Marcus's strategy and question

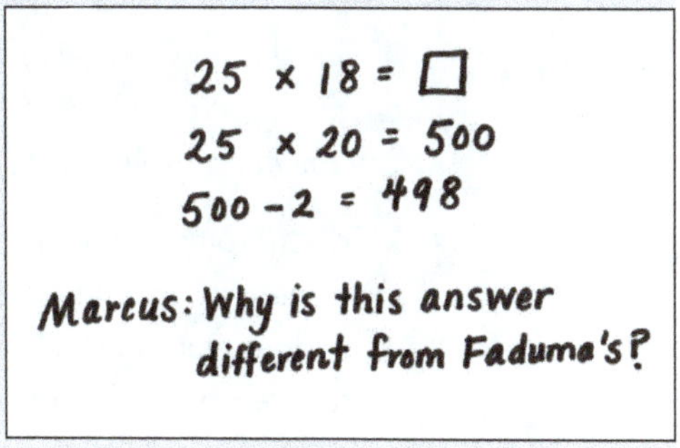

$$25 \times 18 = \square$$
$$25 \times 20 = 500$$
$$500 - 2 = 498$$

Marcus: Why is this answer different from Faduma's?

Ms. Lind: So you're really trying to make sense of Faduma's strategy through your own way. I'm writing your question up here, but before we take up your question, let's see if we can put one more strategy up here and maybe that will help us think about what is going on here.

Ms. Lind makes this move given her goal of eliciting a range of ways to solve the problem. She also knows that Marcus's strategy, trying to round up and compensate for the difference, is not yet widespread in the class and may need some special attention. We can see Marcus trying to make sense of his own strategy in relation to Faduma, which is a regular challenge of listening within Open Strategy Sharing.

Celia: *(Raises her hand to add to the discussion.)* I used what I know about quarters. Four quarters make one dollar. So 16 makes 400 and then 2 more makes 450.

Ms. Lind: *(Orienting the class to Celia.)* Celia, you gave us a lot to think about. What do you think Celia means when she says that quarters helped her solve the problem? And if you're not sure, you can ask her to repeat what she said.

Ms. Lind invites other students to be responsible for making sense of Celia's idea. She reinforces the idea that it's okay to ask Celia to share her idea again. This is an important norm in the class because listening well doesn't mean that you immediately understand a sharer the first time they speak. Encouraging repetition helps listeners process a new idea inserted into the discussion and gets several students to explain that Celia is thinking about the problem as eighteen quarters, because quarters are worth twenty-five cents. Since four quarters make one dollar,

Celia is thinking about four groups of twenty-five at a time. Ms. Lind puts Celia in the role of confirming or clarifying what her classmates say until they understand what Celia did. Ms. Lind writes Celia's strategy on the board (Figure 1.5).

Figure 1.5 Celia's strategy

25×18 is like 18 quarters
Every 4 quarters is $1.00
So every 4   25s is 100
$4 \times 25 = 100$
18 can be broken up into $4+4+4+4+2$
$100 + 100 + 100 + 100 + 50 = 450$

Ms. Lind: *(Prompting students to think about the strategies shared so far.)* We seem to have three different strategies and two different answers. Could you turn and talk to your elbow partner about which strategies convince you and what questions you have?

This partner talk allows students to process what they have heard and gives Ms. Lind the chance to monitor the pairs and potentially select a few ideas to close out the discussion for the day.

Ms. Lind: I'm noticing as I listen to you that you are thinking about how your classmates broke up the numbers to multiply. Some of you are looking hard at Marcus's strategy and thinking that he changed the numbers. Marcus, can we come back to your strategy tomorrow and spend some focused time on it? We can help you think through it more and see whether or not there's something we need to revise.

Ms. Lind ends this warm-up listening to the students' ideas and questions and tells them that in the next few days they will address the questions that arose today. She's out of time to help the class think more about what went awry in Marcus's strategy, so she assures them she will return to his strategy in the next few days. This one problem, 25×18, generated many different ideas (which was Ms. Lind's goal for the discussion) and, as this short excerpt demonstrates, took the class into a broad mathematical terrain of interrelated concepts, procedures, representations, explanations, and mathematical practices. The nature of this problem, and its many strategies, provides students opportunities to listen to interesting thinking, too. In order to create a listening culture in mathematics classrooms, we need to pose problems and tasks that are interesting to listen to. Using the structure of Open Strategy Sharing allowed the class to express and draw upon their ideas but not to linger extensively on any one idea. To spend more time on individual ideas, Ms. Lind needs to plan for targeted discussion.

Targeted Sharing: Two Follow-Ups to Mental Math

The *Open Strategy Sharing* allows Ms. Lind to size up what ideas she needs to work on further with her students and to plan for a targeted discussion. She makes these decisions in the context of her unit and grade-level goals. For example, her students might benefit from dissecting a compensation strategy (i.e., rounding one of the numbers and adjusting the product, as Marcus attempted to do) or developing their skilled use of arrays to produce a representation about why Faduma or Celia's strategies worked. Ms. Lind wants her students to ground their use and justification of numerical strategies in both array and grouping models. She also wants them to learn to contextualize their strategies in story problems. Modeling mathematical quantities, analyzing structure, and developing arguments are several ideas emphasized in the Common Core State Standards for Mathematical Practice (2012). She recognizes that she cannot meet all of her goals in one discussion, and her students could benefit from a focused discussion on using models and creating story problems. These observations lead Ms. Lind to plan for targeted discussions, which bring to the foreground particular ideas and practices.

To illustrate a bit more deeply what we mean by targeted discussion, we offer two brief examples. Ms. Lind could use the targeted discussion structures *Why? Let's Justify* and *Troubleshoot and Revise* to highlight important mathematics that emerged from the *Open Strategy Sharing* discussion. You'll be able to read more about *Why? Let's Justify* and *Troubleshoot and Revise* in Chapters 4 and 7.

Example 1: Why? Let's Justify

Connecting numerical strategies to a visual model is one way of making sense of why a strategy works; the model serves as a resource for children to verify their attempts at breaking apart a problem into smaller chunks. The goal of the *Why? Let's Justify* discussion structure is to figure out why a particular mathematical strategy works. Let's drop in on Ms. Lind's class as she leads a discussion to go further with the class in explaining the steps Faduma took.

> **Ms. Lind:** Yesterday as we were listening to people solve 25 × 18, I realized it has been a while since we worked with arrays. I thought an array would be useful to explain what is happening when we break apart numbers to make a problem easier and how to make sure we've accounted for 18 groups of 25.

Ms. Lind puts an array on the board with Faduma's solution beneath it (see Figure 1.6) and asks students to draw, mark up, and label the array in their journals so that it matches this numerical strategy.

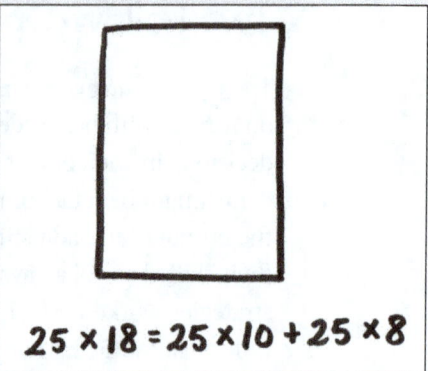

Figure 1.6 Ms. Lind draws an open array to show Faduma's strategy

By walking around the room as students are working with the array in their journals, Ms. Lind can make purposeful choices about which students she will invite to share. She lingers over the shoulder of Celeste, who is dividing up the 18 into tens and ones, and thinks this idea will provide good fodder for agreement and possibly disagreement about how the array can match Faduma's solution. She is interested in inviting Celeste to share not only for her interesting ideas but also because Celeste tends to be quieter during discussions, and Ms. Lind is working to help her see herself as someone with good ideas. She kneels down next to Celeste and asks her if she'd be willing to share her drawing of the array with her classmates. Celeste nods, and Ms. Lind calls the group back together.

Ms. Lind: Celeste has an idea about the array to offer us. Please look up to the screen at this drawing of the array for 25 times 18. I want you to see if you can make sense of how she divided up the array.

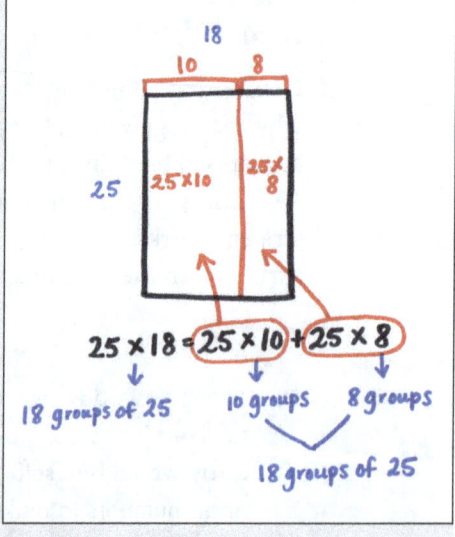

Figure 1.7 The annotated array of Faduma's strategy looks like this by the end of the discussion

Celeste shares her drawing, explaining how she thought about breaking up the 18 into 10 and 8. As students engage in whole-group and partner sharing about the array, the discussion evolves, with students adding on to prior contributions until a full annotation of the array is shared and it corresponds to the numerical recording of Faduma's strategy (see Figure 1.7).

Chapter 1 Introduction

> Ms. Lind's goal is to get to a place where students can see that Faduma's approach began with figuring out 10 groups of 25 and then adding on 8 more groups of 25 to end up with 18 groups of 25 altogether. This targeted sharing asks the class to focus on one solution and explicitly map the connections between the symbolic and visual representation. In Chapter 4 we dig more deeply into how the teacher navigates these discussions to support student sharing and orient students to one another and the mathematics.

Example 2: Troubleshoot and Revise

It can be quite powerful for a classroom community when students share ideas that aren't quite right yet and seek the help of their classmates. A student seeking peer feedback is valued as having a good kernel of an idea that needs to be developed, and their classmates can be motivated to work through the situation. Ms. Lind could use the *Troubleshoot and Revise* discussion structure to help Marcus and his classmates make sense of where Marcus's strategy went astray and how to revise it to make it work. This lesson could take place the same or next day. After asking Marcus if he felt comfortable conferring with his classmates to find an answer to his question, Marcus willingly recapped his strategy aloud. We can't emphasize enough how important it is for students to think through the logic of their approach. Students get wrong answers all the time. After all, they are learning mathematics, so their development is not reflected in the final answer they get but in the decisions they make along the way. We have to make it okay to share ideas as they unfold in order to benefit from each other's ideas. Ms. Lind purposefully takes up this opportunity to support Marcus in thinking through his strategy and also to support all students in knowing troubleshooting and revising thinking is a common practice in this classroom community.

Marcus: I did 20 times 25 to get 500 and then I subtracted 2 to get 498. I kind of think it should work because 20 is just 2 more than 18. But I'm not sure why I'm not getting the same answer as Faduma. I think I should be.

> Ms. Lind could ask students to use an array model to help students Troubleshoot and Revise Marcus's strategy, and if this discussion actually followed on the heels of the first vignette in this chapter, it would be

appropriate for Ms. Lind to use the same model. However, to provide an example of how contextualizing the numbers and operation in a situation that's familiar to the students can also be helpful with the revision process, we are going to ground this next vignette in a problem context that Marcus knows a lot about.

Ms. Lind: Marcus had a great way of beginning this problem. By changing the 18 to 20, he started by making the problem easier for himself. It might help us to put these numbers into a story. When I was thinking about the numbers I gave you, I wondered if any of the collections we had shared with the class would make sense with these numbers. I realized they fit perfectly with something that Marcus shared with us—his baseball card collection. Remember when Marcus shared his collection with us?

Garvey: He has an album and he protects his cards in sleeves so they don't bend and so he can see them. That's what I do too with football cards.

Sadie: He sometimes organizes them by players' positions, like all the pitchers together. Or sometimes by team.

Ms. Lind: Yes! Marcus, remind us more about your collection.

Marcus: Okay, yeah. My brother and I are huge baseball fans. We have been collecting baseball cards for a couple years because our dad used to collect them and he gave us his cards and so we decided to add on to his collection.

Ms. Lind values Marcus's idea that he needed to make an adjustment when he rounded one of the factors to 20. Often students are not completely wrong, and we can highlight their good thinking. She is also intentionally selecting a problem context in order to help Marcus and the class think through the changes to the numbers. Problem contexts are not something to shy away from; contextualizing and decontextualizing the numbers are essential in the process of reasoning mathematically. She was also thrilled that she could build on a context that mattered to Marcus. Taking a strength-based or asset-based view of mathematics teaching and learning includes opening up space for children to bring their lived experiences, and their funds of knowledge to the classroom.

Ms. Lind: It's pretty special to be able to take care of your dad's collection. Remind us of some of your favorite players.

Marcus: Julio Rodríguez, Shohei Ohtani, Fernando Tatís Jr., Mike Trout, so many …

Chapter 1 Introduction

Ms. Lind: I was thinking of one of the albums you brought into class for us to see, which was so cool. And I looked back at the photos I took and I realized that your album really fits with our math problem. So, let's imagine your baseball cards inside one of your albums. What if the album has 25 pages and if you open up a page, there's 9 cards on one side and 9 on the other. So there's 18 cards altogether. Everyone with me? Can you picture that? Let me show this picture of his album to remind you. What would the 25 × 18 mean if we are thinking of Marcus's album? *(Ms. Lind shows an image of Marcus's baseball card collection in an album; see Figure 1.8.)*

Figure 1.8 Marcus's baseball card collection

Marcus: Oh yeah, that's so cool. So 25 times 18 is like having 25 pages of cards. The 18 comes from the 9 cards on one side and the 9 cards on the other side of the page.

Ms. Lind: Yes, when we open up the album and see 9 on one side and 9 on the other, we can call those facing pages because they face each other. So, there would be 25 facing pages.

Andre: Oh, I see. When Marcus changed the numbers to 25 × 20, it made it like there were 25 pages with 20 cards altogether. But, you can't put 20 cards on the pages, only 18 fit!

Ms. Lind: Yeah, it's like he put 2 extra cards in the last sleeve or something like that. Let's draw the 25 facing pages with 20 cards on them so we can look at it together.

Drawing the album pages can help the class keep in mind what happened as Marcus's numbers changed from 18 to 20. A public record of what is being talked about that grows as students contribute can help with listening and processing what is being discussed. Students can see the ideas being discussed and make sense of them through the drawing and discussion.

Ms. Lind: So, what needs to be removed from each set of facing pages to go back to having 18 cards instead of 20?

She uses partner talk to engage all the students in considering how to take 2 cards away from the pages and how to change the drawing to make it match 25 × 18 (see Figure 1.9). Ms. Lind circulates among the

Figure 1.9 These notes on the board supported Marcus in revising his strategy

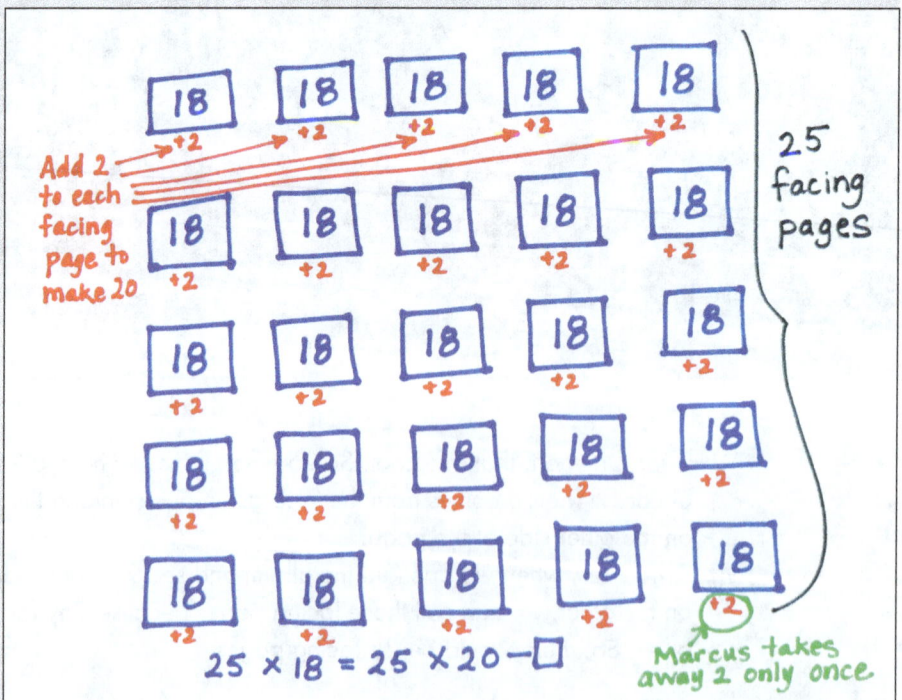

students as partners discuss this problem to select who should alter the drawing on the board. The drawing can be annotated to show that 50 cards altogether need to be removed from the product. This will clarify what happened when Marcus subtracted 2 from only 1 of the pages instead of removing 2 from all 25 facing pages.

Ms. Lind ends the discussion by asking the class to revise Marcus's strategy.

Ms. Lind: Okay, we have worked together to figure out why Marcus's answer was different. Who can say again why his answer was different?

Together the class concludes that when Marcus changed the problem to 25 × 20, he needed to subtract 25 groups of 2 to make sure each facing page only had 18 cards. Marcus was excited that his strategy could work if he thought through what to subtract and why through the example of his baseball card collection.

Ms. Lind: *(Summarizes the group's thinking as she writes on the board 25 × 18 = 25 × 20 − 50.)* So it looks like we agree that the equation that shows Marcus's strategy should read 25 times 18 is the same as 25 times 20 minus 50. That 50 is the extra 25 groups of 2.

She hands out an exit card posing a new problem: "How would 15 × 20 need to be adjusted in order to solve 15 × 19?" As a formative assessment strategy, the exit cards help her see how this discussion helped students think about using a compensation strategy. Students fill out these exit cards at the close of a lesson. Ms. Lind will review them in order to assess what students are learning and what they might still be grappling with. What she learns from the exit cards will help her plan for subsequent lessons. You can read more about Troubleshoot and Revise in Chapter 7.

Looking Ahead

We believe that the way teachers and students talk and listen with one another in the classroom is critical to what students learn about mathematics and how they come to see themselves as mathematical thinkers. In our classrooms students should feel that they belong and that they can be successful. Sharing and listening are an important part of how we build a sense of community and help children grapple with mathematical ideas. Group discussions can energize children if we are careful about how we teach children to listen to, respond to, and engage with one another's ideas. The time we invest in helping our students learn to participate productively in discussions can result in a huge payoff.

We hope the short vignettes in this chapter begin to help you see our principles at work and the differences between *Open Strategy Sharing* and targeted discussions. In *Open Strategy Sharing*, Ms. Lind and her students came up with several ways of thinking about 25 × 18. Targeted discussion helped Ms. Lind zoom in on a few key ideas that came up in the *Open Strategy Sharing*. In the rest of this book, we dig more deeply into these structures.

Chapter 2 describes *Open Strategy Sharing* in more depth. We discuss situations in which teachers might choose *Open Strategy Sharing* and how teachers can lead the discussion to help students listen and contribute to the discussion without getting bored or lost. In Chapter 2, we invite you to take stock of the mathematical discussions you are currently planning and facilitating, and think more broadly about the ways students may be, and could be, participating. We also provide guidance for working explicitly on sharing and listening and ways to build community by drawing on children and families funds of knowledge (González, Moll and Amanti 2005). We begin our discussion of targeted discussions in Chapter 3 with, *Compare and Connect*, a structure that naturally extends *Open Strategy Sharing*. The important difference between *Open Strategy Sharing* and *Compare and Connect* is that in *Compare and Connect* the teacher asks students to find the mathematical similarities and/or differences among strategies.

We want students to develop a repertoire of strategies, but we also want them to be able to explain why those strategies work. Chapter 4 takes us back to the *Why? Let's Justify* structure. The goal is to generate justifications for why a mathematical strategy makes sense. This type of discussion typically focuses on just one kind of strategy or procedure. The students are all oriented toward producing a viable explanation. This chapter will help you understand the difference between describing the steps in a strategy and justifying them.

While it is possible to solve some problems in many different ways, students also need opportunities to become more selective and strategic about when to use a particular strategy. Chapter 5 takes on this issue by describing a structure we call *What's Strategic and Why?* In this discussion structure, the teacher begins not by eliciting ways to solve a particular problem but by (1) showcasing a particular way of approaching a problem and then asking students to generate a strategic use of it or (2) showing a few different ways to solve a problem and asking students to figure out which is the most strategic strategy for this problem and why.

Teachers often introduce new mathematical models (e.g., number line or array), tools (a tens frame, the hundreds chart), vocabulary, or notations into mathematical discussions. Models, tools, vocabulary, and notations are all considered mathematical objects. Chapter 6 will highlight how those objects could be the focus of a discussion we call *Define and Clarify*. We consider when such discussions could occur (e.g., when models, tools, terms, and notations are first being introduced or when students have had a chance to use, say, a certain model, but the teacher wants to refine its use). The teacher orchestrates these discussions by exploring the use of the new model, tool, or idea and helps students determine effective ways to use that mathematical object.

Chapter 7 more closely deals with how teachers can use errors as opportunities for advancing mathematical thinking through *Troubleshoot and Revise*, a discussion structure you've already glimpsed. This chapter showcases teachers prompting students to reconcile different strategies in order to defend the correctness of one of the solutions or to engage in a conversation with classmates to find where missteps occurred in a problem-solving attempt and what revisions are needed.

We end the book by raising some common questions teachers face when building a productive discussion-based classroom and summarize the big ideas we've shared with you. To support your teaching, we've included a set of planning templates for the various discussion structures (Appendices A–F). You will also find additional examples and a list of texts and videos resources that can help you envision some of the practices and moves you'll see described in the vignettes (Appendices G and H).

CHAPTER 2

OPEN STRATEGY SHARING

Chances are if you've asked children to share their thinking about a math problem, you've led an *Open Strategy Sharing* discussion. *Open Strategy Sharing* is typically the first way to get mathematical discussions going in classrooms. It's like having a good, basic recipe for a soup from which you can make all kinds of variations. *Open Strategy Sharing* allows you to nurture the norms needed for a productive math-talk community. And you can use this discussion structure to model how students should talk and listen with one another.

Too often we associate being good at mathematics with being fast and correct the first time through. We love how Sarah Michaels, Mary Catherine O'Connor, and Megan Williams Hall (2010) describe intelligence:

> *Intelligence is much more than an innate ability to think quickly and stockpile bits of information. Intelligence is a set of problem-solving and reasoning capabilities along with the habits of mind that lead one to use those capabilities regularly. It is also a set of beliefs about one's right and obligation to understand and make sense of the world and one's capacity to figure things out over time. Intelligent habits of mind are learned through daily expectations placed on the learner. By calling on students to use the skills of intelligent thinking—and by holding them responsible for doing so—educators can teach intelligence.* (2)

Over time, as students experience themselves and their classmates as people with good mathematical ideas, you will see a big difference in how much they're willing to persevere and take risks in front of one another.

What Is *Open Strategy Sharing*?

Many mathematics problems lend themselves to multiple solutions. In *Open Strategy Sharing*, students listen for and contribute different ways to solve the same problem. The teacher often asks *how* questions, such as "How did you think about the problem?" and sometimes *why* questions, like "Why did you start with the seven?" Most importantly, the teacher invites children to share by asking, "Who thought about this a different way?" Students are supported to listen to each other, and often invited to repeat their classmates' strategies to make sure they are hearing and understanding the ideas being shared. The goal of *Open Strategy Sharing* is to bring out a range of possible ways to solve the same problem and build students' repertoire of strategies.

How Do You Get Started?

Before you begin *Open Strategy Sharing*, you'll need to decide on a set of norms for doing mathematics in your classroom and you'll need to think about the "talk and listening moves" you want to use to get discussions underway.

Norms for Doing Mathematics

Teachers introduce and cultivate norms in the classrooms in many different ways. Whatever your method, we think it's important to pay explicit attention to the norms you want to foster. We offer the following list of norms as a way of bringing to life the principles we introduced in Chapter 1. This particular list was inspired by the Standards for Mathematical Practices in the Common Core State Standards (2012), norms suggested by one of our favorite books, *Classroom Discussions* (Chapin, O'Connor, and Anderson 2009), and norms we've seen at play in many classrooms with productive and nurturing learning environments.

In this class, we will do the following:

- Make sense of mathematics
    - *We think all children should see mathematics as a subject that needs to make sense to them. We don't want children to follow procedures just because their teachers, parents, or peers tell them to.*
- Keep trying even when problems are challenging
    - *Mathematics often has been seen as a school subject that students excel in because they are fast. Not all mathematics problems can be solved in a split second. Problem solving takes planning, strategizing, and persistence.*
- Remember it's okay to make mistakes and revise our thinking
    - *Children must feel comfortable to take risks, to put out partial ideas or ideas that are still in development, and to stumble when they are learning something new. Being able to revise one's thinking gives students the message that rough draft thinking (Jansen 2020) is welcome in mathematics as much as it is valued in writing instruction.*
- Share our mathematical ideas with our classmates (whether we are using words, numbers, pictures, gestures, or tools)
    - *Words are not the only way to display mathematical ideas. And sometimes informal language, gestures, and diagrams can convey ideas that we cannot yet fully articulate in words. Multilingual students, students new to an idea, students with disabilities, and students who tend to be quiet and participate through active listening can be supported to participate productively by knowing that verbal participation is not the only way to show understanding.*
- Listen to understand someone else's idea; give each other time to think
    - *Listening is as important to learning as is talking and sharing your ideas in other ways. Teaching children what to listen for and how to listen to*

- Ask questions that help us better understand the mathematics
  You'll notice that we care a lot about the messages students receive regarding what it means to be "smart" or capable. Asking questions of one another is a way to show that we are listening and trying to understand the ideas being discussed. Asking questions also shows that we are curious about mathematics and that we care that children are making sense of the ideas. We want to frame questions as an important part of the learning process and help students to understand that asking a question doesn't mean they are wrong or that we are revealing something that they should have known.
- Agree and disagree with mathematical ideas, not with each other
  Being able to agree and disagree with the mathematics being discussed is an important part of examining or questioning mathematical ideas. But disagreeing with an idea can be socially uncomfortable. Knowing that it is the mathematical idea, not the person, you are disagreeing with can make disagreeing feel safer and productive.
- Remember that everyone has good mathematical ideas
  In a classroom community, all members bring important thinking and ideas to the discussion. Helping students recognize their own and their classmates' thinking and remembering that there is logic within each person's idea is important for a thriving mathematical community. It's important for students to have experiences where they are able to solve problems by putting their minds together to verify ideas. The teacher is not the sole authority of knowledge.

There are many different ways to set up norms in our classrooms, and this list is by no means the only or the best one. But we hope it will inspire you to collaboratively generate norms with students that will support your classroom community. Figure 2.1 shows a similar list developed by a school we have worked closely with. It is used across all kindergarten through fifth-grade classrooms. It may be powerful for you to work with your colleagues to nurture a set of expectations that students experience consistently across classrooms in your school or grade level.

Talk and Listening Moves

We find the talk moves described by Suzanne Chapin, Catherine O'Connor, and Nancy Anderson (2009) in *Classroom Discussions* enormously useful in helping us think about getting discussions off the ground. The beauty of the authors'

Figure 2.1 Discussion expectations

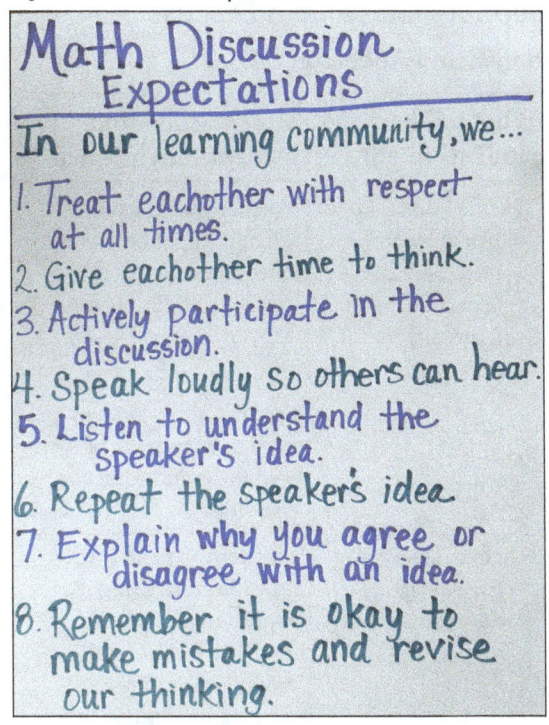

five talk moves is that they can guide both teacher talk and student talk. In the first edition of *Intentional Talk*, we added two additional talk moves, "turn and talk" and "revise your thinking", to help round out the list.

In this second edition, we have further revised the talk moves to include listening moves. By paying close attention to how to listen in discussions, we hope to make the underworld of talk—listening—more visible. In order for talk moves to be effective, we believe that paying close attention to the listening that is entailed in talk is an important next step in deepening our classroom discussions. Specifically, the Talk and Listening Moves (see the table on pages 28 and 29) integrate a focus on what teachers and students might say and how teachers and students might listen for each move. For example, when a teacher uses the talk move of "repeating", they may be using this move to repeat an important idea and slow down the conversation to consider the idea being discussed. That may sound like "Can you repeat what she said (about __) so we can hear it again?" Leading up to this move, the teacher was listening to consider when it might be useful to slow down and hear the same idea multiple times. While the idea is being shared, students are listening closely to hear, understand, and be able to repeat all (or part of) another person's ideas. This sophisticated work requires students to listen, make sense of, and generate questions they may have, and keep track of their own ideas and how they may be similar to or different from the idea being repeated. By paying attention to how teachers and students may listen, we can better understand and explicitly support the demands listening poses for teachers and students in discussion. In Figure 2.2 you will find a classroom poster that can help students consider what it might sound like when they use talk moves and what they may be thinking about when they are listening within each move. We hope this poster may inspire your classroom community to develop their own poster to support students' use of talk and listening moves. We will hear the talk and listening moves in action throughout vignettes across the book. If you're interested in delving deeper into classroom listening for teachers and students, see Appendix H for resources about listening in classroom discussions.

Talk and Listening Moves to Support Classroom Discussions
Adapted from Chapin, O'Connor, and Anderson (2009)

Move	Purpose	What teachers and students might say	How teachers and students might listen
Repeating Asking someone to repeat what another person said	Repeating important parts of an idea in order to slow the conversations down and consider the idea(s) being discussed	**Teacher:** *Can you repeat what she said so we can hear it again?* **Student:** *She said …*	Teacher listens to consider when it might be useful to slow down and hear the same idea multiple times. Students listen closely to hear and repeat another person's ideas. Student will need to keep track of their own ideas and someone else's ideas.
Revoicing Restating in their own words some or all of what another person said	Revoicing can be used to clarify, amplify, or highlight an idea for further consideration	**Teacher:** *Do we hear you saying …?* **Student:** *So are you saying …*	Teacher listens to track how ideas are being expressed and when it might be useful for the group to hear more clarification and/or zoom in on an idea in the discussion. Students listen in order to rephrase what they heard.
Reasoning Thinking aloud about the idea(s) being discussed	Reasoning—individually and collectively—to understand and consider the ideas being discussed and how they are related	**Teacher:** *Do you agree or disagree with that idea; why? Can you connect those two ideas?* **Student:** *I respectfully disagree with that idea because … I was thinking about that idea in a different way … This idea makes sense to me because …*	Teacher listens for important and emerging ideas to invite deeper reasoning, to compare and connect ideas. Students listen to the ideas being discussed in order to understanding another's reasoning and consider their own and the collective sense making.

Adding on Inviting someone to build on what is being said	Adding on allows students to build on others' and their own ideas	**Teacher:** *Would someone like to add on to what we're hearing?* **Student:** *I want to add on to what is being said, I also think that …*	Teacher listens for opportunities for expanding on and building out an important idea in the discussion. Students listens to another's thinking in order to build on their idea.
Wait time Pausing to allow time for thinking	Wait time allows students a pause in the discussion to think, gather their thoughts, and reason	**Teacher:** *Take your time. Let's give everyone a minute to think to yourself.* **Student:** *I need more think time.*	Teacher listens for where think time would help with sense making. Students listen to their own thinking as they make sense of their, and the group's, evolving understandings.
Turn and talk Turning and talking in small groups or pairs	Turning and talking in small groups or pairs allows students to consider, clarify, and engage with emerging ideas. It helps students rehearse and try out their own response and listen closely to one peer's ideas. It is an important time for more student voices to emerge than possible in whole-group discussions	**Teacher:** *Turn and talk to your neighbor about …* **Student:** *Can we talk with a partner about this idea?*	Teacher listens for when smaller discussions would benefit the whole-group discussion. Teacher listens in while students discuss with peers or in small groups to hear what students understand and are coming to understand in order to make decisions about the current or future discussions. Students listen to their peers' ideas, their own thinking, and engage in sense making.
Revising	Revising supports students in understanding that changing your thinking and reconsidering your ideas are important parts of discussion and sense making	**Teacher:** *It sounds like you are starting to wonder … Do you want to revise your thinking?* **Student:** *I thought … But now I think … I'd like to revise my thinking.*	Teacher listens for shifts in understanding to create space for sense making. Students listen to their own and each other's ideas to consider where their thinking is shifting and changing.

Figure 2.2 Classroom poster of talk and listening moves

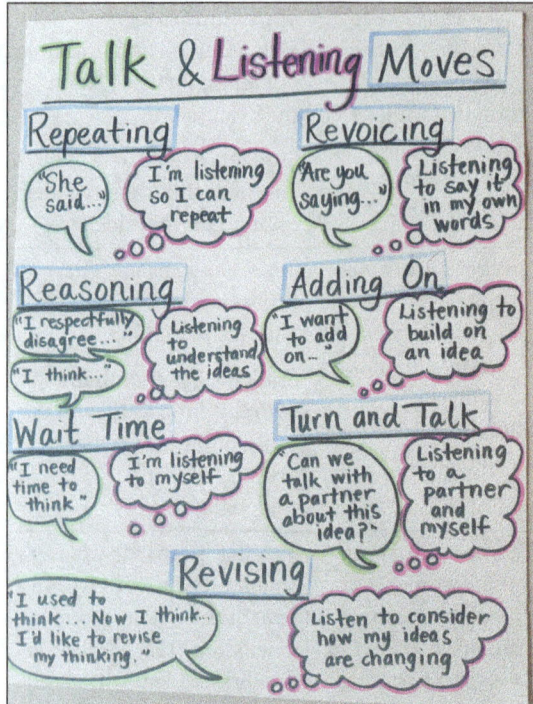

Planning for *Open Strategy Sharing* in Your Classroom

Getting started planning an *Open Strategy Sharing* discussion is rather straightforward. You begin by selecting a problem or task that has multiple viable solution paths. Listing possible strategies for your own reference can help you anticipate what you might hear from students. You could choose to give students time to solve the problem and share ideas on paper or with a partner to allow you to listen in or observe, giving you advanced notice of your students' strategies. Or you could call on students and learn about their strategies for the first time along with your students.

Here's a protocol to help you plan and facilitate the discussion (see also the planning template in Figure 2.3 and Appendix A):

- Select or design a problem or task that can be solved in more than one way. Anticipate how children may approach and solve the problem.
- Decide whether you want children to work on their own, in partners, or in groups to solve the problem.
- Pose the problem, making sure students understand the problem and have a way to get started. Take anecdotal records while they work individually, in pairs, or in small groups as you circulate to listen in or observe their thinking.
- Have students share two to four different ways to solve the problem. Use talk and listening moves and clear representations to help students understand what they hear.
- Close by highlighting the different ways students thought about the problem.

It's important to note that you do not begin an *Open Strategy Sharing* discussion by modeling a particular way to solve the problem. Instead, your job is to select a problem, or a problem context, that students will be able to solve in a number of different ways. Choosing such a task honors the principle that children are sense makers.

Figure 2.3 *Open Strategy Sharing* planning template

Planning Template for *Open Strategy Sharing*

Open Strategy Sharing		
Problem to pose		
Why I chose this problem	**Math Goal**	**Social or Community Goal**
Opening the lesson		
How might my students solve this problem?	**Who I saw solve it this way?**	**Share today?**
Notes to myself about what I'm trying to notice and listen for		
Other strategies that emerged during the lesson		
Closing the lesson		

Open Strategy Sharing provides a good opportunity to set up norms and practice talk and listening moves. Students learn how to talk about their ideas and how to hear and engage with others' ideas. Students can be supported to learn how to share and listen by what the teacher says or what the teacher attends to. For example, a teacher might say, "Did you all just hear what Elijah said? He said he wanted to 'revise his thinking.' That's one thing we can say in our classroom when we want to change our idea." By saying this, the teacher is supporting students in knowing that revising ideas is something mathematicians do in this classroom and that it's easy to signal a change by saying, "I'd like to revise my thinking." You can also give support by posting sentence stems that help students know how to share mathematical ideas in a discussion (see the word bubbles in Figure 2.2).

Open Strategy Sharing In Action

Kamaliʻi Elementary School, located on the island of Maui in Hawaiʻi, is home to a diverse population of students and families who identify as Native Hawaiian, Filipino, Hispanic, white, Tongan, Micronesian, and as being from various Pacific Island nations. In this school community, where children, families, and teachers hold deep cultural connections to the land, lessons are driven by students' questions and often provide openings for children to bring forward, and learn more about, their families' cultural and linguistic funds of knowledge (González, Moll, and Amanti 2005).

As we join the Kamaliʻi community through two vignettes in this section, students and teachers have recently engaged in a school-wide reading of the children's book, *'Ohana Means Family*, written by Ilima Loomis and illustrated by Kenard Pak (2020; see Figure 2.4). This story, a celebration of Hawaiian land and culture, follows a family, or ʻOhana, as they harvest taro. Taro, a root vegetable, is a culturally significant plant, essential to Native Hawaiians not only as a food source but also for its role in traditional stories and spiritual ceremonies. Teachers selected this story because many of their students have knowledge about harvesting taro and discussing this story will deepen their understanding of life in their local community.

Reading the same story school-wide is a common practice at Kamaliʻi. Together, as a school community, children and adults select a story to read in every classroom on the same day to build a school-wide culture of belonging and connection across the school. Reading the same story allows for children and adults in the community to have a common experience. It's typical to hear stories, such as *'Ohana Means Family*, referenced throughout the school's breezeways, playground, and even car and bus rides among siblings, cousins, classmates, teachers, and families. At this school, read-alouds are used as a tool to support both literacy and math learning for children.

Let's join two classrooms at Kamaliʻi as they engage in an *Open Strategy Sharing* discussion the day after reading *'Ohana Means Family*. Both classes, one intermediate and one primary, are discussing what students noticed and

Figure 2.4 *'Ohana Means Family* book cover

wondered while reading the story the previous day. The first classroom we will visit is a fourth-grade class where the teacher and the school math coach are collaboratively teaching. They are working to broaden participation among students and supporting students to engage in deep listening to each other and themselves. The second classroom is a first-grade classroom where the teacher is supporting young mathematicians to learn how to share their thinking and listen to others' thinking in math discussions.

Open Strategy Sharing Through Children's Literature in a Fourth-Grade Classroom

After reading *'Ohana Means Family* the previous day with the prompts of "What do you notice?" and "What do you wonder?" and charting students' ideas, Mrs. Carrasquilla (the school math coach) and Mr. Lee (a fourth-grade teacher) study

Figure 2.5 Two-page spread in 'Ohana Means Family

students' ideas to collaboratively plan an *Open Strategy Sharing* discussion. They notice students wondering within the kalo field context about questions such as "Does kalo always grow in bunches?", "Does kalo grow in combinations of five or three stalks and leaves like in the illustration?", and "How many kalo plants are in a row and in the patch?"

Mrs. Carrasquilla and Mr. Lee reflect on students' active noticing and wondering on a particular illustration (see Figure 2.5). Thinking about mathematical goals of supporting students' repertoire of counting strategies and sense making

Figure 2.6 Mrs. Carrasquilla and Mr. Lee's planning template for an *Open Strategy Sharing* discussion

Mrs. Carrasquilla and Mr. Lee's Planning Template for *Open Strategy Sharing* Discussion		
Open Strategy Sharing		
Problem to pose How are you counting plants, leaves, and stems in the kalo field illustration?		
Why I chose this problem	**Math Goal** Support sense making about mathematical modeling and the relationship between addition and multiplication	**Social or Community Goal** Ground sense making in family and community contexts Broaden participation and support students in deep listening to one another and themselves

Chapter 2 Open Strategy Sharing

Figure 2.6 (continued)

Opening the lesson	"Yesterday we heard you noticing and wondering about this illustration as we were reading, we noticed these themes in the questions you're curious about -- 'How many kalo plants are in the illustration?' and 'How many leaves are on the page?'" • Invite students to gather in small groups who had same wonder/question. • Hand out copies of the book. • Make counting tools available. • Kneel beside students as they discuss counting strategies to listen and observe.

Notes to myself about what I'm trying to notice and listen for
- Listen in while students discuss their questions and strategies.
- Notice and listen for the range of ways students are counting, and their addition and multiplication strategies.
- Jot notes of students (with names and examples for closing) as they engage in sharing and listening with each other

How might my students solve this problem?	Who I saw solve it this way?	Share today?
Counting all by ones	Malia, Mya, and Aukai	
Counting on by ones or skip counting in groups		
Multiplication and addition	Kai, Aiden, and Nalani Lailani, Kainoa, and Sebastian	
Other strategies that emerged during the lesson		
Closing the lesson	• Thank students for sharing their questions, range of counting strategies, and reasoning about addition multiplication. • Name students for their good work in student-to-student talk and listening with a few examples. • Let students know we will continue this thinking tomorrow.	

Figure 2.7 Mrs. Carrasquilla and Mr. Lee co-facilitate an *Open Strategy Sharing* discussion

about mathematical modeling and the relationship between addition and multiplication, they decide to return to this illustration the next day with students. They focus on two themes of questions students are curious about: "How many kalo plants are in the illustration?" and "How many leaves are on the page?" They hope the context of the kalo plant, which has cultural meaning to these children, and the illustration help ground complex ideas about addition and multiplication in sense making for students.

They use the planning template to jot notes for how they will open the discussion, what they will listen for, ways their students may solve, and how they anticipate closing the discussion. They decide Mrs. Carrasquilla (the math coach) will open the discussion so Mr. Lee (the classroom teacher) can listen to his students. They plan for Mr. Lee to then take the lead within the discussion (see Figure 2.6). With a sketched-out plan, they call students to a whole-group discussion. Within the following vignette, italicized narration provides insight into the teachers' thinking about the decisions they make while facilitating discussion. Their considerations span social and mathematical dimensions of classroom discussions.

Mrs. Carrasquilla holds up a two-page illustration that shows people farming taro, also referred to as kalo (see Figure 2.5). She begins by recapping the students' noticings and wonders from this page and narrows upon the two questions students are curious about (see Figure 2.7). They invite students to gather in small groups with people who had similar wonders and further discuss and investigate their questions. As students spread out around the room, Mr. Lee hands out copies of the book (open to the illustration of the kalo patch) and makes counting tools (such as centimeter cubes, markers, and white boards) available.

While students discuss their questions and strategies, both teachers kneel to listen to students' thinking. As Mrs. Carrasquilla and Mr. Lee listen to students' small group discussions, they jot notes about students' strategies. They confer, using their notes to discuss the strategies they hear students using. They plan to invite sharing today and do not decide ahead of time which strategies will be shared in which order. They do plan to elicit three different strategies because that is how much time they believe they have today.

Mr. Lee: Class! You are having fascinating conversations about the kalo illustration. You are counting plants, leaves, and stems using a range of counting, addition, and multiplication strategies. Let's come back together as a whole group to have an *Open Strategy Sharing* so we all can hear and understand the different counting questions you are investigating and the ways people are counting in our classroom. Please turn your bodies to face and listen to the students who are sharing. Your job is to listen to other people's ideas so that you can understand their thinking and see what questions you may have to make sense of their reasoning. It is ok if you counted something different than the group who is sharing. Maybe you counted kalo but the group sharing counted leaves. Or, maybe you counted leaves but the group sharing counted kalo. What is important is that we are sharing counting strategies, whether kalo or leaves, and we are helping each other know how to count. Kai, Aiden, and Nalani, can you get us started by sharing what you are counting and how you are counting? *(See Figure 2.8.)*

Kai: We are counting how many leaves are on the kalo plants. Nalani noticed that some kalo plants in the picture have five or four or three stems. We decided to count how many plants had 5 leaves first and then we saw 8 plants. So we did multiplication to know that 8 plants with 5 leaves was 40 leaves all together. And then we counted how many kalo plants had 4 leaves and so on. We added up how many plants have the same number of leaves and then we have to multiply them, so if 10 plants have 4 leaves that's 40 leaves. First we do multiplication, then we do addition to combine all the leaves. We're not done yet. There are a lot of leaves!

Figure 2.8 Kai, Nalani, and Aiden counting kalo leaves (left) and their sticky notes and table (right)

Nalani: I agree with Kai and we also are using sticky notes to keep track of how many plants have the same number of leaves and our multiplication totals so we can add up all the leaves at the end.

Mrs. Carrasquilla: Thank you Kai and Nalani for sharing your group's counting strategy. I really like the way you jumped in when Kai was done sharing to add on to his thinking, Nalani! Aiden, what would you add on about your group's counting strategy?

Chapter 2 Open Strategy Sharing

Mrs. Carrasquilla and Mr. Lee are working on broadening participation and creating student-to-student discourse, specifically encouraging students to add on to and engage with each other's thinking without the conversation going through the teacher with each exchange. Mrs. Carrasquilla is deepening attention to this norm by naming it as something Nalani did and also inviting Aiden into the discussion.

Aiden: We see that some plants go off the page. We have been in a kalo field and we know that the rows go on for a really long time and there are also kalo that are under the mud and water. We are counting the leaves we can see but there are probably more we can't see and for some plants we can only see part of the plant. It is getting tricky because we have to add on leaves like there's one leaf here (*pointing to the illustration*) and two leaves here. Those are not in groups of 3 or 4 or 5, they are ones and twos.

Kai: We will add those ones and twos on to our total at the end.

Mrs. Carrasquilla: (*Turning to the whole class to repeat the group's strategy.*) Aiden, Kai, and Nalani are counting the leaves. They are paying attention to how many plants have the same amount of leaves and then they are multiplying how many plants by how many leaves. Then they will add up their total of all leaves at the end. They know there may be kalo they cannot see but they want to count all the kalo they can see. (*Turning back to the small group who is sharing.*) Did I repeat your idea correctly? Did I understand what you are telling us?

Mrs. Carrasquilla pauses to ask if she is repeating the students' ideas correctly. She wants to use talk moves herself, such as repeating, to continue to seed the move in discussions. Specifically here, she wants to reinforce the norm of checking in to make sure that students' ideas are heard and understood accurately when repeating. She is also slowing down the conversation a bit to make sure everyone has a second chance to hear this strategy. She makes eye contact with Mr. Lee to see if he is agreeing with her moves and if he wants to ask or add anything. He nods to continue and students jump in.

Aiden, Nalani, and Kai: (*Nodding yes and all talking at once.*) Yeah that's it. Yes. Yep!

Mrs. Carrasquilla: Ok. Can you tell us a bit more about why you are using a combination of multiplication and addition to answer your question?

Nalani: We started counting all the leaves by ones and then we thought it was going to take a really long time so Aiden had the idea to just count how many plants have the same number of leaves and then multiply the number of plants by the number of leaves. And add on the ones and twos of leaves at the end. We are making a table to show how many of each plant has the same number of leaves and then we are going to add them all together.

Aiden: (*Pointing to the table they are making.*) In this column, we say how many leaves, and in this column how many plants that have that number of leaves, and in this column the total number of leaves for all the plants that have that number of leaves on them.

Mrs. Carrasquilla: We hear you saying that multiplication can be a way of counting a lot of items more efficiently because you grouped the leaves into equal sized groups—you have plants with five leaves, four leaves, three leaves. Nalani, in addition to your math thinking, we also hear you spotlighting something Aiden noticed. You said he had the idea to add on the leaves of ones and twos at the end. What I appreciate about what you did was honoring another classmate, Aiden, for their thinking. Everyone brings important ideas to our discussions and you highlighting a classmate for their ideas is something we do for each other in our discussions. (*Turning to the class.*) Can I invite someone to ask the question, "How does your table help you?"

Mrs. Carrasquilla makes many important decisions here to deepen and seed classroom discussion norms. She chose to repeat Nalai's mathematical thinking and also to highlight the way Nalani honored Aiden's thinking. She is working on reinforcing the norm that everyone has good math ideas and that all members bring important thinking to discussions. By calling out the way Nalani honored Aiden, she is naming that attributing another's thinking is a valued practice in their classroom. Lastly, she invites someone to ask a question and provides the question to ask. She wants to create openings for students to ask each other questions and to know what questions might sound like. She is working on the norm that students listen actively to understand each other and they are active in asking questions during discussions.

Mrs. Carrasquilla: (*Noticing Jane's hand up.*) Jane, do you want to ask the question?

Jane: Yes. How does your table help you?

Aiden: (*Chiming in and continuing his earlier explanation of the table.*) It gives us columns to record how many leaves, how many plants have that many leaves, and the total number of leaves for that row in the table. It is kind of a way to organize how we are counting leaves and plants and keeping track of totals.

Mrs. Carrasquilla: (*Turning to Aiden.*) Thank you for this additional detail, Aiden. (*Turning to Jane.*) Jane, thank you for asking a question. As you listen to each other, you will have questions. Please know you can ask each other questions! (*Continuing with the strategy share.*) Did anyone think about counting in a similar way to Nalani, Kai, and Aiden?

Leilani: We did.

Mrs. Carrasquilla: Ok, great. (*Turning to the whole class.*) Mathematicians, as you listen to Leilani and her group share, please listen to make sense of their strategy. Listening to understand others' reasoning is an important part of being in a community.

Leilani: We also counted leaves. We each looked for plants with the same number of leaves. I had a blue marker and I circled all the plants that have 5 leaves. Sebastian has a purple marker and he is looking for groups of 4 leaves. Kainoa has a green marker and he is circling plants with 3 leaves. (*See Figure 2.9.*)

Figure 2.9 Lailani, Kainoa, and Sebastian lean over the *'Ohana Means Family* book illustration, circling kalo plants (left). Close-up of their hands circling kalo plants using different colored markers (right)

Kainoa: I am thinking about the table that Kai, Nalani, and Aiden made. That might help us, too.

Sebastian: Yeah we need a way to organize how many plants have 5 or 4 or 3 leaves.

Mrs. Carrasquilla: We can hear that you are using a similar strategy of grouping and counting and that making a table to organize your counting may help. I really like the way Kainoa is thinking about Kai, Nalani, and Aiden's table and then Sebastian added on more details. Adding on is one of our talk moves—it helps us deepen our explanations and reasoning. Adding on requires us to listen carefully so we can expand others' thinking with our thinking! (*Turning to the whole class.*) What questions do you have to make sense of the strategies shared so far? Asking questions that help us better understand the reasoning is important.

Classmates ask a few questions about the strategies that have been shared. Mrs. Carrasquilla and Mr. Lee continue to encourage student-to-student talk, orienting students to each other by physically positioning themselves to the side and with explicit support (e.g. "In our classroom discussions, you can talk directly to each other. You can ask each other questions, answer questions, and talk with each other without me calling on you."). After a bit of discussion among students about the reasoning within the two strategies shared so far, the teachers confer and decide to surface one more strategy today. They want to build a repertoire of counting strategies and hear the wide range of ways students are counting. Mr. Lee takes the lead next. He has appreciated listening to his students as Mrs. Carrasquilla took the lead and now he is ready to facilitate.

Mr. Lee: Did anybody think about a different question OR solve in a different way?

Asking "Did anybody solve in a different way?" is a common question teachers ask during Open Strategy Sharing. Since the goal of the discussions is to surface a range of ways of thinking and solving, asking for different ways of thinking allows many different ideas to surface.

Malia: Our group—me, Mya, and Aukai—were trying to figure out how many plants were in the kalo field, not how many leaves. We started by talking about when we have been in kalo fields. We know that there are many, many plants and you can see in the picture, the rows go on for a long way.

Mya: And the plants are close together so some plants and leaves overlap.

Malia: Yeah, so we put a cube (*pointing to centimeter cubes*) on each plant. *(See Figure 2.10.)*

Chapter 2 Open Strategy Sharing 43

Figure 2.10 Malia, Mya, and Aukai's counting cubes on the kalo plants in the illustration

Aukai: We started counting the cubes on the paper but then Mya said, "Why don't we …" and she scooted the cubes off the paper with her pencil.

Mya: And we said, "Oh yeah!" We pushed all the cubes off the paper and made a pile of cubes. We started counting the cubes.

Mr. Lee: You put cubes ON the illustration and then pushed the cubes off the page! How did that help you?

Malia: It was really hard to count the cubes on the page because we were accidentally moving them and counting over each other. But when Mya pushed all the cubes off the page, it made a pile of cubes. We each took a chunk of the cubes to count.

Aukai: We each got our totals for cubes in our piles. Then we told our total number of cubes to each other and we each added the totals together using mental math or paper and pencil.

Aukai: But that is where it got hard to count because when we each added the total for all the plants, we got different amounts.

Mr. Lee: It sounds like you disagreed with each other's total number of cubes, or plants in the field. That is something we can do—we can disagree with people's ideas in this classroom. We can also keep at it when problems are challenging and revise our thinking. How did you resolve this dilemma?

Mya: We are actually still disagreeing but we need to add a few more times and see what is happening.

Mr. Lee and Mrs. Carrasquilla notice the time and decide they will wrap up for today. Mr. Lee thanks students and says they will continue this thinking tomorrow. A lot has happened in this Open Strategy Sharing. Mr. Lee and Mrs. Carrasquilla have had a chance to hear a range of ways students are counting and reasoning about addition and multiplication. They also got to reinforce norms, working on broadening participation and student-to-student talk and listening.

Open Strategy Sharing Through Children's Literature in a First-Grade Classroom

Open Strategy Sharing discussions are not just for older students. Let's take a look at *Open Strategy Sharing* in a first-grade classroom also located at Kamaliʻi Elementary School. Kumu Yoshida, a beloved first-grade teacher in the community, routinely creates math problems grounded in students' lived experiences and in connection to the topics they are studying across the curriculum in their classroom. Kumu, the Hawaiian word for teacher, is how students address their teacher in this classroom. On this day, down the breezeway from Mrs. Carrasquilla and Mr. Lee, Kumu Yoshida is also facilitating an *Open Strategy Sharing* discussion after the school-wide reading of ʻ*Ohana Means Family*. She has mathematical and social goals for the discussion. Mathematically, she wants to support students to listen to and make sense of different counting strategies. Socially, she is focused on building classroom norms for math talk and listening with young mathematicians who are learning how to share their ideas and understand other people's ideas.

Kumu Yoshida: Students, you have so many questions about the story we read yesterday, ʻ*Ohana Means Family*. (*Holding up the book and thumbing through the pages; see Figure 2.11.*) You wondered why people plant and pick kalo and what they do with the leaves, and why leaves are shaped like hearts. You wondered how old the farm is and why the people are putting the kalo roots into boxes. What else do you remember people wondered about?

Chapter 2 Open Strategy Sharing 45

Figure 2.11 Kumu Yoshida holding up *'Ohana Means Family* with children gathered on the carpet

Sofie: People wondered how many kalo balls or roots are in the boxes (*pointing to the three boxes in the illustration*).

Kumu Yoshida: Yes, Sofie! What else?

Leo: It's not on our poster, but I started wondering if the people in the farm are family or do they live together.

Kumu Yoshida: That is a great new wonder, Leo, and I am glad you are continuing to ask questions about this story. (*Turning to the class.*) I have a copy of the book for you to work with today. A question that many of you had is "How many kalo are in the boxes?" (*pointing to*

Figure 2.12 Two-page spread in 'Ohana Means Family

the three boxes in the illustration; see Figure 2.12). Your job today is to work with a few classmates to count how many kalo roots are in the boxes. We will share our counting strategies and total number of kalo roots with each other in a while.

Kumu Yoshida organizes students into small groups around the room, passes out copies of the book, and reminds students there are counting tools (such as cubes, clipboards with blank paper, pencils, colored markers) around the room for them to use if they are helpful.

As students get underway counting, she walks around the room with her *Open Strategy Sharing* planning template to make notes about what she is hearing (see Figure 2.13). She hears some students counting each kalo root by ones,

Figure 2.13 Kumu Yoshida's planning template for Open Strategy Sharing

Open Strategy Sharing		
Problem to pose How many kalo are in the boxes (the three boxes in the illustration)? Students will work with a few classmates to count how many kalo roots are in the boxes. We will share counting strategies.		
Why I chose this problem	**Math Goal** Support students to listen to and make sense of different counting strategies	**Social or Community Goal** Grounding mathematics in students' lived experiences Building classroom norms for sharing ideas and understanding other people's ideas. Using talk and listening moves to build the class's ideas and sense making together

Chapter 2 Open Strategy Sharing

Figure 2.13 (continued)

Opening the lesson	"You have so many questions about the story we read yesterday, 'Ohana Means Family. You wondered why people plant and pick kalo and what they do with the leaves, and why leaves are shaped like hearts. You wondered how old the farm is and why the people are putting the kalo roots into boxes."
	• Invite discussion -- "What else do you remember people wondered about?"
	• Pass out copies of the book
	• Reminds students there are counting tools (cubes, clipboards with blank paper, pencils, colored markers) around the room for them to use if they are helpful.

How might my students solve this problem?	Who I saw solve it this way?	Share today?
Counting all kalo by ones	Vivi & Sophie	
Counting on from one box to the next to figure out a total across the three boxes	Leo and Sofie Henry & Jasmine	Begin with Leo and Sofie
Circling groups within boxes and then counting on	Ellis and Addie (counting by 2s) Izzie & Fiona	Addie and Ellis share third

Notes to myself about what I'm looking for
• Listen for how students are reasoning about the total number of kalo -- counting all using one-to-one correspondence, counting on and their sense of the number sequence, counting items in groups, etc.
• Record all answers at the beginning of the discussion

Other strategies that emerged during the lesson		
Counting each kalo root by ones within each box and laying out cubes	Aiden and Aria Abby & Violet	Aiden and Aria share second

Closing the lesson	Summarize the different ways students counted

box by box, and laying out cubes. She hears some students counting on from one box to the next to figure out the total number of kalo root across the three boxes. She sees some students circling groups of two kalo within each box and then counting on by twos across the boxes. She hears students counting all kalo by ones and adding together the box totals. She makes decisions about which counting strategies to surface in the discussion and in which order. She is thinking about how to support students in reasoning about counting on and the number sequence, and beginning to count items in groups (such as twos). She can hear her students are ready to begin using what they know about subitizing, or seeing items in groups, to count by groupings (such as twos) and skip count by twos. This is an important insight for her understanding of students' strategies. She calls students together for a whole-group discussion. She has a copy of the book illustration to hold up for students to point and represent their strategies. She chooses to begin with counting on and to spotlight the work of Leo and Sofie. Sofie is a new class member and she wants to position her as someone with important ideas in the classroom community. Thinking carefully about which ideas and whose ideas are shared is a consideration Kumu Yoshida takes to heart.

Kumu Yoshida: Mathematicians! You are thinking in such interesting ways about how many kalo are in the boxes. I'd like for us to come together to share the different ways people are counting through an *Open Strategy Sharing* discussion. Let's share our ideas about ways to count the kalo and listen to the ways our classmates counted similarly or different than you. First, let's get out the answers we have and I will record them. How many kalo did people count in the boxes? You can say your numbers out loud and I will write them here on our board.

Students: 35! 35! 36! 34!

Kumu Yoshida: (*Recording all the answers.*) We have different answers. Let's talk about your counting and learn more. Leo and Sofie, can you get us started? (*Talking to Sofie and Leo.*) I want you to face your classmates and to speak loudly so everyone can hear your strategy. (*Turning to the whole class.*) Our job as listeners is to hear and understand what Leo and Sofie are telling us about their counting.

As Kumu Yoshida asks Sofie and Leo to speak loudly, she is supporting students in knowing how to share so their ideas are understandable to others. As she reminds students of their job as listeners she is also supporting students in knowing how to listen.

Figure 2.14 Sofie points to the illustration as she counts kalo

Sofie: We counted and we touched each brown round kalo when we counted it.

Kumu Yoshida: Can we hear what it sounded like when you counted? You can point here (*motioning Sofie to point to the illustration while she and Leo count aloud*).

Sophie: (*Pointing to the illustration with her finger, starting with the biggest box in the foreground of the picture; see Figure 2.14.*) 1, 2, 3 … 14.

Leo: Then we went to that one (*adding on from the carpet and pointing to the next box to the left*) and we counted starting at 15, 16, 17 … 24.

Sofie: Then we went to this box (*pointing to the smallest box on the left*) and we kept counting (*Leo joins in and they count aloud the final box together*) 25, 26, 27 … 35.

Kumu Yoshida: Ok so we can hear that you counted all the kalo by ones and you counted on beginning with this box, and then this box, and finally this box. Your answer is 35 kalo plants.

As the first pair shares their counting, Kumu Yoshida supports Sofie and Leo in several ways—from explicitly telling them how to speak ("speak loudly so everyone can hear your strategy"), to how to show their thinking ("You can point here"), to using the repeating talk move to

recap their idea so they, and their classmates, can hear again how they counted. These are ways of getting discussion going in classrooms; it is clearly directed by the teacher and generally goes back and forth between the teacher and students. This type of back-and-forth exchange can begin to show students what it means to share their thinking and allow the teacher, over time, to work toward teaching children how to share, listen, and talk with each other without it going through her each turn.

Kumu Yoshida: Let's hear another strategy. Aiden and Aria, tell us about how you counted the kalo.

Aiden: We put a cube on each kalo and then we took them off and lined up the cubes.

Aria: And we counted all the cubes in the line. We got 36.

Kumu Yoshida: You used cubes to help you count. After you took the cubes off the page, you put them in a line and you counted them all. Class, can you gather around where Aiden and Aria are working so we can see their line of cubes? Let's count their cubes together. Aria, will you point to them for us while we count?

Class: 1, 2, 3, 4 … 36.

Counting aloud connects to other classroom math routines such as choral counting and counting collections. Counting aloud is a way to work on knowing number names and the counting sequence and is a regular part of daily life in this classroom.

Sofie: They got 36 kalo but we got 35.

Kumu Yoshida: That is an interesting noticing, Sofie. I wonder where this difference is coming from in your answers. Let's hear one more strategy and see how it helps us count and if it helps with your noticing of different totals or sums. Ellis and Addie, can you tell us about your counting?

Addie: We circled 2 kalo together and then counted by twos. *(See Figure 2.15.)*

Kumu Yoshida: Ellis, do you want to add on to Addie's explanation?

Ellis: We started circling in this box *(pointing to the box in the foreground and circling twos with his finger)* and then this box *(pointing to the next box to the left)* and then finally this box *(pointing to the box on the far left)*. But this box was a little tricky because the kalo are squished together a bit.

Addie: Yeah we thought these ones were squished together *(pointing to two overlapping sets of kalo in the box)*.

Ellis: And we didn't know if this is 1 kalo or 2 kalo. We think it's 2 and 2.

Addie: We think there are 11 in this box.

Kumu Yoshida: (*Turning to the class.*) Okay, let's stop here for a moment to make sure we all understand how you see the kalo. Can you point again to where you're unsure how to count? (*As Addie points.*) Class, look closely at what Addie is showing us. Can someone repeat what Addie and Ellis are trying to figure out?

Joseph: In this box, the kalo are squished together (*pointing to the box furthest to the left*).

Figure 2.15 Addie circles kalo by twos

Halia: It might be a kalo that is long or it might be 2 kalo.

Kimo: They think it's 2.

Kumu Yoshida: (*Turning to the class.*) I want you to turn and talk with your neighbor—what is happening when Addie and Ellis count the kalo in this box? Make sure both you and your partner share and you both listen to each other.

Kumu Yoshida is using repeating and turn and talk to slow down the conversation and to practice sharing and listening. The turn and talk also gives her a chance to listen to the sense making about how many kalo are in the third box. As students turn to talk, students have time to reason and she has a chance to listen and decide where to go next. While students are talking, Sofie comes up to Kumu Yoshida to say she thinks sees something about why they got different answers.

Kumu Yoshida: (*Pulling the class back together.*) Class, while you were talking with partners, Sofie discovered something she wanted to share with us. Sofie?

Sofie: We got 35 but we thought these squished kalo were 1 long kalo and now we think it might be 2, like Addie.

Kumu Yoshida: So you are starting to change your mind? Do you want to revise your answer?

Sofie: (Turning to Leo.) Leo?

Leo: Yeah I think so.

Kumu Yoshida: Sofie and Leo are revising their answer. That means they got more information and they are starting to think in a new way. Mathematicians often change their thinking and when we do that in our class we can say, "I want to revise my thinking." Do any other pairs want to revise?

Ali: We do. Mia and I got 34 and we think it may be different now too.

Kumu Yoshida: Ok! I notice how you are listening to understand other people's ideas and considering revising or changing your thinking when you see something differently.

Kumu Yoshida had originally planned to close the lesson by summarizing the different ways students counted. When the conversation around revising naturally emerged, she decided to revise herself! She decided during the lesson that it was important to normalize revising ideas as a critical part of the sense making process. She closes by naming and supporting the talk move of revising thinking and offering students language to do so.

In this discussion, Kumu Yoshida makes strategic use of turn and talks, repeating, and revising in order to broaden student participation in the discussion. Being mindful of using the talk moves in this way can keep students engaged in the conversation and build the class's ideas and sense making together.

What Is My Role as a Teacher When Leading Mathematical Discussions?

We can see in the vignettes in this chapter that discussions thrive when students take on active roles and their ideas are at the heart of the talk. But when discussions are student centered, teachers often wonder about their role. While the teacher in student-centered discussions may appear more like a "guide on the side" than a "sage on the stage," the teacher's role in leading productive mathematical discussions cannot be minimized.

For example, consider all the decisions that we saw the teachers in this chapter make. Mrs. Carrasquilla, Mr. Lee, and Kumu Yoshida made many important moves and decisions in order to reveal the details in students' strategies and to help children follow and make sense of each other's ideas. When children stumbled or got confused, the teacher normalized slowing down and persisting through uncertainty. If you glance back through the vignettes, you may notice some of the teachers' actions: they decided how to select and sequence which ideas—and whose ideas—were shared in the whole group and why, when, and how to repeat ideas being shared; they listened in during a turn and talk to think about where to go next and why; they revoiced important ideas that emerged and invited students to repeat; they provided tools to aid in thinking; they recorded and discussed all ideas; they made norms for discussion and the reasons for particular talk moves explicit; and they pointed out the importance of persisting through confusions, asking each other questions as an active listener, and the value in revising thinking. Different from modeling strategies, teachers make many decisions in order to facilitate conversation amongst students.

Reading the vignettes with an eye for the moves and decisions the teacher makes will help underscore the critical role a teacher plays in fostering productive mathematical discussions. In each vignette, the teacher is working hard to monitor what students are doing and understanding, who is engaged and how, who needs more time or different supports to stay actively thinking in the discussion and to be positioned competently. The teacher makes intentional choices about the mathematical objects and tools that are used in the discussions, how to begin and close math talk, how to assess the success of the discussion, and next steps to continue to build understanding and fluency. You may have noted additional things that a teacher is doing in these discussions. Their role is anything but passive!

Building a Respectful Community Through *Open Strategy Sharing*

Building a community through discussion entails many noteworthy elements, from attention to tasks to self-reflection and student voice.

Finding Good Open-ended Tasks that Invite Wide Participation

As you think about developing richer discussions in your classroom, think about what sharing and listening sounds like right now. The first thing to consider is whether your students have opportunities to work on open-ended tasks that invite multiple solutions. In this chapter, we grounded the examples of *Open Strategy Sharing* in a problem context inspired by children's literature that is deeply connected to a local school community. We encourage you to consider contexts that are meaningful and relevant to your local school community. Whether embedded in a context or not, we encourage you to look for mathematical problems that can be approached in multiple ways. It's especially important in fostering good listening that we pose tasks that generate ideas that are interesting to listen to. It's vital to have problems that build your students' understanding and investment in the norms for mathematical discussions and in the purposeful use of talk and listening moves. One way to do that is to fill your classroom with examples of home and community mathematics. Ask your students and families to regularly share and talk about the things they like to do outside of school. What mathematics is important to those everyday contexts? Encourage families to share stories, artifacts, and photographs from these contexts. Notice what community places are important to and frequented by students. What do students do at local parks and community centers, shopping centers, health centers, and sports fields? Think about what you're studying and reading about in other subjects. In what ways might mathematical questions provide depth to understanding something new that you're learning about?

While not specifically related to your own classroom community, your mathematics textbook will also be a good source of problems, although you may have to adjust the prompts to make sure they don't suggest a particular way to solve a problem. Number talks, all kinds of word problems, images, or representations of data can all be good starting points for finding multiple solutions to a problem.

Here's a list of tasks that lend themselves well to *Open Strategy Sharing*.

- **Counting activities** such as choral counting or counting collections where students share different ways to count and represent their thinking (see Franke, Kazemi, and Turrou 2018 in Appendix H)
- **Number talk images, tasks, and routines** that allow students to share how they see images numerically or spatially (see Figures 2.16, 2.17, and 2.18)

| Figure 2.16 Number talk images | Figure 2.17 Math tasks and routines | Figure 2.18 Mathematizing the world routine |

- **Quick Images**, also called dot images, are a powerful daily routine for *Open Strategy Sharing* and fostering norms for talk and listening in the classroom. To read a vignette around this routine, and view the accompanying planning tools, visit Appendix G where Mr. William's fifth-grade classroom participates in the familiar classroom routine of Quick Images. Here you can join a classroom community, gain insights into a teacher's thinking in planning for and facilitating a number talk through Quick Images, and view a planning template with Mr. William's notes and a blank planning template for your own use.
- **Computational number talks** also provide good starting points to share different arithmetic strategies.
- **Word problems** from textbooks or teacher or student-generated problems typically can be solved in multiple ways.

What Does it Sound Like When Students Talk with One Another?

Having good tasks for *Open Strategy Sharing* is necessary to capture student interest. But how the conversations actually play out depends on the discussion expectations that you cultivate and your commitment to persisting through the challenges of helping students listen and talk with one another productively. It might be helpful for you to take stock of what a discussion sounds like right now.

Here are a few exercises to try in your own classroom:

- Record a discussion for five to ten minutes. Listen to what questions you pose and how the students respond. What questions generated the most interest from students? What do you think the demands of listening and talking were for students? In other words, to be an active participant, what did students have to do?
- Invite a colleague who is also interested in deepening their discussion practice to jot notes as you lead a discussion. Look over the notes together to notice themes and consider what you may want to try next and why.
- Invite a colleague to collaboratively plan, facilitate, and reflect on teaching similar to the way Mrs. Carrasquilla (a math coach) and Mr. Lee (a classroom teacher) collaborated. Collaboration allows both a teacher and a coach to partner in decisions before, during, and after the discussion. This model provides each partner a chance to listen to children while the other takes the lead and builds collegiality. Instead of entering a teacher's classroom with the pressure of observing a "perfect" lesson, you can work together and hold joint curiosity for what students will tell you.

- Try something new. Sketch out some questions and talk and listening moves on the planning template for *Open Strategy Sharing*. Pay attention to the talk and listening moves and questions that help surface children's thinking and support students in sense making. Are there any questions or comments that may fall flat or be clunky that could be tweaked? What might that sound like? You can highlight or put a check mark by particularly helpful comments during the lesson if you're pressed for time.

How Do Students Feel About Participating in These Discussions?

Although we are writing this book from the teachers' perspectives, giving you insight into what the teacher is thinking and trying to accomplish, it's vital to elicit how students feel about participating in mathematical discussions. While working closely with teachers to learn how to foster productive classroom discussions, we have always paid attention to how students feel about listening to and sharing ideas. After all, these discussions can be intellectually and socially risky. We want students to know that they have good ideas, that ideas in formation don't always come out in perfectly comprehensible ways, and some ideas need to be revised. How we set and maintain norms for engaging in classroom participation is important. When we asked the students we described in this book how they felt about participating in discussions and what they listen for, we heard comments like the following:

- *When I share my thinking about what I'm confused about, it helps me revise my ideas. We say, "I want to revise my thinking." I don't feel ashamed because I know a lot of people revise their thinking.*
- *Sometimes I forget my idea when I'm listening to another person, but it comes back.*
- *When I'm listening to my classmates, I think about how they got their answer. If I don't understand how they got it, I ask them to explain it again.*
- *When my classmates repeat my ideas, I'm thinking about how my idea can help other students learn. When I hear my idea repeated again, I can learn from that, too.*
- *During a turn and talk I'm thinking about what my partner said and how their math idea connects with mine.*

These types of comments can help you know whether students are taking on and buying into the norms that you want for them. We've also heard students new to discussion be frustrated if someone starts to use or build on their ideas. One student said that he didn't like it when his classmates stole his idea. Reframing for students that it's not about being the one with the idea, but that honoring each other's ideas, and building the collective ideas is our goal. The skill of learning from one another's ideas was clearly an important idea to discuss. It can feel risky and challenging to share ideas in progress, and it's not uncommon for students to quickly and sometimes unkindly correct each other. Many students worry about being embarrassed in front of their peers or are not sure how to step into a conversation. All of this can be steeped in the pressures students feel when math is perceived to be about speed and accuracy. To give you insight about how your students are feeling about participating in discussions, and how and when to frame productive norms, it might be useful to survey your students regularly about their perspectives. Their thoughts and feelings can provide good launching points for classroom meetings as you monitor how they are doing as a group. You might like to ask students to rate their feelings with statements like the following:

I like to share my math strategies in class.
most of the time   **some** of the time   **a little** bit   **never**

My classmates can learn from my math strategies.
most of the time   **some** of the time   **a little** bit   **never**

Listening to other students' math strategies helps me.
most of the time   **some** of the time   **a little** bit   **never**

You might also like to pose some open-ended questions like the following:

1. What does it mean to be good at math?
2. What's it like for you to listen to other people's strategies during math class?
3. How do you feel about being called on to share your thinking?
4. How do you feel about revising your thinking?

With younger students, we have found that drawing and writing or talking about pictures can provide great insight for teachers. A prompt like "Draw a picture of yourself in math class and tell me about it" can open up dialogue about being listeners and sharers. For intermediate-aged students, short surveys can provide information about students' experiences with whole-class discussions (see Appendix H).

Summary and Reflection Questions: When Do I Want to Have an *Open Strategy Sharing* Discussion?

Open Strategy Sharing provides a strong foundation for mathematics discussions. It helps teachers build wide participation by creating opportunities for students to share and hear how problems can be solved in different ways. It's important to choose a task that students can make sense of in multiple ways, and by facilitating the conversation you can meet the mathematical goal of recognizing multiple valid strategies. Many classroom routines, curriculums, children's literature, and word problems lend themselves to multiple strategies. Charting multiple strategies also helps students begin to understand and build a repertoire of strategies. For example, in the *'Ohana Means Family* examples, students counted by ones, twos, threes, fours, and fives. They counted all, counted on, used addition and multiplication, and created tables to organize their thinking. Sharing these initial ideas can help students begin to think about when, how, and why these strategies work, and produce the fodder for more targeted discussions.

Socially, *Open Strategy Sharing* can help you build the norms and discussion expectations that bring to life the principles of productive mathematical talk to life. Children experience themselves and their classmates as competent. They see that their teachers are interested in their ideas, and with the intentional use of talk and listening moves, they learn what it means to hear and make sense of their own and each other's ideas, to take risks, and to revise their thinking.

We invite you to keep thinking about these questions as you move on to the next chapters:

1. What norms do I want to foster in my classroom?
2. Which talk and listening moves seem alive in my classroom? Which talk and listening moves do I want to start using or deepen in my classroom? How can I become more curious about the ways I model listening as a teacher and the ways children listen to one another? How can I make displays that will help my students and me engage as speakers and listeners in math discussions?
3. In next week's lessons, where do I see opportunities for *Open Strategy Sharing* discussions?
4. What challenges have I encountered when I have tried to support my students to share their mathematical thinking and to hear others' thinking? How could I use the talk and listening moves, or the classroom discussion expectations, to work through these challenges with students?

CHAPTER 3

TARGETED DISCUSSION: COMPARE AND CONNECT

Now we're rolling! After asking students "Who solved the problem in a different way?", a logical next step is to think about what makes strategies the same and different. In this chapter, we will transition from *Open Strategy Sharing* discussions, where we surface a range of solutions and strategies, to targeted discussions where we narrow upon particular strategies with intention. Specifically, we will focus on a targeted discussion structure,

Compare and Connect, that invites a closer look at a couple of different strategies. Before we shift our focus from open discussions to targeted discussions, let's take a moment to consider what sharing sounds like in your classroom right now, and how to continue to build a thriving discussion community.

Developing Thriving Discussion Communities

When you close your eyes and imagine what a thriving classroom discussion community looks like, what do you see? Perhaps you see students engaged in problem solving, using manipulatives to tinker with and revise their ideas. Now shift from observing to listening in a thriving classroom discussion community; what do you hear? Maybe you hear students asking each other questions or sharing their ideas-in-progress. As you "see" and "hear" this thriving classroom, what do you imagine supports this thriving for students? What norms may be in place?

Pausing to imagine a thriving classroom discussion community and reflecting on where your classroom discussions are currently (and may go next) is important for deepening your teaching practices. Since writing the first edition, we have learned from teachers, instructional coaches, and leaders that adding support into Chapter 3 to help readers take stock of how mathematical discussions are going would be helpful. Additionally, readers asked for support in thinking about the many ways students can participate in discussions. In this second edition, we will illuminate the many ways students can be active participants in discussions and help teachers think about what's happening for all of their students in a thriving discussion community. For example, how are "quiet" students often actively participating through listening, more than speaking? We will continue to think about how to build on students' active forms of sharing and listening during discussions.

To begin with reflection on your current classroom, here are a few prompts and exercises you can explore with colleagues and students to take stock of where you are now and to support deepening your discussion community.

Taking Stock of Where We Are With Mathematical Discussions

Here are some questions to think about individually or together with colleagues.

- **Nature of the tasks and problems we work on**
    - Do some of our tasks or problems lend themselves to multiple solutions?
    - Do some of the tasks reflect students' lived experiences and interests?

- When students work at their desks, tables, or on the rug, do they have a chance to solve a problem using their own strategies?
- When looking at student work, is there variety in how students have solved and/or represented their thinking?

- **Norms for ways of being in our community**
    - What norms do we use to guide and ground our discussions?
    - Do we actively use, refer to, and refine our classroom discussion norms and expectations?
    - Which norms seem especially helpful for thriving discussions?
    - What norms do we have for framing mistakes during discussions? How do we tend to navigate student mistakes and in-progress thinking? How do students respond to themselves and/or their peers when they share incorrect or in-process thinking?
    - What is missing from our norms?

- **Ways of participating actively in our discussions**
    - Do our discussions include turn and talks for pair or small-group processing? For what purposes and how often?
    - Which students tend to participate by talking, or sharing their thinking aloud, in classroom discussions? Who do we tend to hear from the most?
    - How would I describe the range of ways students tend to participate in discussions?
    - How do I create openings for, and support, students' active participation?
    - Which students tend to participate as active listeners in classroom discussions? Who do we not tend to hear? What is powerful about this form of participation? How can we find ways to highlight the thinking of quieter students? What are the challenges?

- **Looking ahead to next steps**
    - What am I curious to better understand about developing thriving discussions?
    - What is a next step to explore in strengthening our discussions?

Being curious about classroom discussions, reflecting on current ways of being, and exploring new practices is a way to deepen our practice and grow as teachers. As we move into targeted discussions, specifically *Compare and Connect*, we invite you to carry these noticings and wonders with you.

Planning for a *Compare and Connect* Discussion in Your Classroom

When you are planning any targeted discussion, it's important to think carefully about your instructional goal. Since not all discussions have the same goal, a targeted discussion is an opportunity to focus upon particular strategies. For the targeted discussion of *Compare and Connect*, the goal is to focus upon selected strategies to examine what makes them similar and different. Often, a *Compare and Connect* discussion comes after *Open Strategy Sharing*, perhaps the following day. Once many strategies have surfaced through *Open Strategy Sharing*, teachers have a chance to step back and reflect on the ways their students are making sense of the mathematics. Then, the teacher can decide where to go next to deepen sense making. We begin with the targeted discussion structure of *Compare and Connect* because it is a natural and accessible way to start planning for and facilitating targeted discussions. By placing a couple strategies together and asking students "What connections do you notice?", we have an easy way into targeted discussions.

When planning for *Compare and Connect*, begin by considering mathematical connections you want your students to make between strategies. It may be helpful to begin by focusing students on comparing two strategies (working toward possibly comparing more than two strategies over time). What do *you* as the teacher notice makes the strategies similar and/or different mathematically? What do you anticipate *students* may notice about what makes them similar or different? Make sure you are clear about why it's important for students to notice those similarities and/or differences; they need to know the mathematical value of doing so. As in any discussion, the students should listen to and contribute ideas in order to move toward shared understanding.

You can use the template found in Appendix B to think through the following instructional decisions:

- Decide which strategies you want your students to compare and connect.
- Identify connections that you believe are important for students to notice between the two or more strategies.
- On your planning sheet, write out the strategies as you imagine they will be recorded on the board. (Add more columns to the planning sheet if you are comparing more than two strategies.)
- Anticipate what students may notice as they compare and connect the strategies and how you might respond to support their ideas.
- Jot a note to yourself about the mathematical idea you want to target during the discussion and highlight at the end of the discussion. Put

the note in your pocket so you can quickly remind yourself during the discussion.
- If it's helpful, jot a note to yourself about the social goal you want to work on through the discussion.

As you facilitate the discussion, stay focused on the targeted strategies, the key mathematical idea, and your social goal(s). It can be tempting to pursue other interesting mathematical ideas that may emerge (as we do in *Open Strategy Sharing*); however, a *Compare and Connect* discussion is all about delving into the connections between the strategies of focus. As you will see in the upcoming vignette, Mr. Delgado keeps two particular strategies (counting on by ones and counting on by bigger increments) at the heart of the discussion. He is focused on supporting students in expanding their strategies for addition. He is also curious to better understand the range of ways these first-grade students participate in discussions. For a social goal in this discussion, he is going to pay attention to how he can create openings and support for students' active participation.

First Graders *Compare and Connect* Two Strategies for Adding

Let's drop in on the *Compare and Connect* discussion in Mr. Delgado's classroom. After listening to his first graders share their ideas about 7 + 5 in an *Open Strategy Sharing* session, Mr. Delgado stands back that afternoon after school to think about their ideas. Reviewing the chart he made during their *Open Strategy Sharing*, he can see students added the two numbers in a range of ways, including counting all by ones, counting on by ones using fingers or a number line, and decomposing five or seven into quantities that allowed students to make ten (see Figure 3.1).

He decides to design a follow-up *Compare and Connect* discussion focusing on counting on by ones and counting on by bigger increments to make ten; he wants to highlight the idea that decomposing the second quantity into chunks to make ten is a strategic way to think about adding numbers. He sits down to quickly sketch out his plan for the next day's discussion. As Mr. Delgado prepares, he targets particular solutions to help students think about how they can make decisions about making bigger jumps. He jots himself a note to pay attention to supporting students' active participation.

Mr. Delgado is using a previous class discussion as fodder for the *Compare and Connect* discussion (see Figure 3.2 for his planning notes); this helps us see how *Open Strategy Sharing* can lead to targeted sharing. Throughout this book, for each of the targeted discussion structures, we provide a planning template to help you anticipate and think through key mathematical ideas for each

Figure 3.1 Students' strategies for 7 + 5 are noted on this classroom chart

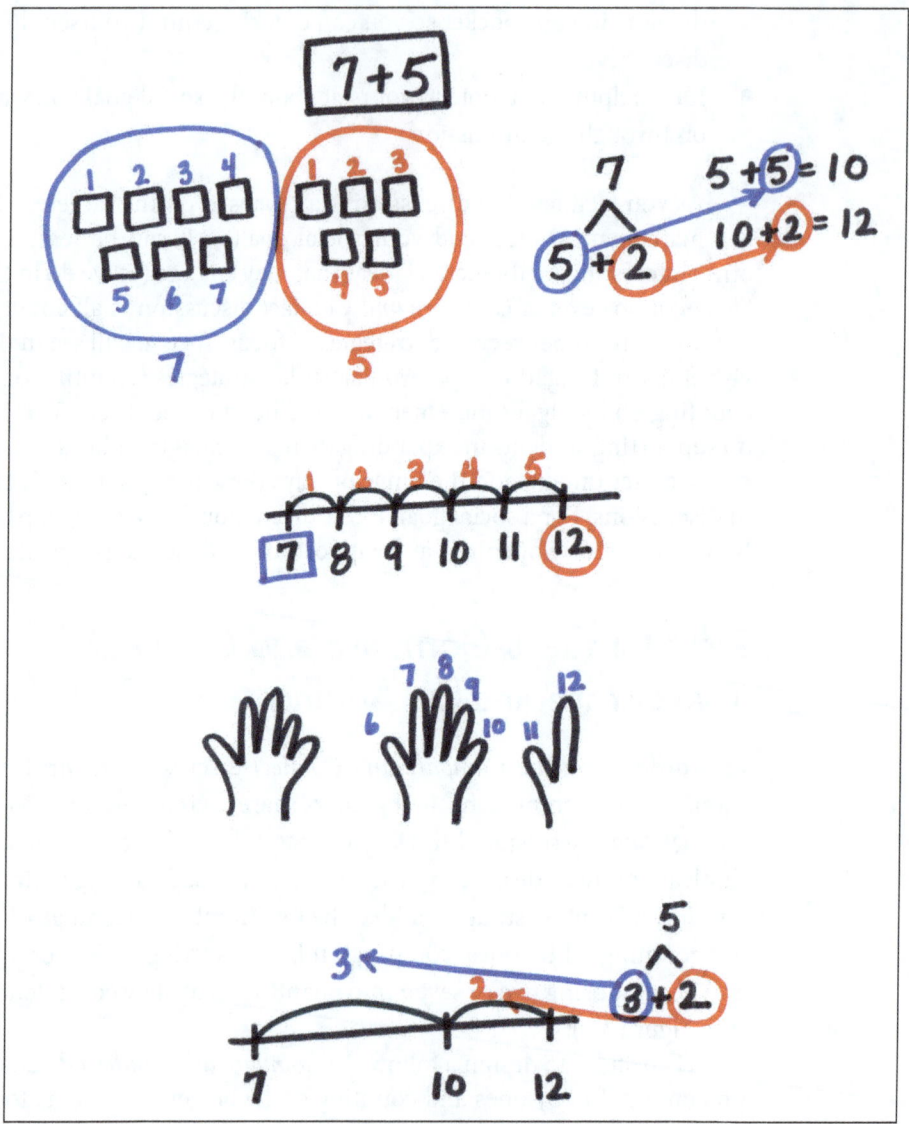

discussion. The planning templates are a place to sketch your ideas about the mathematics your students are learning. We hope you will use your valuable experiences with lesson planning strategies to use and adapt these templates in ways that are useful for you. Like the teachers in the vignettes, nurturing social goals is woven into every discussion. If you find it helpful, like Mr. Delgato does, you can jot a note for particular social goals you're working on. The teachers in the vignettes provide insights into how they think carefully about nurturing social community in their planning and facilitation of discussions.

Figure 3.2 Mr. Delgado's planning template for a *Compare and Connect* discussion: Counting on strategies

Compare and Connect	
Strategy 1	**Strategy 2**
7 + 5 Counting on by ones on fingers or a number line 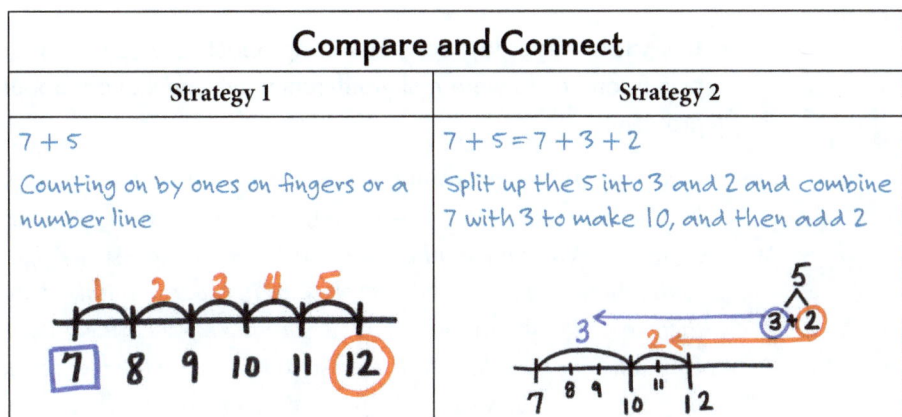	7 + 5 = 7 + 3 + 2 Split up the 5 into 3 and 2 and combine 7 with 3 to make 10, and then add 2
What are the connections that are important for students to notice?	
You can start with 7 and count on the 5 one by one. Or we can break up the 5 into chunks that allow us to easily make tens.	
Supporting Students' Thinking	
What students might notice	**How I might respond to their thinking**
Both started at 7.	Why does starting at 7 make sense? How did the strategies use the second number?
Both got 12.	How did the strategy help get to 12?
One broke up 5 and added three numbers: 7, 3, and 2.	Where would the 7, 3, and 2 be in the second strategy? Could you break up the 5 into a 4 and a 1? Why was it useful to break the 5 up that way?
What is the key mathematical idea I want to highlight?	
Breaking up the second number into chunks that easily make tens makes counting the total efficient. Social note: Pay attention to supporting students' active participation.	

Mr. Delgado: Yesterday we were talking about how you might add 7 plus 5, and there were many different ways you thought about this problem.

Referring to the chart from the previous day's discussion, Mr. Delgado briefly recaps each strategy. In doing this he is orienting students to each other's ideas and the mathematics. As he shares each strategy, he looks to the students who shared the solutions in order to thank them for their contribution and to ensure he is capturing their ideas accurately. He glances at the other students also to make sure they understand the solutions so they can delve further during today's discussion. He recognizes that hearing your own, and others', strategies aloud requires active listening and participation from all students as they make sense of their own and each other's ideas.

Mr. Delgado: There is a lot we can learn from thinking more about each of these strategies. Today, I would like us to focus on two particular solutions. Keisha, you solved this problem by counting on by ones. *(Pointing to her solution on the chart.)* Can you model this for us again? *(Looking at the other students.)* Your job right now is to listen to Keisha explain her idea and make sure you understand her thinking. This means you are setting your own thinking aside so you can understand Keisha's thinking. If you worry that it may be challenging to remember your strategy after setting it aside in your brain, there are white boards and markers available for you to jot down your solution. You will have a chance to ask her questions if that helps you understand her strategy.

Mr. Delgado starts by inviting Keisha to share her strategy because he is working toward the mathematical goal of counting on by numbers larger than one. By starting with an example of counting on by ones he hopes to come to a collective understanding of this strategy, name the strategy as "counting on by ones," and use it as a launching point to move to counting on in larger jumps. He is also explicitly naming that the students' job is to actively participate as listeners. This helps him name both for himself and for students that listening to another person is active and we listen to understand another's thinking. From listening to his students describe their experiences, he knows active listening is demanding work and that jotting your solution down before setting it aside to listen to another's

Chapter 3 Targeted Discussion: Compare and Connect

idea may be helpful. He provides materials so that students can self-select if they want to jot down their idea before actively listening to another's idea.

Keisha: *(Carrying her number line to the front of the room.)* First I pulled out my number line.

Mr. Delgado: Can we watch you do that and listen to how you counted using the number line?

Keisha: Okay. *(Putting her finger at 7 and jumping ahead by ones.)* 1, 2, 3, 4, 5.

Mr. Delgado: Go on, what did you do next?

As Mr. Delgado asks Keisha questions such as "Can we watch you do that and listen to you count?" and "What did you do next?" he is supporting Keisha and her classmates in knowing what and how to share.

Keisha: Then I saw that I landed on 12. So my answer is 12.

Mr. Delgado: Thank you, Keisha, we see just how you counted. *(Taking out a new piece of paper to re-record strategies for discussion.)* And let me draw a picture of the number line to show what you did *(see Figure 3.3)*. How many other people are comfortable using Keisha's strategy? *(Many hands go up.)* Yes, this strategy makes good sense. You started at 7 on the number line and then you counted on by ones 5 more numbers and landed on 12. *(Turning to Keisha's classmates.)* What questions do you have for Keisha about her strategy?

Even though Mr. Delgato senses from the students raising their hands that they understand Keisha's counting on strategy, he is thinking about his social goal for this discussion—creating openings,

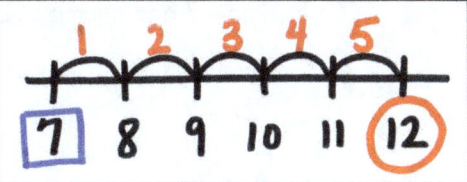

Figure 3.3 Keisha's strategy for counting up by ones

and support, for students' active participation. By asking students what questions they have, he is making space for students' active participation through student-to-student discussion. He hopes that practicing student-to-student discussion through an opening for questions will encourage student participation and support student-to-student discussion when the ideas become more complex.

Mr. Delgato: Great, we have a few questions to understand Keisha's strategy. Let's hear from Nathanie, Carrie, and Yue—you can ask your questions directly to Keisha, and Keisha, you can reply to Nathanie, Carrie, and Yue. The rest of us will listen in.

As the class and Mr. Delgato listens to the student-to-student discussion, he is careful to allow students to lead the talking and listening. He names the strengths of their active listening and making sense of each other's thinking. He then turns to the second strategy they are comparing and connecting today because he wants to leave the bulk of the discussion time to focus on the relationship between the two strategies.

Mr. Delgato: Xavier, you thought about the problem a little bit differently. I'd like you to tell us again how you thought about 7 plus 5.

Xavier: Well, I kind of thought about how I could make the problem a little bit easier for me. I broke the 5 into a 3 and a 2.

Mr. Delgado points to the number line on the chart from the previous day, tracing his finger along two jumps on the line showing the 5 broken into a 3 and a 2.

Xavier: I looked at the 7 and I looked at the 3 and the 2 and I decided to start with the 7 and make a jump of 3 because that gets me to 10. And I always like to get to 10!

Mr. Delgado: Okay, I'm going to try to show what you did here, and I'll make a new number line. You started at 7 and then you made a jump of 3 and that got you to 10 (*draws jumps on the number line*). Did you know 7 and a jump of 3 is 10?

By drawing an open number line in order to show Xavier's jump of 3, Mr. Delgado uses a representation to orient students to each other and the mathematics—in this case Xavier's strategy for adding on in increments, or jumps. He anticipated using this particular representation ahead of time because an open number line is a clear tool for seeing jumps. Anticipating ahead of time allowed him to make fewer decisions in the moment.

Xavier: Kind of. I said it real fast in my head, like 7, 8, 9, 10 (*bobbing his head as if making jumps on the number line for 8, 9, 10*). Ten! But now I know 7 … 10, I don't have to say each number.

Mr. Delgado: Let me show the 8, 9, 10 that you're talking about on our number line also. (*Fills in dash marks for 8, 9, 10; see Figure 3.4.*)

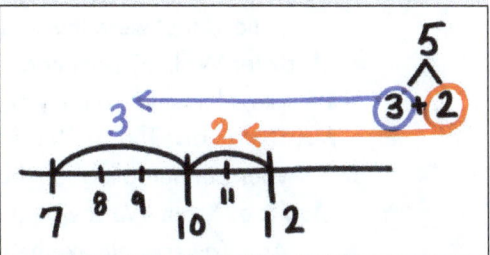

Figure 3.4 Mr. Delgado represents Xavier's incremental strategy on a number line

Mr. Delgado: So when you jump from 7 to 10, you're making a jump of 3, and those three numbers are right here (*pointing to the number line*): 8, 9, 10. Let's count those 3 all together … 7 …

Class: 8, 9, 10

Mr. Delgado: So 7 and 3 more is 10. Xavier, what did you do then?

Xavier: I still had the 2 I hadn't used yet so I added that on to the 10, like 10, 12. (*As he says this Mr. Delgado returns to the number line and draws the jump of 2 to land on 12.*)

Mr. Delgado: So, now we have these two strategies that Keisha and Xavier have shared side by side. With your partner, find three things that are similar and/or different about their strategies.

As students talk in pairs, Mr. Delgado listens in on several conversations and tries to pick out what students are noticing and how it connects or not to what he anticipated they might notice. He calls on Kenji to begin the "Connect" phase of the discussion.

Kenji: Alex and I talked about how they both started at 7. We also said that you can see their strategies on a number line.

Mr. Delgado is pleased that Kenji is reporting back his conversation with his partner rather than reporting only his own ideas. Being able to repeat another's thinking is evidence of active listening, and therefore active participation. Mr. Delgado is also listening for whether the pair is noticing the mathematical features of the problems that are similar and different. As Kenji comments about the number line, Mr. Delgado notices a place to probe more. He wants to be sure he allows students to share what they noticed but also needs to orchestrate the discussion so they reach the planned goal of the discussion.

Mr. Delgado: I heard many of you talk about the number lines that are up here in both strategies. Keisha used the number line herself. Then,

I used the number line to show what Xavier did. Before we talk about how their strategies were different, were there other things that you noticed that were the same?

Maddie: Well, my partner and I said that they counted up from 7, and, well, like, I know you didn't ask this but that's also what's a little different.

Mr. Delgado: Thanks, Maddie. It's okay, we can go there. Did you and your partner talk about how their counting was different?

Maddie: Yeah. We saw that Keisha counted each one or each number. And Xavier, well, like he made jumps. He skipped over some numbers.

Mr. Delgado thinks about bringing Keisha and Xavier back into the conversation, and he also notices that sometimes when students explain, they need support in helping describe the mathematical differences. He thinks of asking a question that will help the class articulate why Xavier's choice of breaking up 5 into 3 and 2 was strategic when combining with 7.

Mr. Delgado: *(To Maddie.)* Can you use our number line up here to show what you mean about skipping over some?

Mr. Delgado had drawn the number lines intentionally to help students show how counting by ones and counting by 3 and then 2 are related. Maddie uses the open number line to show how Xavier didn't count each one but counted 3 and then 2.

Mr. Delgado: Maddie and her partner notice that Xavier made two jumps, a jump of 3 and a jump of 2. Everyone, think about this question: Why did Xavier choose to break 5 up into 3 and 2? Why didn't he break up the 5 into 4 and 1? *(Mr. Delgado gives the class ample wait time.)* So, let me go back to Xavier and Keisha. Keisha, before we check with Xavier, do you think you can predict why Xavier might have done that? Share with him what you think he did and then ask him, "Is that what you did?"

Mr. Delgado tries to insert into class conversations small prompts to help students learn how to talk to one another and this aligns with his social goal of opening up and supporting students' active participation in today's discussion.

Keisha: Well, if he broke up 5 into 4 and 1, then maybe he would have to count by ones, like 7, 8, 9, 10, 11. But we know that 7 and 3 is 10, so it seems like that's a good jump. Is that what you did?

Xavier: Yeah, if I am starting at 7, jumping 3 gets me to 10. So I broke the 5 into a 3 and a 2. But, like, if the problem was 6 plus 5 I would have broken the 5 into a 4 and a 1, because starting at 6 and adding 4 would get me to 10. I always like to get to any number that ends in zero—like 10! It all depends on the numbers in the problem, and that tells you how to break apart the other number.

Mr. Delgado: I like how you talked to one another. What we are noticing is that Xavier was strategic in how he chose to break up 5 because of the numbers he was adding. So, let's make sure we have a way of thinking about what's the same and what's different. Try to sum up with your partner what's different about how Xavier and Keisha counted up from 7. Then I'll ask a few partners to share what we're learning about the strategies.

By asking students to summarize what they thought was the main difference, Mr. Delgado gives them a chance to stay focused on the main goal of noticing that adding the second quantity in increments that make 10 is a useful strategy. He purposefully invites Keisha to predict why Xavier might have broken 5 into 3 and 2 because he wants to support her mathematically and socially in this discussion. Mathematically, he wants to support her—and the class's—learning about how to add in strategic increments by giving her the opportunity to explain this strategy. Socially, he wants to position her as an important contributor—both for her offering of the common strategies of counting on by ones and also for her understanding of her classmate's different strategy. Mr. Delgado continues the discussion by giving a few students time to help sum up their observations in front of the class. Then, he summarizes the discussion and gives students an exit task so that he can check whether they are able to use the idea in a new situation.

Mr. Delgado: Today we focused on two different ways to solve 7 plus 5. We can solve this problem by counting by ones. We can also solve this problem by making jumps that are bigger than 1, especially strategic jumps that will get us to 10. I have a new problem I would like for us to solve. I want you to try making jumps bigger than 1 and I want you to think about what size jumps to make given the numbers in the problem. (He poses 8 + 6 to the class, and children begin working.)

The *Compare and Connect* discussion structure helped Mr. Delgado's students notice similarities between two addition strategies; from there Mr. Delgado was able to invite his students to try new strategies and to add on in increments, or larger jumps than one number. We offer the next example to show that the *Compare and Connect* discussion structure could also apply to the use of mathematical tools. Sometimes students become really comfortable with a particular tool or representation and need to be pressed to consider how a different one works.

Third Graders *Compare and Connect* the Use of a Number Line to a Hundreds Chart

In this next vignette, Ms. Mason focuses her *Compare and Connect* discussion on the similarities and differences between a number line and a hundreds chart. Figure 3.5

Figure 3.5 Ms. Mason's planning template for a *Compare and Connect* discussion: Number line and hundreds chart

Compare and Connect	
Strategy 1	**Strategy 2**
Using a number line to compute 82 − 57 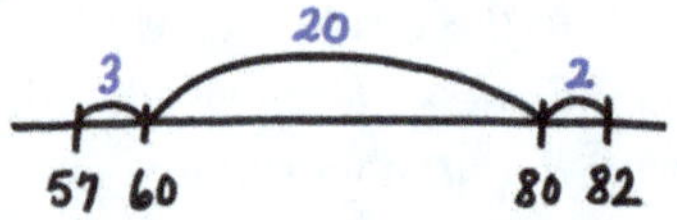	Using a hundreds chart to compute 82 − 57 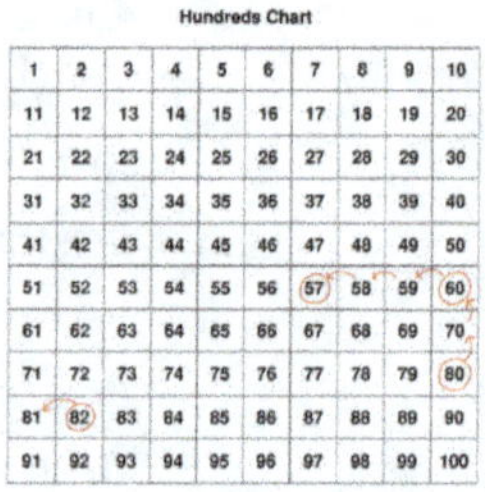
What connections are important for students to notice?	
Because the hundreds chart wraps the numbers, keeping track of jumps means moving from right to left when going backward. On the number line, you can keep track of jumps on the arcs above the numbers.	
Supporting students' thinking	
What students might notice	How I might respond to support their thinking
Seeing the jumps is easier on the number line.	How can we mark up the hundreds chart to show the jumps?
You can use the same strategy on both the number line and the hundreds chart.	What's the same? What's different? Which direction do you go on the hundreds chart if you go backward?
The numbers are all marked on the hundreds chart. You use only some numbers on the number line.	How do those differences help you keep track?
What is the key mathematical idea I want to highlight?	
The jumps on the number line can be mapped onto to the jumps on the hundreds chart.	

shows her planning template for the discussion. Because the open number line can be used regardless of the magnitude of the number, it can offer more flexibility in keeping track of computations. In the case of the problem Ms. Mason poses for her third graders, the hundreds chart presents challenges in keeping track of the direction the numbers are going, because they wrap around from one line to the next. Mathematically, it's important to help students translate between these two strategies so they thoughtfully attend to how they use the models to support their work with, in this vignette's example, subtraction. She sketches her ideas on the planning template. Socially, Ms. Mason considers how to support student-to-student questions so the talk does not always go through the teacher. Similar to Mr. Delgato, Ms. Mason is working on broadening participation in math discussions and across the school day. She is coming to more deeply recognize active listening as an important form of participation. She is curious to better understand how active listening shapes the questions students ask one another and how asking questions requires listening attentively.

Ms. Mason: Mathematicians use tools. You use many tools as a mathematician inside and outside of school! I see you using manipulatives, counting cubes, rulers, and hundreds charts in our classroom. I hear you talk about using tools outside of school like measuring cups or spoons when baking, a timer for calculating how many minutes left in a video game, a meter or yard stick for measuring length or distance. I want you to think to yourself about a tool that is helpful to your thinking in school or at home. Once you have an idea and example, turn and talk with a partner to share and listen. I'm going to listen to your pair discussions.

Ms. Mason listens in, allows students to share and listen, and brings them back together.

Ms. Mason: It is important to have discussions focused on how we use tools to help us in sense making. You had a mini-discussion with your partner and now I want to have a whole-group discussion focused on two different mathematical tools students in our class used to solve a subtraction problem.

Ms. Mason launches the discussion by making a connection between sense making, tools, and students' everyday lives. She intentionally designs this launch to foster making connections—in this case connections to students' lives inside and outside of school—which is at the heart of Compare and Connect.

Ms. Mason: If we look at the poster of strategies that students used yesterday when solving 82 minus 57, we can see that both Yahya and Simra counted back in order to find their solution. They both started at 82 and counted back to get to 57. Both strategies involved jumping to landmark (or decade) numbers. What was different was the tool they used to keep track of their jumps. Yahya used an open number line, and Simra used the hundreds chart. An open number line is a tool. A hundreds chart is a tool. (*Turning to Yahya and Simra.*) I'd like to invite both of you to describe your thinking to us and how the tool you used helped you solve the problem. While they are sharing their thinking, I want the rest of us to be listening to and considering how they used the open number line and hundreds chart to support their thinking and how these tools are similar. Yahya, why don't you start?

Yahya: Counting back makes a subtraction problem easier for me. I like to think about subtraction as finding how far away one number is from the other one. I draw a line. Then I draw the starting spot. Here it is: 82. Then I start making jumps on the line, like I'm jumping backward, and I make jumps to get to landmark numbers because that is easiest.

Ms. Mason: Okay, let's pause here for a moment to use an open number line on the poster to think about what Yahya is telling us. Yahya, will you show us each jump on the poster as you describe it? (*Pointing to the poster where Yahya's open number line is recorded.*)

By asking Yahya to point to the open number line on the poster, Ms. Mason is orienting the students to each other and the mathematics. She wants to make sure everyone understands the way Yahya used the open number line as a tool (see Figure 3.6). Ms. Mason also wants to support active listening.

Yahya: My first jump back was 2 to get to 80. Then I made a big jump from 80 to 60. That was a jump of 20. And finally I had to jump back just 3 more to land on 57. That was a jump of 3.

Figure 3.6 Yahya's use of the number line to compute 82 – 57

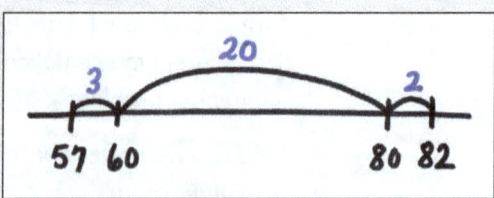

Ms. Mason: (*Turning to the class.*) So, let's turn and talk to repeat what you hear Yahya saying and discuss where Yahya's answer came from.

Students talk with and listen to their partners. Ms. Mason's use of turn and talk invites everyone into the conversation to make sense of Yahya's strategy and how she used the number line representation to subtract. Her use of a turn and talk also creates an opportunity for all students to actively process Yahya's thinking so they repeat her idea and begin to generate any questions they may have for their classmate.

Ms. Mason: Let's have a few people describe what they heard or said in your turn and talks. You can jump in without being called on. You can add on to what you're hearing or say something different.

Rafe: My partner said that the answer is in Yahya's jumps. She had to add up the size of her jumps to know how much she went back.

Lee: (*Pointing to Yahya's jumps.*) It looks like Yahya jumped back 2, then 20, then 3. So that's 2 plus 20 plus 3, or 25. Is that what you did?

Yahya: Yes, that's what I did!

Maria: She jumped backward on the open number line. Like here (*getting up to point to the poster*), she jumps back 2 and gets to 80 and then 20 to get to 60, and then 3 more to get to 57.

Ms. Mason: (*Using wait time.*) Who can add on to Maria's description or has a question for Yahya? James.

James: Yeah, and the answer is in her jumps. The answer is (*tracing the arc of the jumps with his finger*) 2 plus 20 plus 3. Or 25. Why did you make the jumps in that way?

Ms. Mason is using talk moves—repeating, adding on, wait time, and turn and talk—to support all students in making sense of how Yahya solved the problem using the open number line. Repeating gives all students (including the sharer) an opportunity to hear the idea again. Adding on allows the description of the strategy to be fully flushed out. Turn and talk ensures all children try repeating the solution being discussed and it also allows the teacher to listen in to hear if there are any ideas that need to be clarified. Wait time gives space for students to jump into the discussion without being called on by the teacher. Their class is starting to have more student-to-student talk without all turns going through the teacher. Ms. Mason listens in to the partners and decides that returning to James' questions as a whole group would be helpful both mathematically and socially.

Ms. Mason: Okay, I heard you all repeating Yahya's solution using the open number line. I saw you pointing to her jumps and I heard you adding up her jumps. I want to consider James' question about why Yahya made those jumps. It is important that you are asking each other questions and James' question is something we want to consider. Yahya, can you tell us, how did you know where to start your jumps and when to stop your jumps and why did you make those jumps?

Yahya: I started at 82 because the problem starts with 82. And then I knew I needed to land on 57 so I jumped until I got there. But I was smart about how I jumped and the numbers, or distances, were on purpose to get to landmark numbers.

Ms. Mason: Thank you, Yahya. We can hear that you were strategic in how you jumped on the open number line. And thank you everyone for listening to and making sense of Yahya's strategy. I'd like to hear from Simra now. Simra, you also counted back and you also made jumps to landmark numbers, but you used a different mathematical tool. You used the hundreds chart. I tried to record your solution on our poster but because we are discussing your solution further, I'd like to ask you to point to our actual class hundreds chart as you describe to us in more detail how this tool helped you solve the problem 82 minus 57.

Simra: I will try. I started on 82. And then I counted back. I didn't want to count every one (*pointing to each square on the chart*) so I thought about if I could make jumps that are bigger than 1. (*Looking at Ms. Mason.*)

Ms. Mason: Keep going, Simra. What did you do next?

Simra: I jumped back from 82 to 80, and then it was easy to jump from 80 to 60 (*pointing to the 80, 70, and 60 on the chart and traveling vertically up the chart*) and finally from 60 to 57. (*See Figure 3.7.*)

Savion is raising his hand and then jumps up to the chart. This is exciting to Ms. Mason because it is paving the way for a student exchange that she is supporting more than initiating.

Savion: So you jumped back too. But I can't see your jumps. How big were your jumps?

Ms. Mason: Who can help us with Savion's question? Simra, do you want to tell us or ask for help?

Simra: That's what I need help with.

Ying: I see you jumped back 1, 2, 3 (*pointing to 82, 81, 80*), then 10, 10 (*pointing to 70 and 60*) and then 1, 2, 3 (*pointing to 59, 58, 57*).

Chapter 3 Targeted Discussion: Compare and Connect 77

Figure 3.7 Simra's use of the hundred chart to compute 82 − 57.

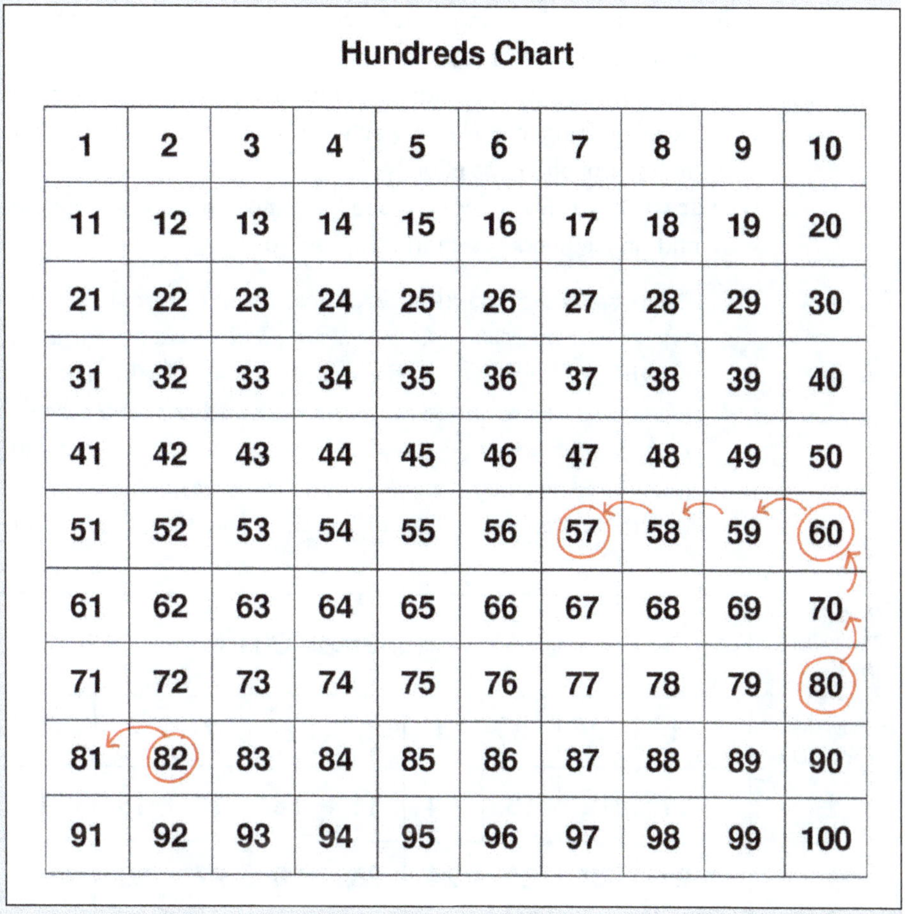

Hundreds Chart

1	2	3	4	5	6	7	8	9	10
11	12	13	14	15	16	17	18	19	20
21	22	23	24	25	26	27	28	29	30
31	32	33	34	35	36	37	38	39	40
41	42	43	44	45	46	47	48	49	50
51	52	53	54	55	56	57	58	59	60
61	62	63	64	65	66	67	68	69	70
71	72	73	74	75	76	77	78	79	80
81	82	83	84	85	86	87	88	89	90
91	92	93	94	95	96	97	98	99	100

(*Retracing the jumps again to herself and adding mentally she whispers.*) 1, 2, 3, 13, 23, 24, 25, 26. Twenty-six.

Ms. Mason can see that Ying is counting the number she started on, 82, as well as the number she ended on, 57, and can see the logic in Ying's thinking. She anticipated this confusion with the hundreds chart and wants to raise the issue of whether you count the number you start on and end on or not. She now knows it is her work to support Ying through her misstep, which is common, and position her competently in front of her classmates as Ying does the brave work of coming alongside Simra to try to explain her thinking.

Ms. Mason: Ying, can I try that again while you watch? *(Pointing to the hundreds chart, Ms. Mason reenacts Ying's strategy and then pauses, using wait time, for students to weigh in.)*

Ying: Something is wrong there. It should be 25. I think I want to revise my idea but I can't say how yet. I need help.

Ms. Mason: A classmate has asked for help with her thinking. That's an excellent thing to do when you're unsure. Who can help Ying as she thinks through her solution?

Fardosa: It was just so easy to see the jumps on the open number line and on the hundreds chart it isn't so easy.

Ms. Mason looks intently at Fardosa as she shares and uses more wait time to leave an opening for another student to add on. She is using wait time as a talk move to give children time to think and also to bring more student voices into the discussion. She doesn't want the talk to travel through her every time. She is focused on her social goal to support students to know they can talk directly with one another about their ideas. After twenty seconds, which can feel like a long time, Savion joins in.

Figure 3.8 The hundreds chart is annotated to show the jumps of 10

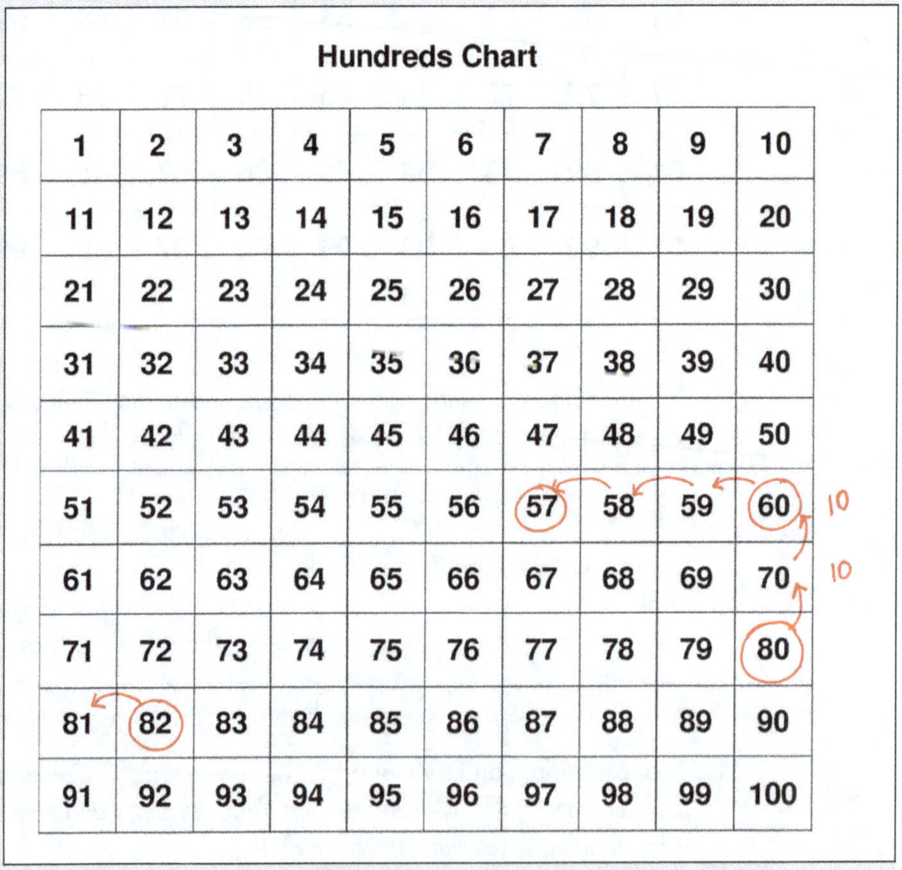

1	2	3	4	5	6	7	8	9	10
11	12	13	14	15	16	17	18	19	20
21	22	23	24	25	26	27	28	29	30
31	32	33	34	35	36	37	38	39	40
41	42	43	44	45	46	47	48	49	50
51	52	53	54	55	56	57	58	59	60
61	62	63	64	65	66	67	68	69	70
71	72	73	74	75	76	77	78	79	80
81	82	83	84	85	86	87	88	89	90
91	92	93	94	95	96	97	98	99	100

> **Savion:** Um, yeah, Fardosa said, like, the jumps are hard to see on the chart. But some of the jumps are easy to see.
>
> **Ms. Mason:** Which jumps are easy to see?
>
> **Savion:** When Simra jumped from 80 to 70 to 60. Those are big jumps of 10. And she jumped straight up on the chart. *(See Figure 3.8.)*
>
> **Ying:** Yeah, I was sure about *those* jumps too!
>
> **Ms. Mason:** So let's mark them. That might be one way to keep track better. Who can keep us going here?
>
> **Savion:** It's the jumps at the beginning and the end.
>
> **Ms. Mason:** Could we look at the open number line to help us think about this?

We leave Ms. Mason's discussions here, and hope you've noticed the careful work she's doing to help the students use one representation to reason about another representation. She has worked toward her mathematical goal of comparing and connecting two different tools—the open number line and the hundreds chart—as tools mathematicians use when subtracting, or finding distances or differences in numbers. She has simultaneously worked on the social goal of creating more student-to student discussion, through active listening, questions, and wait time. It's helpful to look back at the conversation and think about how Ms. Mason used each of the talk moves to create purposeful discussions.

Summary and Reflection Questions: When Do I Want to Have a *Compare and Connect* Discussion?

In the *Compare and Connect* discussions shared in this chapter, we can notice the ways the teachers and students focus on similarities and differences among strategies and tools. For example, Mr. Delgado chose to focus on two different counting on strategies, counting on by ones and counting on by strategic increments. Mr. Delgado focused on comparing and connecting these two strategies because he was trying to support his students thinking about how they could make decisions about bigger jumps in order to make their counting on more strategic. Similarly, Ms. Mason focused on two different mathematical tools (an open number line and a hundreds chart) that students used in order to solve a subtraction problem. They both worked on socially supporting active student participation and expanding what counts as active participation—specifically active listening.

Compare and Connect is one type of targeted discussion. You may be wondering what types of lessons lend themselves to a discussion about comparing and connecting strategies. You may want to have a *Compare and Connect* discussion in these situations:

- The problem can be solved in more than one way, and you know, based on your students, that they will have a variety of ways to approach it.
- You want to support your students in making sense of the different strategies that they have generated in order to make sure students don't see the mathematics in the solutions as disconnected.
- You're prompting students along in their understanding and selection of strategic approaches to a problem.
- You want to compare the use of two different mathematical tools or representations to solve the problem.

Before you continue to the next chapter, reflect on these questions:

1. When do you think a *Compare and Connect* discussion would be most useful in a unit you are currently teaching or are about to teach?
2. This discussion structure could be useful in helping students see connections between their invented strategies and standard algorithms. How might the *Compare and Connect* discussion structure help students really make sense of the notation in standard algorithms?
3. What kinds of anchor charts or displays could you keep after a *Compare and Connect* discussion to support students' work as you move through a unit?
4. What norms currently support thriving discussions in your classroom? What may be a next step in deepening your classroom discussions?

CHAPTER 4

TARGETED DISCUSSION: WHY? LET'S JUSTIFY

During math discussions, we regularly ask our students to explain their thinking. As teachers, hearing students' thinking helps us know what they understand and what they are coming to understand. For students, producing explanations is an important part of making sense of mathematics, and students should always be asking themselves, "Does this make sense?" It is also important for students to learn how to push further and ask themselves, "*Why* does this make sense?" Asking *why* challenges students to reason about mathematics and to develop, use, and justify how mathematical ideas work (Russell 1999). Reasoning and justifying are complex and important practices of being a mathematician.

When students reason and justify they are simultaneously engaging in both mathematical content and practices, specifically the mathematical practice of argumentation. As students individually and collectively make sense of mathematics, they make conjectures, justify their conclusions, communicate with and to others, and engage with the arguments of others. As the Common Core State Standards for Mathematical Practices tell us, "Elementary students can construct arguments using concrete referents such as objects, drawings, diagrams, and actions … Students at all grades can listen or read the arguments of others, decide whether they make sense, and ask useful questions to clarify or improve the arguments" (Common Core State Standards Initiative 2012).

As students listen and contribute to the arguments of others, we are reminded that justifications are often collaborative in nature. Students share their arguments and build on the justifications of others—which works to broaden participation. As Russell and her co-authors describe in *But Why Does It Work? Mathematical Argument in the Elementary Classroom*, "All students can participate in a discussion about proving, each student bringing her or his own resources and engaging at the edge of her or his understanding" (2017, 9). In other words, our collective arguments are stronger because of the varied lived experiences children bring to our discussions. In this chapter, we focus on discussions designed to spotlight reasoning and argumentation; we call these conversations *Why? Let's Justify*.

There are natural times in the elementary curriculum when *Why? Let's Justify* can come in handy, as students reflect on general ideas, concepts, or strategies. Why do you simply append two zeros to a number when we multiply by 100? When can you break up the divisor in a division problem to make the problem easier? What happens when you add two even numbers? Why are four-tenths and two-fifths equivalent to one another? When you are multiplying two numbers, and you multiply one factor by two and divide the other factor by two, why does the product stay the same?

Planning for a *Why? Let's Justify* discussion requires us to identify the main idea or generalization we want students to examine. We need to anticipate and think through how the justification will sound as students share ideas over the course of the discussion. During the discussion, we need to listen for procedural descriptions that students might give and be sure not to have the conversation stop there. When we press beyond procedural explanations into explanations that include reasoning, we are supporting students in justifying their ideas. For example, if students say that order doesn't matter in addition because that's a turnaround fact, we need to think about how students might use an understanding about the behavior of addition as an operation to justify the commutative nature of addition (Russell, Schifter, and Bastable 2011). How do we plan for a discussion that helps students create those convincing models or explanations? First, it is helpful to consider the forms justifications may take.

Forms of Justification

Students encounter and generate many mathematical generalizations throughout their elementary years. Research into children's thinking has helped us think about the forms of justification that children use when they are trying to convince themselves of an idea. (See Lannin, Ellis, and Elliott 2011 for a nice discussion of mathematical reasoning in the elementary and middle school years.)

Let's go back to the idea of turnaround facts in addition to explore different kinds of justification.

1. *Justification through appeal to authority*
   Students may justify an idea because someone or something else told them it was true: "My Mom showed me that it doesn't matter what order you add numbers; it's always the same" or "The book says so."
2. *Justification through examples*
   Once we show students that they can't just rely on the word of an expert, they might try to convince themselves that a mathematical statement is true by giving lots of examples that work. If order doesn't matter in several examples (5 + 6 = 6 + 5; 3 + 4 = 4 + 3, and so on), then you can be convinced that it must be true. As students become more familiar with our number system, they might try special cases—fractions or negative numbers, for example—to test if an idea still holds. This kind of play with examples can be quite useful for students because it gets them to try out the generalization and be sure they understand what the statement is saying. Of course, examples alone can't necessarily justify that something is true; all that it takes to refute a mathematical statement is one example where the idea doesn't hold. Order does matter in subtraction, because 5 − 3 is not the same as 3 − 5.
3. *Justification through a generic example*
   As students gain more experience, specific examples might be replaced with a generic one. The idea of commutativity might be explored in the context of a specific case, but students might say it wouldn't matter what numbers were chosen: the same idea would still hold. Students may also develop models that help them make their case. For example, to explain commutativity,

students might make a model with two different-colored unifix cubes, showing the specific case of adding 7 and 5. They use the model to show that since addition means combining quantities, the sum is 12, whether 7 is added to 5 or 5 is added to 7. When students start playing with a generic example, they use a specific model but talk about it in more general ways. Students would say they could link together any number of unifix cubes of one color and any number of another color. Whatever the addends, the sum wouldn't change. When they do that, students are using the example of 5 and 7 generically. Susan Jo Russell, Deborah Schifter, and Virginia Bastable (2011), in their book *Connecting Arithmetic to Algebra,* call these forms of justification representation-based proofs, and they are particularly powerful ways for elementary-aged students to engage in justifying claims.

4. *Justification through deductive argument*
   In mathematics, justifications are always based on logic. When students are convinced by the truth of one statement, they can use that agreed-upon understanding to connect to other statements that follow by logical deduction. So, once we are convinced that order doesn't matter in addition with two numbers, students can begin to extend that idea logically to the idea that order doesn't matter in addition regardless of the number of addends. Younger students may rely on physical or visual models more than on symbols to show the way several ideas logically build on each other.

Thinking about the power of justifying through generic examples can be helpful as you plan for and facilitate a *Why? Let's Justify* discussion.

Primary Vignette: "Why Do We 'Append Zeros' When We Multiply by Multiples of 10?"

Ms. Latimer's third-grade class has been happily working on skip-counting tasks. They have noticed a pattern that the tenth, twentieth, and thirtieth multiple of a number all end in zero and have started to notice that when you multiply by 10, you "add" one zero to the number, as the students say. Ms. Latimer decides to make this a focus of her next targeted discussion. She wants to make sure students understand what is happening when a zero is added to the end of a number and can reason about why. She has a hunch that "adding a zero" is becoming a "trick" students can use, but she knows that in order for students to generalize to bigger numbers and more complex mathematics in the future, reasoning about place value is important now. You can see her notes in the planning template in Figure 4.1. She uses a problem context inspired by *Mini Lessons for Extending*

Figure 4.1 Ms. Latimer's planning template for a *Why? Let's Justify* discussion: Appending a zero when multiplying by 10

Why? Let's Justify
What mathematical strategy or idea are we targeting in our discussion? • "Adding a zero" when multiplying by 10. It's not a trick... why does this work?!? • Use a specific example: 2 × 3 and 2 × 30 • Will invite students to generate stories for 2 × 3 and will build on those for 2 × 30
What is the explanation I want students to come up with? (Include sketch of any representations that might be helpful for the explanation.) You attach or append a zero (not "add") because the product is 10 times larger. 2 × 3 = 6 Ten of these will fit in here. It is 10 times bigger. 2 × 30 = 60 When you multiply by 10, something gets 10 times bigger. So, 2 × 3 ten times is 2 × 3 × 10, or 2 × 30
Supporting students' thinking (If students say this... then I may ask them this to work toward stronger justification.)

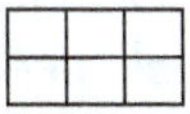

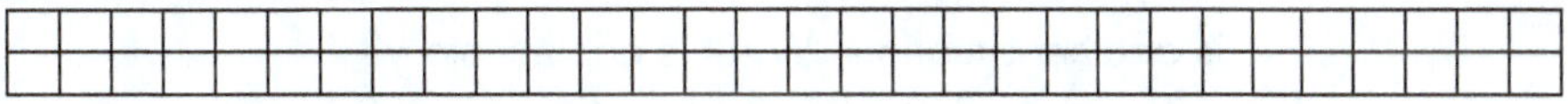

What students might say	How I might respond
"Add a zero."	"If I 'add a zero' to 6, I just get 6. Do you mean append or attach a zero?" "Connect the quantities back to the array model or the story situation. How many 2 × 3s do you think fit into 2 × 30?"

Multiplication and Division (Uttenbogaard and Fosnot 2008). On her planning template, Ms. Latimer writes down the representations that she'll use and the questions she might ask students in order to get to the explanation she is aiming to produce. A blank version of the planning template can be found in Appendix C.

Ms. Latimer: Today I want us to gather together on the carpet so we can have a discussion and try explaining what it means to multiply by 10. You have been working on multiple towers and you've been working on finding the twentieth multiple or the thirtieth multiple of a number. Today we are going to figure out what it means when you multiply by 10. I have some problems we are going to work on. We are going to start with a problem that feels familiar to you. *(Writing 2 × 3 on the whiteboard.)* What does 2 times 3 mean if you put it in a story? In your own words? What does it mean?

Iris: It is 6.

Ms. Latimer: You want to tell us what it is, what it equals? It's 6. Iris is telling us 2 times 3 is the same as 6. What I want us to think about now is what does that mean? What is a situation for 2 times 3?

Tessa: There are 2 roller coaster cars and 3 people can ride in each car.

Ms. Latimer: Wow, that would be so awesome! Can you imagine that? I love roller coaster rides. There are 2 cars and 3 people in each car. That's one way of thinking about what 2 times 3 means. 2 times 3 means having 2 groups and there are 3 in each group. Or, in our story, there are 2 roller coaster cars and 3 people in each car. What is another situation? What is another story?

Josh: There are 2 children and each one had 3 toys.

Ms. Latimer: Okay, 2 children and they each have 3 toys to play with.

Since the mathematical goal for this discussion is to be able to generate a justification for why attaching a zero works in multiplication, Ms. Latimer is starting the discussion by inviting students to think through an explanation for a specific example for 2 × 3; understanding what 2 × 3 represents will be an important step in understanding what 2 × 30 represents. She hopes this will lay the groundwork for producing a more general justification.

Ms. Latimer: I'd like to show you a picture of 2 times 3. *(Holding up a cutout array that is labeled 2 × 3; see Figure 4.2.)* I want to know why I can hold this up as 2 times 3. How does the array show 2 groups of 3? Can you point and show us? Listen for what

Figure 4.2 Ms. Latimer uses this array to depict 2 × 3

Chapter 4 Targeted Discussion: Why? Let's Justify

is the 2 and what is the 3 as we hear people's ideas. *(Holding the array out near the children.)*

Riley: *(Pointing to the array and tracing a finger across the 2 rows of 3.)* Across there are 2 different groups.

Ms. Latimer: Across there are 2 different groups? You have a good idea starting. There is something across. What is it across?

Riley: Three.

Ms. Latimer: Could you imagine that being the 3 people in our roller coaster story example? *(Tracing her finger across the top row of three, then the bottom row of three.)*

Riley: Yes.

Ms. Latimer: Or the toys in our other story example? *(Again, tracing her finger along two rows.)* Here are 3 toys and here are another 3 toys. There are 2 groups of toys.

Riley: Yes.

Ms. Latimer: This array shows that there are 3 kids in one roller coaster car and 3 kids in a second car (sweeping her finger across each row as she points out the 2 groups of 3), or the top row is one set of 3 toys and the row below it is another set of 3 toys. I'd like you to think about what 2 times 3 means and see if you have any questions. If you have a question, you can ask us. Take your time … we'll wait.

Wanting to make sure students have a moment to take stock of their understanding of 2×3 before moving on in the discussion, Ms. Latimer chooses to pause here. She offers wait time so children can notice what they understand and ask questions if they feel unclear about what they've discussed so far. She waits for 10 seconds, observing the students' thinking, thinking herself, and making sure she's supporting the expectation that learners in their class give each other time to think.

Ms. Latimer: I can see you're thinking. Does anyone have a question? *(Pausing for 5 seconds of wait time.)* Okay, it is important that we try to think about what 2 times 3 means. Keep thinking about our story situations as I write out the next problem. *(Places 2×3 array on the whiteboard and then writes 2×30 on the board.)* So, 2 times 30—what do you think that it is going to be? If 2 times 3 is 6, what is 2 times 30 going to be? You can shout it out.

Students: Sixty!

Ms. Latimer: Sixty. How did you figure that out? Who haven't we heard from yet today? We need everybody's ideas to help us figure this out.

Ms. Latimer uses the phrase "Who haven't we heard from?" in order to draw new voices into the discussion. She is establishing the expectation that all students have important contributions to the discussion and that through wide participation—through sharing and active listening—we can reach our goal.

Cooper: You just put a zero on the end of it.

Ms. Latimer: You're right, I can just put a zero on the end of it. But can we explain why that works? How can we explain putting a zero at the end of it? What does 2 times 30 look like? Let's go back to our roller coaster cars. What has changed about the roller coaster story? Let me hear you tell your neighbor what would change in the roller coaster picture.

Cooper: (*Speaking to his neighbor*) You have to put 30 people in the car instead of 3 people. It would be crowded!

Ms. Latimer: What kind of roller coaster would it turn out to be? A giant car! That's exactly what 2 times 30 means. You would have 2 *huge* cars, and there would be 30 people in each car. What about the toys story?

Calli: Each kid would get 30 toys! Yeah!

Ms. Latimer: And each of these 2 children would get 30 toys. Wouldn't that be so fun? We can see, or picture, 2 groups of 30. *(Holding up a 2 × 30 open array).* This is an open array for 2 times 30. I didn't fill in all the little squares because that would be a lot of lines. So let's make sense of why this is 2 times 30. Show us where one of the 30s is. *(Kneeling down next to the children on the carpet and holding out the array for a student to point to. Jeremiah pauses to look at the array and then traces his finger along the top of the open array while Ms. Latimer describes what he is doing.)* Okay, Jeremiah is showing us where the 30 is on our open array. And where is the other 30? *(Jeremiah traces his finger along the bottom of the open array as Ms. Latimer narrates to the class what he is doing.)* There are the kids in one roller coaster car and here are the kids in another roller coaster car. Here are the toys one child has; here are the toys the other child has. *(Ms. Latimer now traces her finger along what would be the 2 rows of 30 if the open array was filled in.)* Okay, I have a new question for us to consider now. How many 2 times 3s do you think fit into 2 times 30? How many 2 times 3s are there in 2 times 30? *(Wait time.)* Everybody think of an idea. Think about what is making you come up with that idea. I'm going to ask many different people to tell us what they think so we can hear each other's ideas. *(Pointing to individual students and eliciting many different answers.)*

Atoosa: Twenty.

Marci: Ten.

Christopher: Six.

Kristine: I'm not sure.

Ms. Latimer: We are hearing many different ideas. *(Records 20, 10, 6 on the board.)* We are hearing some people are still thinking about this. If you need more time you can add in your idea when you're ready.

Atoosa: I revised my answer.

Ms. Latimer: Okay, you revised your answer. Great. What is your new answer?

Atoosa: Ten.

As Ms. Latimer records all the answers on the board and allows students to revise their initial ideas, she is treating students as sense makers and valuing their ideas. She is supporting children in offering up their ideas even if they are not sure their thinking is correct yet. She wants her students to feel safe expressing their ideas and to know they can always revise their thinking as they get more information.

Ms. Latimer: *(Pointing to the 10 already recorded on the board.)* So, here are our ideas. We think there might be 20, 10, or 6. Some of us are not exactly sure yet. Let's try to figure this out. So this is the 2 times 3 array *(holding up the array)* and this is the 2 times 30 array *(pointing to the array on the board)*. Let's see how many of these fit inside. I'm going to lay our 2 times 3 array on top of our 2 times 30 array and draw a line. We can keep track by counting out loud together *(see Figure 4.3)*.

Students: 1, 2, 3, 4, 5 …

Figure 4.3 Ms. Latimer helps the class visualize 2 × 30 by placing the 2 × 3 array within a 2 × 30 array.

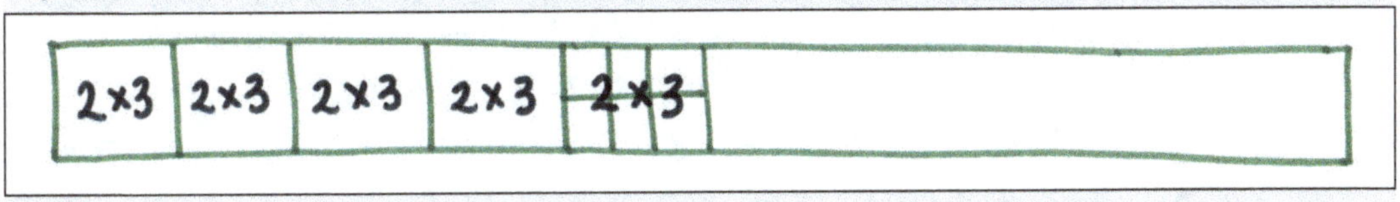

Ms. Latimer: Let's pause here *(the students have counted out five 2 × 3 arrays within the 2 × 30 array).* We can see how many 2 times 3s we have marked so far and how far we have to go. Does anyone want to revise their idea about how many 2 times 3s will fit into 2 times 30?

Kristine: I want to revise!

Ms. Latimer: What do you want to change to?

Kristine: Ten!

Christopher: Me, too.

Ms. Latimer: *(Looking around.)* Anybody else?

At this point in marking the 2 × 30 array, the students have more information. They can see what has been marked and what has not yet been marked and they can use that information to make a new prediction of how many 2 × 3s will fit in 2 × 30. Ms. Latimer chooses to pause and offer students the opportunity to revise their thinking.

Ms. Latimer: *(Pointing to the five 2 × 3s they have already accounted for.)* Okay, here is 1, 2, 3, 4, 5 groups of 6, or five 2 times 3s. Let's keep going. 6, 7, 8, 9, 10.

Students: There are 10!

Ms. Latimer: There are 10. Hmm. Now, that is curious—there are ten 2 times 3s in a 2 times 30 array. Hmm. *(Giving 5 seconds of wait time.)* What do you think about that? Tell us your thinking so we can hear how your thinking is developing *(Giving 5 more seconds of wait time.)*

Elliott: I think it is 10 because 2 times 3 is 6 and 2 times 30 is 60.

Ms. Latimer: Interesting. We hear you saying you think that it is 10 because 2 times 3 is 6 and 2 times 30 is 60. If you take the 6 *(holding up the 2 × 3 array)* and multiply it by 10 you would get 60. Interesting. Hmm. *(Giving wait time.)* Did we change the 2?

Students: No.

Ms. Latimer: What did we do to the 3? Can you look up at those numbers?

Kendra: You added a zero.

Ms. Latimer: I did put a zero there. 'Append' is another way to say we put a zero in the 1's place. Roy, you look like you want to say something.

She repeats Kendra's words to value her idea and then brings in different language, "append," that is more accurate to what happens mathematically when students use this strategy.

Roy: If you do 3 times 10 you get 30.

Chapter 4 Targeted Discussion: Why? Let's Justify

Ms. Latimer: Do other people agree with this? Do you see the multiplication in this picture? *(Holding up the array for 2 × 3.)* If I want to get to 30, how many of these do I need? To get from 3 kids in the car to 30 kids in the car, we multiplied by 10.

Roy: And to get the 6 to 60 we multiplied it by 10.

Ms. Latimer: You know what you're telling us? You're saying we multiplied by 10. I'm going to write these same problems over here in a different way. *(See Figure 4.4.)*

Ms. Latimer: We can write 2 times 3 times 10, and that is the same as 2 times 30.

Lynsey: I never knew that!

Ms. Latimer: Lynsey said she is learning something new. Let's all take a moment and see if you can explain to your partner—after thinking and listening to each other today—what we mean by 2 times 30 being the same as 2 times 3 times 10. Try to put it into your own words, and let's see what sense you're making of this.

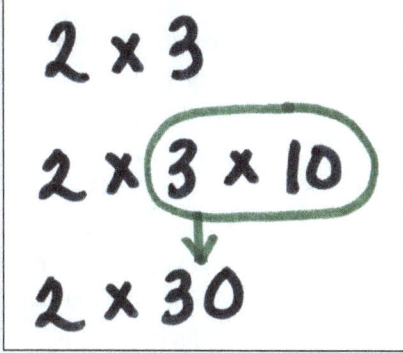

Figure 4.4 Ms. Latimer uses this notation to show the relationship between 2 × 3 and 2 × 30 numerically

This quick turn and talk (see Figure 4.5) allows students to make sense of the idea Roy has just offered. Making sense of 2 × 30 being the same as 2 × 3 × 10 is essential in understanding multiplying by 10; therefore,

Figure 4.5 Ms. Latimer's students engage in a turn and talk to discuss the idea that 2 × 30 is the same as 2 × 3 × 10

Ms. Latimer chooses to highlight the idea in a turn and talk and give children a chance to try saying what they understand. As they talk, students can be overheard saying, "Because 3 times 10 is the same as 30," "Because 2 times 3 is 6, but now we are multiplying by 10, which is 30 plus 30, which is 60, and you can do it 2 times 3 times 10. You don't have to do 2 times 30," and "Because there are ten 6s, that's why! That's why!" Listening in to students' turn and talk gives Ms. Latimer valuable insights into the sense her students are making and helps her think about where to go next.

Ms. Latimer: I would like you to share some of these ideas you are thinking about in your own words. We are on the cusp of being able to explain what it means to multiply by 10 and why you can put a zero in the one's place! That is our goal today. If you say to someone, "It is really easy to multiply by 10; you just attach a zero," it sounds kind of like magic, like it is a trick. But it really isn't a trick. There's a reason why a zero gets put—or appended—at the end, and that is what we are making sense of today. How come when you have 2 times 3 you have 6 and when you have 2 times 30 you have 60? Let's really listen to your classmates here to understand their ideas.

Marie: Three times 10 equals 30, and 2 times 30 is the same as 2 times 3 times 10.

Greg: I would say that 2 times 3 is 6, and that is similar to 2 times 30 is 60.

Rebecca: Like 60 is 10 times bigger than 6. Remember when we counted ten 2 times 3s in the 2 times 30 array? The 2 times 30 array is 10 times bigger. So, like 2 times 3 and then 2 times 3 times 10 or 2 times 30.

Ms. Latimer: Okay, we are hearing lots of good thinking. Rebecca, can you repeat your idea so we can listen again?

Rebecca: Sixty is 10 times bigger than 6. We counted ten 2 times 3s in the 2 times 30 array. The 2 times 30 array is 10 times bigger. We did 2 times 3 and then we did 2 times 3 times 10, and that is 2 times 30.

Ms. Latimer: What do you hear Rebecca saying? Did you understand Rebecca's idea? If there is a part you're not sure about, you can say, 'Rebecca can you explain that part again?'

It can be hard to make sense of complex mathematical ideas and the ways your classmates are thinking about those ideas. Ms. Latimer is thinking about this challenge for her students and she is giving them a second chance to hear an explanation and the language to ask for help from one another. She is supporting students in knowing how to participate as active listeners, especially when they have questions about the idea being discussed.

Stella: Rebecca, can you say the part about 2 times 3 times 10 again?

Rebecca: It's like we know this is 2 times 3 *(taking the array)* and then we see that it takes us 10 times to fill up to 2 times 30. So, that is like 2 times 3 ten times, or 2 times 3 times 10.

Ms. Latimer: Stella, does that help? Do you want to try to say Rebecca's idea?

Stella: Not yet.

Ms. Latimer: Okay. Stella, I like the way you are thinking through Rebecca's idea and saying what you need as a sense maker. Let me add on to our thinking and try saying our thinking out loud. When we multiply by 10, we are making something 10 times bigger. In our problems today, we made 2 times 3 10 times bigger, and 2 times 3 10 times, or 2 times 3 times 10 is 60. So you can attach a 0 to the 6, because *(wait time)* …

Beau: Because … It is 10 times bigger! There is a zero on the end of the 6, because it was 6 but then it was 10 times bigger, so it is 60.

As the conversation concludes there is great energy around the newly emerged justification for why you can "attach a zero." Ms. Latimer invites many more children to say out loud what is happening when you multiply by 10 and take their own try at using words to justify why attaching a zero works. If a student is still feeling uncertain, she invites them to repeat the idea of someone who is feeling more certain, and praises their sticking with a complex idea. She concludes by posing a new set of problems, 4 × 3 and 4 × 30, and challenges students to justify why 4 × 30 is 10 times bigger and why you can append a 0 to the product of 4 × 3 when solving 4 × 30. As the students begin tackling this new set of numbers, they are testing their justification through examples, the second level of justification, to make sure their idea still holds true with different numbers.

During this *Why? Let's Justify* discussion, students in Ms. Latimer's classroom were able to collectively generate a justification for why adding a zero works when you are multiplying by 10. It is important to know that sometimes it may take more than one discussion to generate a justification. Perhaps it will take several discussions to work toward a justification, and each discussion will be an important step in being able to justify with understanding.

Intermediate Vignette: Fourth Graders Reason About Decomposing a Factor in Multiplication

Mr. Crandall wants to support his fourth-grade students in thinking about why it works to decompose a factor by its place value when you are multiplying a one-digit number by a two-digit number. He chooses to pose a true/false equation to

Figure 4.6 Mr. Crandall's planning template for a Why? Let's Justify discussion: Decomposing a factor by its place value to multiply efficiently

Why? Let's Justify
What mathematical strategy or idea are we targeting in our discussion? $$6 \times 19 = 6 \times 10 + 6 \times 9$$ True or false? Remember to ask "Why?"
What is the explanation I want students to come up with? (Include sketch of any representations that might be helpful for the explanation.) Choose either 6 groups of 19 or 19 groups of 6. Stick with one interpretation for today's lesson. Six groups of 19 is the same as 6 groups of 10 and 6 groups of 9—and be able to use the picture to see, understand, and prove why. Draw picture on the board so that groups of 10 and groups of 9 are in line. This will help students see groups of 19. Could also draw a picture of 19 groups of 6. So the picture should be 10 groups of 6 and then 9 groups of 6, which makes 19 groups of 6
Supporting students' thinking (If students say this ... then I may ask them this to work toward stronger justification.)

What students might say	How I might respond
"The numbers are broken up."	"How are the numbers broken?" Establish that it's by place value components.
Read the number sentence using only language of "times."	Ask them to use the language of "groups of." (E.g., 6 groups of 19 is the same as 6 groups of 10 and 6 groups of 9.)

his students to help them develop a justification for this idea. He anticipates that he will ground this discussion in a specific example in order to lay the foundation for students to explore whether decomposing one factor according to place value will be a viable way to multiply a two-digit number by a one-digit number. Mr. Crandall's planning template is shown in Figure 4.6.

Mr. Crandall: Class, we are going to do an activity called a true/false equation. I'm going to write an equation, and you get to think about whether this equation is true or false and how you know whether it's true or false. When I write the equation I don't want you to figure out the answer to it. Instead, I want you to study the numbers and see if you can come up with a reason for why you think it's true or false. Let me give you an example. Let's say I gave you this equation: 3987 + 2365 = 2365 + 3987 (Mr. Crandall writes the equation on the board.) See these big numbers? Think to yourself, is the equation true or false, and can you figure it out without actually adding up those two numbers in your head?

Mr. Crandall pauses for wait time, allowing children to examine the numbers and think (see Figure 4.7). He's purposely given them large

Figure 4.7 Mr. Crandall's students use think time to consider a true/false equation

numbers so that they will examine the quantities instead of automatically computing to compare the two expressions.

Mr. Crandall: Would you do this: Would you check in with the person next to you? Do you have a reason why this is true or false?

Mr. Crandall kneels down to listen as students talk. One can be overheard saying, "It's true! It's true because they are just switched around!" He can hear students are noticing quantities are the same on both sides of the equation. He decides to hear more about this thinking and to press for justification.

Mr. Crandall: I want you to say out loud what you think. Is it true or false? Everybody?
Students: True!
Mr. Crandall: I hear some consensus. That means it sounds like you agree that it is true. But *why* is it true? I heard some people talking about why it is true. Why is it true?

Through his questions, Mr. Crandall is pressing students to explain why. Explaining, or justifying, why a number sentence is true is the goal of this discussion. He's made a note to himself on his planning sheet to ask why often during this talk. His students are learning that a mathematical explanation includes why.

Drew: Because you only switched the numbers around.
Mr. Crandall: I only switched the numbers around. And why does that make it the same?
Lynn: They are the same numbers you switched around, and so it would be the same answers.
Mr. Crandall: Who can tell me something about how addition works that helps me know it would be the same? Can we add on to this idea?

Mr. Crandall is noticing that they are justifying the equation by labeling it as a turnaround fact. Listening carefully to hear and understand students' thinking, Mr. Crandall asks them to think about the behavior of the operation of addition as they try to generate a justification.

Theresa: You get the same answer and you just switch it around.
Mr. Crandall: I'm hearing when you switch it around you get the same answer to the same problem. Here is an example about how you would use the idea about addition: When you are combining two

numbers, if you have some amount here and a different amount here and you put them together you will still get the same total or sum, even if you switch the order of your amounts. We are using the idea of what adding means to explain why.

Mr. Crandall recognizes that it might be hard for students to explain something that seems so obvious to them. He doesn't belabor the point further, except to provide a very brief example of what he wants them to think about today.

Mr. Crandall: Now that you have an idea of what true/false means, I am going to give you a different problem. Before I do that, let's notice, did anyone tell me what the answer to this problem was?

Students: No.

Mr. Crandall: So for the next one, I don't want you to tell me what the answer is. I want you to think about the numbers. *(Mr. Crandall writes the following equation on the board.)* $6 + 19 = (6 \times 10) + (6 \times 9)$

Students excitedly talk. One can be overheard saying, "Yeah! It is true because 10 plus 9 is 19."

Mr. Crandall: I hear people saying this is true. Does everyone think this is true?

Students: Yes!

Mr. Crandall: Is anyone not sure? It is okay if you're not sure. If you're someone who is not sure, let's see how listening to your classmates' ideas can support your thinking. We are trying to explain why this equation is true. Are we convinced by our explanations? Let's listen carefully to how one person starts, and then we will add on.

In order to be able to justify why, you really have to understand the idea. When you are unsure, it can be challenging to know what to listen for in the discussion. Mr. Crandall is explicitly supporting students who may be unsure, or are on their way to understanding why, in knowing what to listen for.

Janine: You broke it by place value.

Mr. Crandall: Janine, thanks for getting us started. You said I broke it by place value. Let's see who can add on.

By offering a student the opportunity to share a kernel of an idea in order to get the conversation started and then inviting classmates to add on, Mr. Crandall is using the talk move of adding on in a unique way. His students know they do not have to have a fully formed idea in order to share. They can share what they do know, and that partial idea can be built upon, or added on to, by others.

Louisa: You know it's true because for the 6 times 9 part you take away the 10 and put the 9 there.

Mr. Crandall: *(Repeats student's idea, then asks a question.)* I want to make sure I'm understanding what you mean, but I'm not sure. Does your idea connect to this idea about place value?

Louisa: Yeah.

Mr. Crandall: Can you tell us how?

Louisa: You make it into more problems when you break it up by place value.

Mr. Crandall: What number am I breaking up?

Louisa: The 10 and the 9 from the 19.

Mr. Crandall: Here is an important part of giving a mathematical reason, a justification. *(Pointing to 6 × 19.)* Let's start with what this part means. Who can tell us what 6 times 19 means? Terrance, you look like you're really thinking. Do you have something to share?

Supporting young mathematicians in justifying their thinking also requires explicit support for what it means to justify. Mr. Crandall is using language all students know ("a mathematical reason") and then the mathematical language they are coming to know ("justification").

Terrance: I'm not sure yet.

Mr. Crandall: Do you want to pass? Do you want to ask another classmate to share? *(Terrance points to a classmate, Grace Marie.)*

Grace Marie: You take one number and you take the other number and you add it that many times.

Mr. Crandall: You said, "You take one number and you take the other number and you add it that many times." Okay, who'd like to take Grace Marie's idea and put it in your own words?

By inviting students to revoice, or put another's idea into their own words, Mr. Crandall supports the other side of talk—listening. When students are encouraged to revoice and add on to others' ideas, they are learning how to listen to understand and build on each other's thinking. Listening is active and must be explicitly attended to within discussions.

Nina: Grace Marie said you take one of the numbers and you take the other number and then you add it that many times. Like, for 6 times 19, you add 6 nineteen times.

Mr. Crandall: Okay, who else can add on to what we're hearing?

Janine: Or you add the 19 six times.

Mr. Crandall: We have two ideas out. *(Turning to all students.)* Do you agree with these ideas? You add the 6 nineteen times or we can have 19 sixes. We need to pick one of these for our work today. Which one should we pick for this problem? *(Students point to 6 ×19.)* Okay, let's try this one. So if this means 6 groups of 19, I'm going to give you some time to think about this with a partner. We started with the idea that this is broken up by place value. How do I finish this by putting words to what this part means? Six groups of 19 is the same as ... Put some words here ... what is this saying?

Pointing to the $(6 \times 10) + (6 \times 9)$, he motions for the students to turn and talk. He then circulates around the room, kneeling down to listen in on students' ideas (see Figure 4.8). He pauses to sharpen the focus on "groups of."

Figure 4.8 Mr. Crandall kneels next to his students to listen during their turn and talk

Mr. Crandall: I hear some people finishing my sentence by saying that 6 groups of 19 is the same as 6 times 10 and 6 times 9. I'm going to challenge you; that's not the sentence I want to hear. I want you to keep this language of "groups of." Try again and see what you can come up with.

He continues to monitor by listening to students' reasoning and then pulls the whole group back together.

Mr. Crandall: What did you come up with?

Dominic: Six groups of 19 is the same as 6 groups of 10 and 6 groups of 9.

Mr. Crandall: Do people hear what Dominic is saying? Dominic, can you say your idea again?

Dominic: I think that 6 groups of 19 is the same as 6 groups of 10 and 6 groups of 9.

Mr. Crandall: Who can repeat Dominic's idea? Jessica?

Jessica: He said that 6 groups of 19 is the same as 6 groups of 10 and 6 groups of 9.

Mr. Crandall: Agnes?

Agnes: He said that 6 groups of 19 is the same as 6 groups of 10 and 6 groups of 9.

By having students repeat Dominic's idea, Mr. Crandall is providing multiple opportunities for students to hear that 6 groups of 19 is the same as 6 groups of 10 and 6 groups of 9, which helps them work toward their goal in today's discussion. He is also choosing to repeat this idea because of the language Dominic is using when he says "the same as." Saying (or reading) the words "the same as" where an equals sign could be placed in an equation is an important part of understanding what equals means, supports students' understanding of relational thinking, and builds a strong foundation for learning algebra (Carpenter, Franke, and Levi 2003).

Mr. Crandall: Let's see if we can draw that in a picture to help us understand this idea. (*Mr. Crandall begins the drawing, narrating what each part of Dominic's idea represents.*) Let's start by making 6 groups. (*Using a black marker, he draws 6 ovals and labels them 1 through 6.*) Now, let's put a group of 10 in each of the 6 groups to show our 6 groups of 10. (*Using a red marker, he adds a 10 to each of the 6 groups.*) And then let's add in our 6 groups of 9. (*He finishes* by using a blue marker to add 9 to each of the 6 groups.) (See Figure 4.9.)

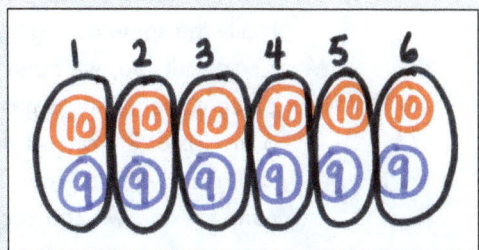

Figure 4.9 Mr. Crandall draws this picture to show 6 groups of 10 and 6 groups of 9

Mr. Crandall: Let's see if this drawing helps us think. I want you to look at this picture and see if you can point to where the 6 groups are *(pause)*. Can you point to where the 6 tens are and the 6 nines? Turn to your neighbor and tell them where you see the 6 groups of 10 and the 6 groups of 9. *(After a few moments.)* Now I want you to tell your neighbor where the groups of 19 are in this picture.

Listening in on the partner groups talking, Mr. Crandall can hear that most students are seeing the 6 groups of 19 as well as the 6 groups of 10 and 9. He decides to bring them back together.

Mr. Crandall: We are creating a mathematical justification. A reason. A reason why this number sentence, 6 times 19 equals (6 times 10) plus (6 times 9), is true. How can you justify that this number sentence is true using this picture? George?

Bringing in a representation and reminding students they are creating a justification are both moves Mr. Crandall is making to sharpen the focus of the discussion and work toward proving why this number sentence is true. With the idea out that 6 groups of 19 is the same as 6 groups of 10 and 6 groups of 9, it is time for the discussion to delve into why these groups are equal, and Mr. Crandall hopes the representation will help support their justification.

George: *(Coming up to the picture and pointing.)* We have 6 groups. In each group we have 10 and in each group we have 9. That is the same as having 19 in each group. So, 6 groups of 10 and 9 is the same as 6 groups of 19.

Mr. Crandall: Who can repeat what George just said? Camilla?

Camilla: He said that we have 6 groups and in each of our groups there is a 10 plus a 9. So that is the same as having 19 in each of our groups.

Mr. Crandall: Do you agree with what George and Camilla are telling us? *(Students use the "me too" signal pictured in Chapter 1 Figure 1.2.)* Why do you agree? Emilio?

> **Emilio:** I agree because I can see it in our picture and I know that 10 and 9 together make 19. And we have 6 of them. Six groups of 19 is really the same as 6 groups of 10 and 6 groups of 9.
>
> **Mr. Crandall:** So, we have proved that breaking the numbers up by place value makes 6 groups of 19 the same as 6 groups of 10 and 6 groups of 9. You just did your first true/false equation! Did we ever talk about what 6 times 19 is? We didn't have to! We can study the numbers and we can prove why the number sentence is true.

Kindergarteners Justify which Items Belong Together

In the above vignettes, we joined a third- and a fourth-grade class to listen to *Why? Let's Justify* discussions. It's important to remember that young children are excellent at reasoning and should also be supported to justify the

Figure 4.10 Ms. Root's planning template for a *Why? Let's Justify* discussion

Why? Let's Justify	
What mathematical strategy or idea are we targeting in our discussion?	
Developing justifications - which lunches belong together and why	
What is the explanation I want the students to come up with? (Include sketch of any representations that might be helpful for the explanation.)	
These lunches belong together because...	
Supporting student thinking (If students say this … then I may ask them this to work toward stronger justification.)	
What students might say	How I might respond
• I /we notice… • These belong together because… • These do not go together because • I disagree with that idea • We agree with that thinking because	• You are paying close attention to details • You are justifying your thinking by saying because • Do you disagree with that thinking? Why? • Do you agree with that thinking? Why? • Do you want to revise your thinking?

mathematics they are learning. Let's join a kindergarten classroom to hear a bit about what it sounds like when young children engage in a *Why? Let's Justify* discussion.

It is early in the school year and Ms. Root plans a discussion with her kindergarten students about the question "What is your favorite food for lunch?" She wants to create an opening for students to begin to share about themselves by posing a question that everyone will have ideas about and she wants to support young mathematicians to develop justifications (see Figure 4.10).

She invites students to a moment of individual think time and then to turn and talk with a partner. As students share with each other, she can hear many different foods—hamburger, peanut butter and jelly, wonton soup, hotdog … She counts down to bring the students back together in a whole group, "5, 4, 3, 2, 1 … okay let's talk in a whole group!"

Ms. Root: A few days ago I was in the lunchroom and you might have noticed that I had my camera. I took photographs of your lunches and all the lunches of the four kindergarten classes! *(Displaying an array of photos of lunch boxes under the document camera, Ms. Root transitions through four slides of lunch box arrays.)* As you look at these lunches, what are your math noticings? What do you notice or see in these photographs? *(See Figure 4.11; students point to the screen as they enthusiastically share.)*

Juno: That lunch is mine! I also had a sandwich that is not in the picture.

Addy: That lunch has 2 strawberries! More lunches have strawberries, too.

Jack: Some of the lunches have my favorite foods—like strawberries and oranges.

Harper: There are foods that are orange but are not oranges—like carrots and cheese. The foods are the same color but they are different foods that don't taste the same.

Rosalie: All the lunches are different because we don't eat the same and people like different things and have different foods in their family.

Lily: *(Jumping up to use the pointer to point to the whiteboard.)* This one has a plate. Some lunches have many compartments but that one has only one place on the plate. Not each lunch box has the same number of spaces for foods! *(See Figure 4.12.)*

Ms. Root: So many noticings! I hear you are beginning to notice foods, colors, and that there is more than food in the pictures. You see spaces

104 INTENTIONAL TALK AND LISTENING

Figure 4.11 Photographs of student lunches and the caption "What are your math noticings?"

and shapes in the lunch containers. Let's look at these lunches more closely using photographs of them. I have copies of all of these lunches for you to look at with friends at your tables. At your table, you will find an envelope that has cut outs of all the lunches. Your job is to take out the photographs and spread them all over your table. Then, you can notice and wonder about the lunches and decide together which lunches belong together and *why*. You might have ideas that

Figure 4.12 Lily points to the whiteboard

are the same or different from your friends at your table and your job is to say why you think the lunches belong together. You might change your thinking after listening to other mathematicians at your table *(see Figure 4.13)*.

Figure 4.13 Students work together to sort lunch box images

As students begin to take out the lunch box photographs, Ms. Root can hear them making more noticings. Shivani exclaims, "Everything is different, this one has big compartments" while Wynn announces, "This one has circles and this one has circles!" Sophie, next to Wynn, adds in, "These have purple!" (scooting three images together that have shades of purple containers and foods). In the background, one table begins clustering a pile of lunches that contain cheese, singing "Cheese group!" Students continue to pass, sort, study, and discuss the lunch images while making emerging noticings about which belong together, which do not belong together, and why. The more they notice, and hear each other's noticings, the sharper their collective noticings become: "Oh yeah, there is a little tiny bit of orange here, see right there!"

Ms. Root circulates the classroom to listen in as students sort the images and justify their claims. She sketches notes about the phrases students are using to repeat their words and nurture language of justifications, jotting down, "*I notice ...*", "*These belong together because ...*", "*These do not go together cause ...*", "*I disagree ...*". After listening to each table group's discussion, she culminates with a brief whole group sharing. With students at their tables, she announces, "Ok, mathematicians, we are going to wrap up today by sharing a bit about what you noticed about which lunches belong together and *why*!" Several groups share and new questions and ideas emerge, for example, "We think all these belong together (*pointing to a cluster of photographs*) because they have some meat in them but we don't know if that is a tomato or meat" and "these ones belong together because they have one compartment for each food but these ones do not belong to that group, or they belong to their own group, because they have many foods in one compartment." Ms. Root thanks them for their careful noticings and as students put the lunch images back into the envelopes, she sketches a few notes about how to continue the discussion tomorrow.

The next day, Ms. Root opens the discussion by briefly recapping the day before, "Yesterday you sorted the lunchbox photographs at your table. You were thinking with others about which lunches belonged together and why. You had important noticings about foods, colors, shapes, and sizes. Today, we are going to continue thinking about which lunches belong together. As you think, say what you think and why. Yesterday I heard you saying things like, 'These belong together because …', 'These do not go together cause …'," Also, say what you think about when you hear other people's thinking. Yesterday I heard you say, 'I disagree …' When you do not agree, you can say 'I think differently than you' and ask people about their ideas, 'why do you think that?', and you can always change or revise your thinking. What is really important is your why—why you think something is your *justification*. Once your group decides which lunches belong together, you are going to use glue sticks and paper to make a poster of the lunches you select. We will share our posters—and your justifications—in a little bit."

Students spread the lunch boxes images out again and continued their exploration (see Figure 4.14). Some groups deepened their own thinking from the

Figure 4.14
A pair of students label their sorted lunch set

day before ("Let's keep looking for blue in the photos"), other groups took up the thinking from other groups that was shared at the end of the previous day ("I want to look for lunches with meat in them now"), and some took up brand new pathways ("Let's look for new things today!"). As they discussed, Ms. Root knelt down next to students to listen in, prompting their discussions ("Do you agree with that thinking? Why?") and to infuse language for reasoning and justifying ("You are not sure. Do you want to revise your thinking?" and "When you have your strong why, that is a justification. You are justifying your thinking with saying why you think that").

With their posters completed, Ms. Root called the students up to the carpet to sit together. Before she displayed the first poster under the document camera, she said, "We are going to look at other group's posters. BUT, I am not going to tell you how they sorted the lunch boxes and they are not going to tell you either. Your job, when you look at their thinking, is to try to figure out—how did they group their lunches? Or, what made their group all the same? Okay, here is the first poster. Look at it! How might they have sorted this? What made this group all the same?" The discussion continued with guesses, lively banter, playful argumentation, and focused discussion about why the lunches belonged or did not belong together, with explicit attention to being mathematicians who reason, argue, claim, and justify ideas.

Summary and Reflection Questions: When Do I Want to Have a *Why? Let's Justify* Discussion?

During a *Why? Let's Justify* discussion, the talk narrows upon a general claim in order to closely examine the mathematics and generate a justification for it. Certain types of mathematical ideas lend themselves to a discussion that generates a justification for that idea. You may want to have a *Why? Let's Justify* discussion in these situations:

- A rule or "trick" is commonly used, but students may not have a conceptual understanding of why that rule works and therefore may struggle to generalize the rule with accuracy when solving new problems.
- You can connect a strategy students are beginning to use to a visual model or a problem context in order to make sense of how a strategy works regardless of the numbers. For example, when you want to add two-digit numbers, you can always combine the tens and combine the ones separately and then add them together. The model or context serves as a resource for children to verify and test their justification for why the strategy works.

We want to share with you the guidelines that Susan Jo Russell, Deborah Schifter, and Virginia Bastable (2011) provide about how to focus students' attention on justifying a general claim:

1. Choose accessible numbers when first trying to make sense of a general idea.
2. Use a set of expressions or a true/false equation (like you read about in this chapter's vignettes) and focus on the meaning of the expressions instead of just carrying out the computation.
3. Ask students to show their ideas using cubes, number lines, arrays, story contexts, or other representations they have been working with.
4. Identify general claims worth justifying by listening for the patterns, mathematical relationships, or underlying structure of numbers your students notice as they do mathematics.

Before you go on to the next chapter, reflect on these questions:

1. Why is it important that students have opportunities to reason about and justify mathematics? What messages about mathematics does a focus on reasoning and justification send to young mathematicians?
2. Reflecting on my teaching experiences, what are some of the rules or tricks that I've always wanted my students to make sense of? Which of these might I be able to target in the coming weeks?
3. What generalizations come up as my students develop strategies for adding, subtracting, multiplying, and dividing? How can these general ideas be fodder for *Why? Let's Justify* discussions.
4. How am I currently supporting my students in reasoning, arguing, making conjectures, and justifying their ideas? What are the next steps I want to take in facilitating discussions that incorporate these mathematical practices?

CHAPTER 5

TARGETED DISCUSSION: WHAT'S STRATEGIC AND WHY?

While it is possible for students to solve some problems in many different ways, they also need opportunities to become more selective about when and why to use a particular strategy. In this chapter we focus on a discussion structure we call *What's Strategic and Why?* Instead of eliciting many different ways to solve a particular problem, the teacher structures the discussion in one of several ways:

1. They may begin the discussion by focusing on one strategy and then ask students to generate an effective use of that strategy.

2. They may display a few different ways to solve a problem and ask students to think about which way might be most strategic for that problem and why.
3. They may display a problem and ask for strategic ways to tackle that problem.

With *What's Strategic and Why?* discussions, we're asking students to analyze situations and decide on the effectiveness of particular strategies in specific situations. We want to invite teachers and students to consider this question: "Given these numbers, given this context, or given my available tools, which approach do I want to take and why?" Often being strategic depends on the task and the particular resources we have at hand. By naming this discussion structure *What's Best and Why* in the first edition of our book, we may have inadvertently sent the message that some strategies are just always better than others. It can be tempting to consider the most "efficient" strategy as best, but we've come to learn over the past ten years that selecting what's best is more nuanced and strategic. We are not trying to send the message that there is a universally best approach. Instead we want our students to consider how the purpose of the mathematical question along with the available resources can help us make choices about which strategies to use.

In this second edition, we offer a new name *What's Strategic and Why?* to better communicate our intention that students discuss when, how, and why to use a particular strategy. A shift from what's best to what's strategic emphasizes sense making and intentional choice. The term "strategic" may not be familiar to students at first, but you'll see in the vignettes in this chapter that the teacher doesn't necessarily need to use the term to help students think about when and why they would use particular strategies.

Our first vignette takes us into a fourth-grade classroom in which students think about adding a list of numbers. The class considers changing the order of the addends and estimating in order to figure out the sum. In the second vignette, third graders study subtraction problems in order to judge whether it's more efficient to use an adding on strategy or a removal one.

Fourth Graders Discuss How to Strategically Add a Set of Numbers

Like Kassia Omohundro Wedekind and Christy Thompson write in their book *Hands Down, Speak Out*, "One of the best ways to know what issues students are grappling with is by listening to them talk to each other" (2020, 192). If we want to bring our students to mathematics, one thing we can do is listen to what sparks their interest and curiosity.

Let's visit Ms. Thomas's fourth-grade classroom. As the end of the year is approaching and the class is busy with celebrations and family events, Ms. Thomas hears three of her students talking about their Japanese ancestry and traveling to Tokyo. One of their classmates says they had heard that in Tokyo, you could

Figure 5.1 YouTube video of Mario Kart tour in Tokyo

participate in a real-life Mario Kart by driving Mario Karts around the city. Ms. Thomas seizes the opportunity to bring many of her fourth graders' love for the Mario Kart video game into a mathematics lesson. She talks with her mathematics coach to design a task that begins with students watching and reacting to a brief video clip she found on YouTube depicting tourists on the Mario Kart tour in Tokyo (see Figure 5.1).

Surprise, laughter, and joy cascades through the room as the students watch adults dress up as Mario Kart characters and be guided through the streets of Tokyo as if they were in the video game itself. Students see the tourists pay for their tickets, put on their costumes, get their safety briefings, and have a lot of fun as they drive by Tokyo's landmarks.

Like many mathematical discussions, Ms. Thomas begins the conversation by asking pairs of students to share what they notice and wonder about in the video (see Figure 5.2).

Figure 5.2 Students share what they noticed in the real-life Mario Kart video

Figure 5.3 Ms. Thomas records what students are noticing and wondering about after watching the real-life Mario Kart video

Chapter 5 Targeted Discussion: What's Strategic and Why? 115

It is not hard to generate conversation around what captured their attention. Ms. Thomas writes the ideas on a chart paper, listing them under columns labeled "notice" or "wonder" (see Figure 5.3):

- Everyone who was driving the go kart was dressed as a main character.
- I wondered how fast the go karts can go.
- I noticed that you had to have a driver's license to drive them.
- Whenever I play Mario Kart I notice there are cool places. I am wondering if it is based off of Tokyo.
- I wonder if the map has important places in Tokyo.
- I wonder how far they drove the go karts.
- I noticed the karts are not the same.
- I wonder how much it costs to do a tour.
- I noticed that there was a guide.
- I noticed that Tokyo copied France. The Tokyo Tower is like the Eiffel Tower.
- I wonder why they don't have seatbelts.
- I wonder how many people can do a tour.

There is so much to delight over in these observations. Jason is just floored to find out that the place names in the game that he loved were actual places in Tokyo. He had no idea that the Rainbow Bridge actually existed! Students are keen on noticing differences in the karts on the video and the karts in the actual game. And of course, when one student notices the drivers weren't wearing seatbelts, they want to play back the video to see if they were wearing lap belts like you would on an airplane. While you have to have a real driver's license to go on the tour, the students are clearly enchanted by the possibility that one day in the future, if they are able to go to Tokyo, they could find themselves on the streets in a real-life Mario Kart. Before they end this part of the lesson, Ms. Thomas asks the students if they thought mathematics could be useful in answering any of the questions they raised. The students readily agree they could use mathematics to figure out the tour's cost and how fast the Mario Karts were going. They are especially interested in the length of the tour, in terms of distance.

Later that day, Ms. Thomas meets with her grade-level team and their mathematics coach to think about the possible ways this initial conversation could be taken further and deeper. As Ms. Thomas and her colleagues brainstorm what to do in the next mathematics lesson, they come up with the idea of finding a map of the tour and sharing data that students could use to answer some of their questions. They make a slide of this information (shown in Figure 5.4) and decide to list the distances between a few of the key places on

Figure 5.4 Ms. Thomas projects this slide with a map and data about Tokyo's real-life Mario Kart tour

Data	
Cars max speed 60,000 meters an hour	
Cost of Ticket: • 9,000 Yen for 1 hour • 16,000 Yen for 2 hours 1 dollar=150 yen	
Rainbow bridge to Tokyo Tower	8,047 meters
Tokyo Tower to Tokyo Dome	9,334 meters
Tokyo Dome to Kaminarimon Gate	7,225 meters
Kaminarimon Gate to Shuto Expressway	11,748 meters
Shuto Expressway to Rainbow Bridge	9,012 meters

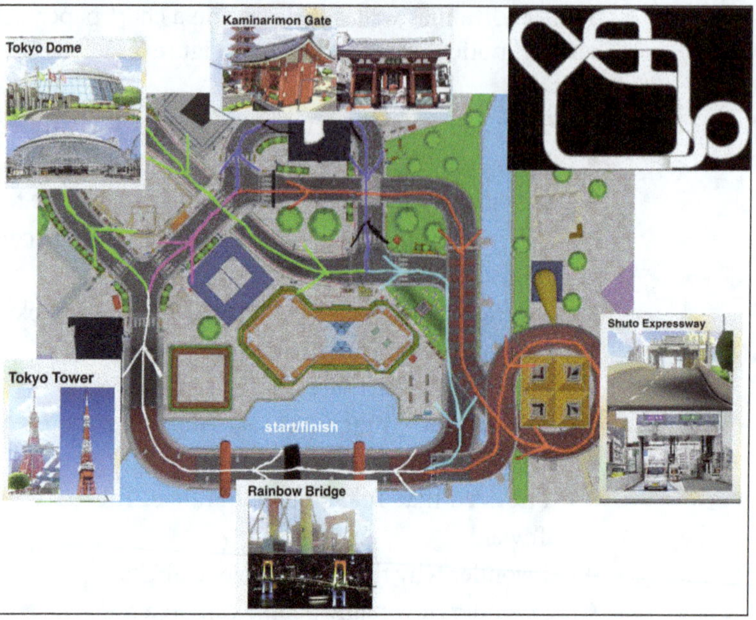

the tour that students were talking about and noticing. Because students work with larger numbers in fourth grade, they use Google maps to approximate the distances in meters. They also list an approximate exchange rate between the Japanese yen and the US dollar for students who might be interested in how much the tour costs.

Ms. Thomas begins the second day of mathematics work on the Mario Kart context by reminding her students what they had done last time.

Ms. Thomas: So on Wednesday, we watched a video about Mario Kart in Tokyo, Japan, and you all talked about what you noticed and wondered in that video. Some teachers and I met after school on Wednesday, and we collected some data that we think would be helpful to answer the questions that interest you the most. So I want to show you that data, and then I want you to be thinking about what you notice and wonder. Maybe you want to start thinking about which of the math questions from the anchor chart we made on Wednesday you could answer using the data that we are giving you. I'll give you a second to do some quiet think time, and then we'll share with the partner *(see Figure 5.5).*

Figure 5.5 Ms. Thomas listens in as students discuss the data she shared with the class

Ms. Thomas begins this discussion in a familiar way, giving students time to return to the context from the previous day's class and process what they are seeing with a partner. This kind of move prepares students to think, listen, and start to share their ideas with one another. After students share what they notice about the data, they sit at their desks with copies of the data to work on whichever problem interests them. As Ms. Thomas and the instructional coach, Ms. Klein, circulate together, they observe some students thinking about the cost of the tour in US dollars. Another student gets interested in trying to figure out how much ground could be covered in one hour versus two given the maximum speed of the Mario Karts. Many students are interested in using the map and data to figure out the total tour distance. It's probably not surprising that many students work on finding the distance by adding the distances in the order they appeared in the table. After observing students at work, Ms. Thomas and Ms. Klein huddle together briefly to consider how Ms. Thomas might bring the whole class back together to have a shared discussion. They decide it might be possible to hold a *What's Strategic and Why?* conversation. They think about asking students to sit back and ponder the list of distances and ask themselves if they could think about whether adding the distances in the order listed made sense, or whether there was a more strategic way of figuring out the total tour distance. As they huddle, Ms. Thomas jots down a few questions she could ask:

- How could you be strategic in deciding how to add these numbers?
- What do you notice about the numbers that would help you rearrange them to add them all up?
- Why would that order help you with the addition?
- Is there another order that makes sense and would be strategic?
- How could estimating help you?

Ms. Thomas and Ms. Klein think that students might start by adding the bottom two numbers because their sum is close to 20,000 meters, and they wonder if students will bring up estimating in their decision making.

Ms. Thomas asks the students to come back to the rug and begins a brief discussion while projecting the map and data (Figure 5.4).

Ms. Thomas: Okay, I have a question for us to talk about. What do you notice about the numbers that would help you come up with the total? Like, you could just go in order, right, and add them all up. That definitely works. But I'm wondering what else you might do to be strategic. Think about this for yourself first and then with a partner.

Chapter 5 Targeted Discussion: What's Strategic and Why?

After some time to contemplate Ms. Thomas's question, Jabari volunteers to share first.

Jabari: I was thinking about if we could just add up the thousands place first, yeah, and take them off the hundreds. And then what I would do is I would add all the hundreds up, and then add that to the answer I got from the thousands place.

Jabari surprises Ms. Thomas and Ms. Klein right off the bat. His response is not one of the ideas they had quickly anticipated but it made good sense. If you add all the thousands up first and then the hundreds, you'd have quite a reasonable estimate. They had considered that estimating might be helpful for the students, but they didn't think of Jabari's idea. This was a good reminder to stay open to the strategies students generate.

Ms. Thomas: Oh wow, I have to tell you I had not thought of that myself. So, let's be sure we're following what you're saying. How are you hearing what Jabari is saying?

Leila: Well, is he just like doing some of the problem? He said he could just add all the thousands and ignore the rest of the number. Then go back and add the hundreds. But what about the rest of the numbers?

Jabari: It would give you a pretty good estimate.

Ms. Thomas: It would give you a pretty good estimate. So, do we need an exact number? What do you think, Leila?

Leila: Maybe. I guess not.

Ms. Thomas: What do you think, Jabari?

Jabari: I just want to know about how long it is. I'm not sure the exact total matters.

Ms. Thomas: I'm thinking you're saying that it depends on your purpose—if I could re-voice what you're saying. If you cared, or if you really needed, the exact total, you could add the tens and ones. But if you didn't, you could just focus on the thousands and hundreds, is that what you're thinking?

Jabari: Yeah, the thousands and hundreds are the most important part. Because like that's the biggest part of the number.

Leila: I see what you're saying.

Cristina: I have another way. You could round the 8047 down to 8000, 9324 down to 9000, 7225 down to 7000, 11,748 up to 12000. I'm basically just going to the nearest 1,000. And then I'll add maybe 1,000 because I know the hundreds make at least 1,000.

Ms. Thomas: So what I'm hearing you say, Cristina, is you might not get the exact answer, but you'll get close because you're going to estimate by rounding to the nearest thousand. And what I also heard you say is you're going to add in 1,000 at the very end to make up for the hundreds and the tens and the ones place that you didn't add in. So far, we've heard two different ideas to find the total of a list of numbers that both involve estimating. I have to tell you that I wasn't thinking about that myself when I asked you that question, but I can see that it's a good use of estimating. Let's just be sure we can restate what these two different ways are and what's strategic about them. If you could turn and talk to your neighbor and see if you have a comment or a question about it.

Ms. Thomas was surprised that her students came up with estimating as a way to be strategic, but given the context of this problem, she thinks it's quite a reasonable choice.

Ms. Thomas: I'm going to ask Nate and Sari to repeat the strategies in their own words.

Nate: You can round up or down to whatever 1,000 you're close to. Like if it's lower than 500, then you keep it at that thousand or if it's higher, then you can go up. That's what Cristina did.

Sari: Or you could add all the thousands like they are and all the hundreds. And then see if you want to add any more. That's what Jabari did.

Ms. Thomas: It seems to be like we're seeing the differences between these two estimation strategies. What other comments or questions do you have?

Jo: Well, I was just thinking that if you wanted to find the exact total, you could use Jabari's strategy and just add the tens and ones exactly as they are.

Ms. Thomas: Oh yeah I see that. Do you all see what Jo is saying? (*Students make the "me too" sign, nod their heads or say, "yeah."*) Thanks for sharing what you noticed. Jabari could adjust his estimating strategy if he wanted to get the exact total. It's time for us to wrap up. I want to say that the ideas we shared are good examples of when estimating is a strategic thing to do. And today, that was our goal, to sit back and look at these numbers to figure out how we wanted to tackle adding them all up.

Ms. Thomas is happy with how this discussion unfolded even though, and maybe especially because, it didn't quite look like what she anticipated. That would not be the first time a class discussion has taken an unexpected turn, and it is a joy of teaching! But Ms. Thomas always learns something from how her students are approaching problems. She found the discussion about estimation valuable and ended it by highlighting that students were really thinking about how, when, and why estimation could be strategic. One thing to notice about this discussion is that they didn't actually complete the estimation themselves to get to the total number. The goal of this discussion was to surface how to go about tackling the problem so it wasn't necessary to fully carry out each strategy.

Third Graders Discuss Counting Back Versus Counting On

Mr. Soeur's third graders have a nice repertoire of strategies for subtraction. They can think about subtraction as removing one quantity from another or as finding the difference between two quantities. His students have been showing flexibility in moving up and down the number line. He'd like for them to think explicitly about when it might be strategic to count backward and remove a quantity from one number in order to find the difference and when to count forward and find the distance between two numbers. Mr. Soeur knows that how far the numbers are away from one another can sometimes make one strategy more efficient than another. He doesn't want to assume that his students have realized this too. So, he uses the *What's Strategic and Why?* planning template to help him raise this issue explicitly (see Figure 5.6).

Mr. Soeur uses a set of problems from the previous day, when he focused only on generating strategies. This particular sequence of computational problems, or "number string," is designed so that the difference between the two numbers in each problem is purposefully exaggerated. He chooses problems where the computation is not that challenging so he could focus their energies on which subtraction strategy to use and why.

Our work with number strings is informed by the research of Catherine Fosnot and Maarten Dolk and their *Young Mathematicians at Work* series (particularly *Constructing Number Sense, Addition, and Subtraction*, 2001). We are taking up their ideas about adding on versus removing to imagine a targeted discussion about finding the distance between numbers and engaging in a discussion with children about what's strategic and why. *Number Talks* by Sherry Parrish (2014) and *Making Number Talks Matter* by Cathy Humphreys and Ruth Parker (2015) are two other helpful resources.

Figure 5.6 Mr. Soeur's planning template for a *What's Strategic and Why?* discussion about counting back versus counting on

What's Strategic and Why?
What are my mathematical and social goals? What are we trying to be strategic about?
To think together about which strategy to use when subtracting numbers. Specifically, counting back when numbers are far apart. Counting on when numbers are close together.
What tasks/problems/prompt will help us discuss what is strategic and why?
Number string 33 − 4 33 − 7 42 − 37 33 − 28 • Return to strategies from yesterday. • Ask students to think about why they chose going backward or taking away for first two and adding up for the second two. Perhaps focus just on what they did for 33 − 4 and 33 − 28. • Ask students to reflect on why those strategies work in relation to how the operation of subtraction behaves.
What questions might I use? What would I like to hear from my students?
When numbers are far apart, it can be easier to go backward from the larger number, to take away. When numbers are close together, it can be easier to go forward from the smaller number, to count on or add up. Either way works because we can think about subtraction as comparing two numbers and seeing how far apart they are from each other or as taking away one amount from another.

Chapter 5 Targeted Discussion: What's Strategic and Why?

Mr. Soeur: Today I want to look carefully at two strategies that you're all using and think about when you might choose to use one strategy instead of the other. We know mathematicians often have many ways to solve a problem and that mathematicians, before solving a problem, stop to think carefully about which strategy to use depending on the numbers in the problem. So let's begin by looking at the number string we were solving yesterday and remember the two main ways you were solving these subtraction problems.

The Common Core State Standards for Mathematical Practice (2012) have given Mr. Soeur some nice language about how to help students learn what it means to do mathematics. Today, he is highlighting the idea of planning a solution pathway before jumping in, as described in the first mathematical practice, "make sense of problems and persevere in solving them." As you will see, he will also help his students think about the meaning of subtraction which connects with the seventh mathematical practice of "analyzing structure." He also wants to keep supporting students to express themselves and show agency when doing math by slowing down and taking the time to notice features in the problem. He doesn't want his students to just quickly get through problems or get bogged down because they think they have to use a tedious strategy.

Figure 5.7 The poster showing the previous day's number string

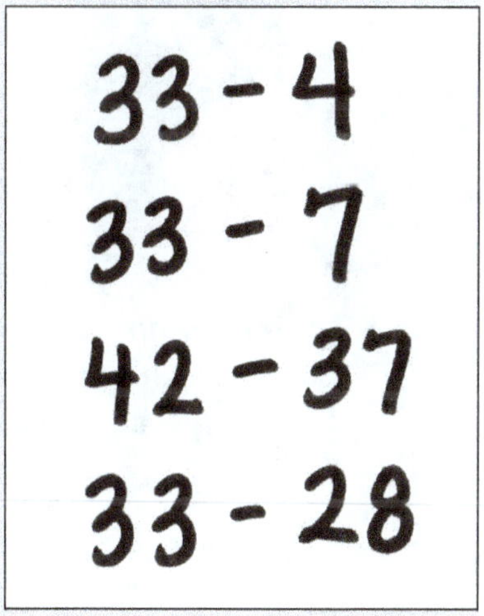

$$33 - 4$$
$$33 - 7$$
$$42 - 37$$
$$33 - 28$$

Mr. Soeur: *(Pointing to the poster shown in Figure 5.7.)* Here is our number string from yesterday.

Mr. Soeur: I want you to look at our poster from yesterday, and I want you to think to yourself about the ways you and your classmates were solving and discussing each of these problems.

Mr. Soeur rests his chin on his hand to model think time and waits for a full minute before inviting the class to share; see Figure 5.8.

Figure 5.8 Mr. Soeur models think time

Mr. Soeur: Let's begin by focusing on the first set of problems. I want you to turn and tell a neighbor what you remember about the way a lot of us were solving the problems 33 minus 4 and 33 minus 7.

Mr. Soeur chooses to use think time and a turn and talk to allow the students to call up the strategies he wants to highlight. Yesterday's chart helps a lot of students dial back to the previous day. He knows which strategies he wants to focus on and is listening in to the turn and talk in order to invite those students who are talking about the target strategies to share. One way to bring up the targeted strategies in a What's

Chapter 5 Targeted Discussion: What's Strategic and Why?

Strategic and Why? discussion is for the teacher to recap the strategies. Another way is to have the students offer up the strategies, as Mr. Soeur is doing here.

Mr. Soeur: As you were sharing, I could hear many pairs talking about the same strategy. Orlando, will you tell us what you and Vivianne were saying?

Orlando: We remembered that lots of people were counting back. Like for 33 minus 4, people were saying they start with the 33 and then say 32, 31, 30, 29. *(Many students are using the "me too" sign as Orlando speaks.)*

Chaz: Yeah, and people were using, like, the hundreds chart or the number line on our wall to think. *(Pointing to the hundreds chart.)* Like what I did was I pointed to 33 and then I hopped back 4 numbers and landed on the 29.

Mr. Soeur: You are saying that people are using tools—like the number line—that we have in our room to help them solve, and we hear you saying that for a problem like 33 minus 4 people you hopped back. Let me put that strategy on the number line. We can all count back out loud together and I will record our hops on the number line.

Students: 32, 31, 30, 29.

Mr. Soeur planned to use an open number line during this discussion because of the way a number line helps show distance between numbers (see Figure 5.9). One way to think about subtraction is to think about the distance between the two numbers. The numbers in this set of problems from yesterday's class were designed to generate discussion about deciding between using a counting back strategy or counting on strategy based on whether the numbers are close together or far apart.

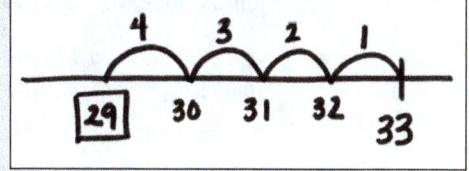

Figure 5.9 A diagram showing counting back strategy on the open number line

Mr. Soeur: We're always working on sharing and listening to one another. I want to add some of the words you were using to describe this strategy. Can you share what you heard so I can add them here?

Jorge: Chaz said he hopped back.

Chaz: Yeah, that's like Orlando saying that he counted back.

Mr. Soeur: Okay, nice listening. Let me just add these phrases here because your words nicely describe this strategy, counting back or hopping back. What I want us to think about is why people were solving this problem by counting back. Take a moment to think on your own, and then turn to a neighbor and explain why you think people were counting back when they solved 33 minus 4. *(After wait time and the turn and talk.)* What ideas do we have?

Marco: It's just easy that way.

Mr. Soeur: Can you say more? What makes it easy?

Marco: It's easy because you just jump back—just jump back 4 times.

Mr. Soeur: Marco says you just jump back 4 times. You only have to make 4 jumps. Ooh, I'm going to add jump back to our list here. Do you agree with Marco? *(Seeing many "me too" signs.)* Why do you agree?

Roshann: I agree with Marco, but you know what's kind of weird? The numbers in the problem are far apart, but on the number line they are close together.

Mr. Soeur: Say more about that, Roshann.

Roshann: *(Getting up and pointing to the numbers in the number string.)* See here the 33 and 4? Those numbers are way far apart *(holding her arms open wide)* but then here on the number line, they are closer *(moving hands together)*.

Mr. Soeur: Roshann, you're noticing something really important. When we jump back only 4 numbers on the number line, where we land is our answer to the subtraction problem. And because we only took 4 jumps back from 33, we land on a pretty close number.

Although it's hard to predict what students are going to say or notice, their ideas can help us make the transitions we need to navigate through a conversation. Mr. Soeur has drawn the counting back strategy (see Figure 5.9) and recorded students' own words. Now he wants them to look at the next two sets of numbers and notice which strategies they used when the numbers were closer together.

Mr. Soeur: I love that Roshann is noticing that it's kind of weird that the numbers are so far apart in the problem but everything looks very close on the number line. Let's take a look at the other problems in our number string. (Pointing to 42 − 37 and 33 − 28.) What do you notice about the numbers in these problems? Zoe?

Zoe: They are bigger.

Tamar: They are close together.

Mr. Soeur: Bigger and close together. Let's focus on 42 minus 37. Do you remember a common way people in our class were solving 42 minus 37?

Kimberlynn: Well, it was more like people were jumping forward.

Mr. Soeur: Can you give us an example?

Kimberlynn: Um, like, for 42 minus 37 people were hopping forward to 40 and then hopping again to 42.

Mr. Soeur: Okay, let me draw that on the number line. Daniel, let's hear what Kimberlynn was noticing. Can you say it again while I'm drawing?

Daniel: For 42 minus 37 she said you could jump forward to 40 and then jump again to 42. *(See Figure 5.10.)*

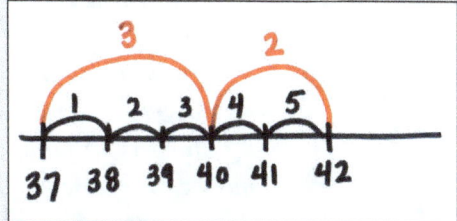

Figure 5.10 A diagram showing jumping forward on the open number line

Mr. Soeur: So, Kimberlynn, you were adding on. You added on by making jumps of 3 and 2.

Kimberlynn: Yeah, 3 gets me to 40 and then 2 more to 42.

Mr. Soeur: So, these two jumps together make 5 jumps altogether. I think you're making a useful choice there to get to 40. I remember from yesterday that some people also counted up by ones from 37 to 42. What can I add here to describe your strategy for 42 − 37?

Isabel: Maybe like Kimberlynn said hop forward.

Mr. Soeur: Okay, let me write that. What else?

Gini: Jump forward or like add on.

Mr. Soeur writes those terms as well.

Mr. Soeur: Let's also add count on, since that will match up with what we have for the first two subtraction problems. So going back to what Roshann said, did anyone first think, oh no, these numbers are big, that's going to make the subtraction problem hard? *(Some students nod in agreement.)*

So let's look at these two strategies that you've described as count back, jump back or count forward, jump forward. When you look at the way we are using these two strategies today, I want you to think about what the numbers were like when you were counting back versus when you counted on? Turn and talk to your neighbor about why you think we counted back for the first two problems but counted forward for the second two? I want to hear what sense you're making of this.

Mr. Soeur uses the turn and talk as an opportunity for students to describe what they are noticing and also to hear their ideas and see, as he says, what sense they are making. As he listens in, he can hear many partners talking about the distance between the numbers, using phrases like "close together" and "far apart." He listens further to hear if they were then using what they noticed about distance to determine which strategy, counting back or counting on, was strategic for which problem. He can hear "close together" and "counting on" often together, and, likewise "far apart" and "counting back" being coupled. He decides for the discussion wrap-up to have children try explaining why they think those solutions are strategic for these problems. He asks the class to come back together, summarizes what he was hearing, and asks several children to say out loud why they think counting back when the numbers are far apart makes sense, and why counting on when the numbers are close together is a good fit. Using repeating and revoicing, they make suggestions for how to decide which strategy to use when they subtract:

> "Look at the numbers. If they are super close together, then just add up from one to the other."

> "If the numbers are really far apart, it would take a long time to jump from one to the other. Try jumping back."

> "When the numbers are close together, add up but try to use as big a jump as you can. You don't have to count by ones."

> "Think first. If the numbers are close and you want to subtract, just add on from the smaller number until you get to the bigger one. If the numbers are far apart, then just go backward using the smaller number."

Mr. Soeur records these strategies and summarizes for the class what they are thinking about, showing students how carefully he's listening to them.

Mr. Soeur: I'm proud of the thinking that you've done today. I want you to look at what you've shared. We're starting to think more about what

> we do when we subtract and I love this last statement, "think first." When you take some time to think first, you're thinking about how to tackle the problem, what strategy to use. So, you're thinking about being strategic. I'm going to keep thinking with you about the meaning of subtraction as we work together.

There's so much to accomplish when we teach mathematics. As we think about this vignette, there's still so much more the students could talk about. For example, do the students believe that if they counted back or counted forward, they would get the same answer? Would 33 − 4 have the same answer if we counted back 4 numbers or if we started at 4 and counted up to 33? What kinds of problem contexts help us think about subtraction as explicitly taking away one quantity from another? For example, problem contexts that have an explicit removal action could involve something leaving, getting dropped and rolling away, or getting separated. What kinds of problem contexts could help us think about the second meaning of subtraction as the distance between two quantities? Perhaps situations where we are comparing how far apart two quantities are like comparing ages or heights could help us think about subtraction as difference. What Mr. Soeur accomplishes in today's discussion is helping students pause and notice the different strategies they tended to use based on what the numbers were. Thinking strategically is important to their mathematical learning.

Summary and Reflection Questions: When Do I Want to Have a *What's Strategic and Why?* Discussion?

We want children to have a variety of ways to solve problems. We also want children to be able to select from their repertoire of strategies in order to make wise choices about which strategy to use for a particular problem. Having a *What's Strategic and Why?* discussion allows us to target particular strategies. Perhaps you will choose to focus on a strategy you think is a next step for your students—such as the estimation strategy Ms. Thomas highlighted. Perhaps you will select a few different ways to solve a problem and ask students to figure out in what situation a particular strategy could be more efficient than another—as Mr. Soeur highlighted in the discussion about counting back versus counting on strategies. You can think about whether or not to use the term strategic. You can introduce the term by connecting it to intentional choices that your students are making, identifying and naming that they are being strategic.

You may want to have a *What's Strategic and Why?* discussion in these situations:

- Many students are on the verge of *transitioning from one strategy to another*. For example, students begin to notice a difference between counting up by ones and counting up by tens when adding 27 + 30.
- You would like students to think about *when a particular strategy is useful*. For example, what quantities really lend themselves to a compensation strategy when you round one number and make up for the difference? (29 × 12 is the same as 30 × 12 − 12. Since 29 is so close to 30, it's a good time to round up.) Younger students might talk about when to use a making tens strategy and when a doubles strategy is helpful. You could try a "Would you rather question?" If the problem was 7 + 5, would you rather make a 10 and do 7 + 3 + 2 or change it to 6 + 6? Or, if you were measuring the side of your desk with nonstandard units, would you rather use a paper clip or a pencil? Again, the goal isn't to declare that there is one right answer but to help children make and explain their intentional choices.
- You notice students are getting lost trying to keep track of something and *need to organize information* in order to tackle a problem. For example, how could a chart help keep track of information? Younger students could discuss how to keep track of objects in order to count them all.

Before you move on to the next chapter, take a moment to reflect on these questions:

1. Facilitating a *What's Strategic and Why?* discussion is different from facilitating an *Open Strategy Sharing* discussion. As teachers of mathematics, we are used to eliciting many different solutions and asking children to explain their solutions, but it is interesting to think about how our questioning and talk moves change when the mathematical goal of the discussion changes. How might the questions you ask or the moves you make in a *What's Strategic and Why?* differ from the questions you ask in an *Open Strategy Sharing* discussion? If it is helpful, you can use the moment when Kimberlynn, in Mr. Soeur's class, shares her solution for counting on by 3 and then 2 (page 127) to imagine what you would say next. What move might you make next if it was *Open Strategy Sharing*? What move might you make next if it was a *What's Strategic and Why?* discussion? Why are your moves different for these two types of discussions?

2. What mathematical strategies are your students working on? Which are particularly well suited to be used in particular situations? Take some notes in the table below to help you identify mathematical ideas at your grade level that might form the basis of a *What's Strategic and Why?* discussion.

Idea or strategy	When is it strategic to use this strategy or idea?	Is this context suitable for a *What's Strategic and Why?* discussion?

CHAPTER 6

TARGETED DISCUSSION: DEFINE AND CLARIFY

Teachers often introduce mathematical objects into discussions such as tools (e.g., hundreds chart, cubes, protractors), representations (e.g., open array, number line), symbols (e.g., +, <, %), and vocabulary (e.g., parallel lines, product, decimal). As these new objects are introduced, or as they naturally emerge, a teacher needs to think carefully about how to support students in using them appropriately and how to create opportunities for students to make meaning and develop usage with understanding. In doing so, a teacher might plan a *Define and Clarify* discussion.

Our thinking about this discussion structure is inspired by what James Hiebert and his colleagues write about the use of mathematical tools in their book *Making Sense: Teaching and Learning Mathematics with Understanding*: "Tools can be used to think with. They can make difficult thoughts easier to manage; they can enable some thoughts that would hardly be possible without them; and they can share the kinds of thoughts we have" (1997, 53). Hiebert et al. also pose the question, "How do students develop meaning for tools?" (1997, 53). We take this question to heart as we think about discussions that serve to define and clarify new objects and support students in using them meaningfully. Discussing *how* and *why* to use mathematical objects is an important part of developing problem-solving skills and number-and-operation sense (Jacobs and Kusiak 2006). It is important to consider when *Define and Clarify* discussions can and should occur (e.g., when objects are first being introduced or when teachers want to help students refine their use).

We share four *Define and Clarify* discussions in this chapter. We start with two kindergarten examples, emerging from questions that students asked. Our first vignette takes us into Ms. Abrahamson's kindergarten classroom, where children are using a new tool, the two-hundreds chart, for the first time. The class is working with the two-hundreds chart in order to identify and learn how to write a new and challenging number, 101. Ms. Turner's kindergarten classroom, in the second vignette, grapples with how to write an equation that matches a story problem one of their classmates created. The situation is a little tricky because it involves determining whether a zero is being added or taken away. In the third vignette, Ms. Allen and her fourth-grade students engage in a discussion about the correspondence between symbolic notations, specifically, clarifying how to write eight and ten-tenths as a fraction and as a decimal. In the fourth vignette, Mr. Tavana and his fifth-grade students use an open array, a visual representation they have used before for multiplication, in a new way to think about how to make meaning of a division strategy for 240 divided by 12. These different examples will show how the *Define and Clarify* structure can be used to support the use of mathematical objects, be they tools, notational systems, or visual representations.

Kindergartners Ask, "How Do You Write 101?"

Ms. Abrahamson's kindergarteners have been interested in counting past 100 and their counting collections have steadily grown in size (Franke, Kazemi, and Turrou 2018). She's anticipating that students will need new tools to help them learn how to write numbers past 100. She knows the class is ready for a new tool when she hears Omar exclaim to his partner Hala, "I don't know how to

Figure 6.1 Ms. Abrahamson's planning template for a *Define and Clarify* discussion

Define and Clarify

What new tool, representation, symbol, or vocabulary are we targeting in our discussion? Is this new to the students or are they using it in a new way?

200s chart. New tool. Introduce to support students in identifying and writing numbers greater than 100, specifically, 101.

What problem or task are we working on? How do I support meaning making? What misconceptions might arise?

How to write 101. Use 200s chart as a new tool—connect it to our use of the hundreds chart. Find 101—discuss how to write 101. Have students share their current ways of writing the number (1001, 101, etc.) Make meaning of why it is written as 101.

write 101!" and she plans a *Define and Clarify* discussion to introduce the two-hundreds chart to the class (see Figure 6.1).

Ms. Abrahamson: Yesterday Omar and Hala were working together counting their collection, and they asked an important question. Omar, can you tell the class what your question was?

Omar: How do you write 101?

Hala: You could maybe write it like one zero zero one. *(He uses his finger to write the number 1001 in the air.)* Because it's like 100 and then you put a 1 at the end to make 101.

Omar: Yeah. Maybe. But I don't know.

Sophie: I want to know too!

Ms. Abrahamson: When we were talking about it yesterday, Lola noticed that we couldn't use the hundreds chart or our number line.

Lola: They only go to 100. And we, we are trying to write a number that is after 100.

Ms. Abrahamson: Hmm, Lola says we are trying to write a number that comes after 100. Let's count together on the hundreds chart starting at 90 and look into Lola's idea.

Ms. Abrahamson points to 90 on the hundreds chart (see Figure 6.2) and to each number after it as the class counts chorally.

Students: 90, 91, 92 ... 99, 100, *(students shouting)* 101!

Ms. Abrahamson: I hear you saying 101. But it is not on our chart. Our chart stops at 100. I began to wonder, is there a two-hundreds chart? We have a hundreds chart, but is there a two-hundreds chart? Guess what? There is! *(Students gasp and giggle.)* I know! Isn't it exciting? And guess what? I have one we can use today to help us all answer Omar's question.

Ms. Abrahamson displays the two-hundreds chart with the document camera (see Figure 6.3).

Figure 6.2 The familiar hundreds chart

Figure 6.3 The two-hundreds chart that Ms. Abrahamson introduces to her class

Hundreds Chart

1	2	3	4	5	6	7	8	9	10
11	12	13	14	15	16	17	18	19	20
21	22	23	24	25	26	27	28	29	30
31	32	33	34	35	36	37	38	39	40
41	42	43	44	45	46	47	48	49	50
51	52	53	54	55	56	57	58	59	60
61	62	63	64	65	66	67	68	69	70
71	72	73	74	75	76	77	78	79	80
81	82	83	84	85	86	87	88	89	90
91	92	93	94	95	96	97	98	99	100

Two Hundreds Chart

1	2	3	4	5	6	7	8	9	10
11	12	13	14	15	16	17	18	19	20
21	22	23	24	25	26	27	28	29	30
31	32	33	34	35	36	37	38	39	40
41	42	43	44	45	46	47	48	49	50
51	52	53	54	55	56	57	58	59	60
61	62	63	64	65	66	67	68	69	70
71	72	73	74	75	76	77	78	79	80
81	82	83	84	85	86	87	88	89	90
91	92	93	94	95	96	97	98	99	100
101	102	103	104	105	106	107	108	109	110
111	112	113	114	115	116	117	118	119	120
121	122	123	124	125	126	127	128	129	130
131	132	133	134	135	136	137	138	139	140
141	142	143	144	145	146	147	148	149	150
151	152	153	154	155	156	157	158	159	160
161	162	163	164	165	166	167	168	169	170
171	172	173	174	175	176	177	178	179	180
181	182	183	184	185	186	187	188	189	190
191	192	193	194	195	196	197	198	199	200

Chapter 6 Targeted Discussion: Define and Clarify

Cruz: *(In the midst of many students saying, "Whoa.")* Look at all those numbers!

Ms. Abrahamson: Yes, look at all the numbers. This is a two-hundreds chart. A two-hundreds chart is a tool that can help us as we think together about numbers up to 200. Let's look together at this tool and share things we notice. First, I want you to look at it all by yourself and see what you are noticing. Keep your ideas inside your mind. *(Ms. Abrahamson gives everyone ample wait time. Then, since the room is so quiet because the students are engrossed in examining the chart, she kneels down and whispers what she wants them to do next.)* Wow, I can really tell you're thinking. Now I want you to turn to your neighbor and tell them one thing you are noticing when you look at the two-hundreds chart.

As Ms. Abrahamson listens in on the children sharing what they notice, she overhears comments such as, "There are lots of 1s on there," "I see a long line of sevens," "I found 101," and "The last number is 200." Since she is just introducing this tool, she is curious about what children are noticing and is listening for ideas she can elicit and highlight in the discussion.

Ms. Abrahamson: Let's all come back together. As I was listening to your ideas, I heard many different things you were noticing about our new tool, the two-hundreds chart. *(She recaps many different ideas and then narrows the discussion.)* I heard Logan say the last number is 200. Logan, can you point to the 200 for us? *(Logan approaches the screen and points to 200.)* Do you see the 200 Logan is pointing to? Let's all say these numbers together. Two zero zero. A 200 is written two zero zero. Let's write 200 in the air. *(Students write the numbers 2-0-0 in the air.)* Yes! This chart has a 200 on it. It is our two-hundreds chart. There are 200 numbers on our chart. I heard another comment. I heard Adelia say that she found 101.

Because of Omar's good question, we now have a new tool that can help us know how to write numbers. Adelia, can you come point to where you see 101? *(Adelia comes up to the screen and points to 101.)* Do you see the number Adelia is pointing to? How do we know this is 101? Carlos?

Carlos: It has a 1 in it.

Ms. Abrahamson: It has a 1 in it. Who else has an idea? Paya?

Paya: It comes after 100.

Ms. Abrahamson: It comes right after 100. Let's think about what Paya is telling us. I have a two-hundreds chart for each of you to hold. When you get your chart, I want you to point to where you see 101. *(Passes out an individual two-hundreds chart printed on cardstock to each child. Children start pointing to where they see 101 and showing their classmates.)* I want us to count out loud again together and point to each number on our two-hundreds chart as we say that number. Let's begin at 90. *(Counting out loud and pointing.)* 90, 91, 92, 93 … 99, 100, 101. Stop! Let's stop. We just counted 100, 101. Yes, Paya, 101 comes after 100. And, Omar, what do you notice about how 101 is written?

Omar: *(Pointing to his two-hundreds chart.)* One zero one.

Ms. Abrahamson: We hear Omar saying 101 is written one zero one. Let's all write 101 in the air. *(Students draw in the air.)* Nice work, kindergartners. We all know how to find and write 101!

Kindergarten Graders Clarify How to Write an Equation to Match a Story Situation

The children in Ms. Turner's kindergarten class discuss the photos she took while they were visiting a local beach as part of their science unit on habitats. They are studying four habitats in their local community: the schoolyard, a river, the forest, and the beach. During their study of beach habitats, they take a field trip to a beach close to their school in the Pacific Northwest in order to study intertidal habitats. They ask questions like:

- Who lives here?
- How are the plants, animals and people connected to each other and to the place?
- What do they need to survive?
- How do the plants and animals use the environment to meet their needs?
- What are some problems in this place? And how can humans help?

Among the creatures they study are moon snails, crabs, barnacles, and starfish. In the days following the field trip, students are buzzing with stories about their observations and experiences. Ms. Turner had taken many pictures as children were exploring the beach and talking about what they saw. To launch

Chapter 6 Targeted Discussion: Define and Clarify

Figure 6.4 Ms. Turner's pictures from the field trip to the beach

Notice and Wonder

the discussion, she projects a collage of photos from the trip on the screen (see Figure 6.4). She creates an opening for discussion, choosing these photos intentionally, because everyone has a story they can tell connected to being at the beach. She knows these shared experiences will continue to nurture the social community in her class.

Ms. Turner opens the conversation saying, "You remember when we went to the beach last week at low tide. And we saw all these animals. Let's have a turn and talk to share what we notice about these pictures from our field trip." The volume in the class quickly grows as children point to the pictures from the carpet remembering what they had seen and touched and held. Ms. Turner invites a few students up to the board to share (see Figure 6.5).

Asami: I notice seaweed in this picture. And I forget what this was called.
Ms. Turner: Can we give her some help?
Many students: Seagrass.
Asami: There were animals in the seagrass so we didn't step in it.
Ms. Turner: Can we see them in the picture?
Many students: No, they're hiding.

Ms. Turner is pleased that Asami feels comfortable to both share an idea as well as say something that she couldn't remember and that her classmates respectfully help her remember the term seagrass. She is also happy to hear Asami begin to elaborate on something she remembered

Figure 6.5 Asami shares what she notices in one of the photos.

about the seagrass. These details could be useful for the mathematical storytelling that she was going to prompt in a few minutes. Ms. Turner continues asking several other students to share something they remembered. With each one, she asks a follow-up question to get more ideas into the public space that could be useful for storytelling and to encourage students to connect their ideas to the previous speaker.

Ms. Turner: Who else can share something different that they noticed?
Miles: I notice these little crabs. It looks like they are on the seagrass.
Ms. Turner: Can you tell us anything else?
Miles: The crabs like to eat smaller animals.
Ollie: I notice a barnacle. I can see inside the barnacle. It's black.
Ms. Turner: Could that be the animal that lives inside that hard shell casing? Can someone else add on to the barnacle picture?
Sandra: I see a shell next to the barnacle. I see more black stuff over here.
Ms. Turner: I see little tiny acorn barnacles on top of that big barnacle. What else?
James: That looks like a moon snail shell

Chapter 6 Targeted Discussion: Define and Clarify

Ms. Turner: Yes, Shelly was holding that up. I took that picture of her holding it.

Now that students are back into the experience of being at the beach, Ms. Turner transitions to the next part of the lesson passing out a copy of the collage for each student. This time, she reminds them about some important things to do in their partnerships as they listen and talk.

Ms. Turner: I printed all those pictures for you. You're going to pick a picture that you want to talk about. You can tell a story of when you saw the animal that you saw on the beach. We're going to remember that you're going to listen to your partner. Their story is important. We can also ask questions. That's one way to show that we are listening. So if your partner is talking about something in their story and you're wondering about something in their story, you can ask them a question. And then you can switch and the next person can tell their story.

Ms. Turner displays these brief ideas on a new slide (shown in Figure 6.6) to support students in their listening and talking.

She listens in as the turn and talks happen, noting the kinds of memories students are recalling and the stories they are telling. She hears stories about the crabs and the spirals students noticed in the shells, how things felt, and how many creatures they saw. Students share some of their noticings, and Ms. Turner charts their noticings next to each picture (see Figure 6.7).

Figure 6.6 Ms. Turner adds information about listening and talking in partners

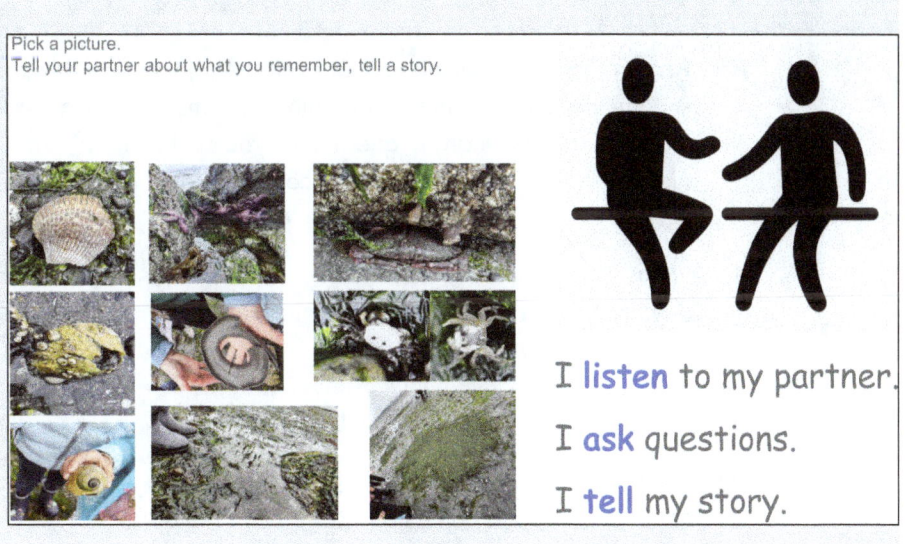

Figure 6.7 Students discuss what they notice and wonder (left) and Ms. Turner records their ideas on chart paper (right)

With a lot of rich memories to work with, Ms. Turner turns the conversation slightly to nudge the students toward some mathematical storytelling.

Ms. Turner: You are noticing so many interesting things in these pictures. And I'm wondering about what math questions you could ask. You could ask a "How many?" question or you could ask a "What if …" question. What kind of math story could you ask? *(See Figure 6.8.)*

Students stay on the rug or return to their seats taking copies of the photos with them. They eagerly begin to construct their stories. Ms. Turner listens in and watches as students draw pictures and build their stories (see Figure 6.9).

She overhears Ben telling a story about the picture of the two crabs and realizes this will make a really good conversation for her class.

Ms. Turner: I am hearing so many good stories. Let's start with one of them. Ben, can you come up and share your story?

Figure 6.8 Ms. Turner asks students to make their own math story problems.

Ben: There are two crabs. And a creature didn't want to eat them. So there's still two crabs.

Ms. Turner: You're really thinking about the memories we shared about our trip to the beach. Let's think together about what Ben just said. There were two crabs and a creature didn't want to eat those two crabs. How many crabs were left?

Josie: Two.

Ms. Turner: Two were still left.

Ms. Turner notices how Ben's story creates an opportunity to work on modeling a word problem with a mathematical equation. This has been a focus in the last half of kindergarten as students were beginning to make sense of the plus, minus, and equal sign and the problem situations that match these symbols. Ben's story is an opening for a Define and Clarify conversation.

Figure 6.9 Students write their own story problems about the beach

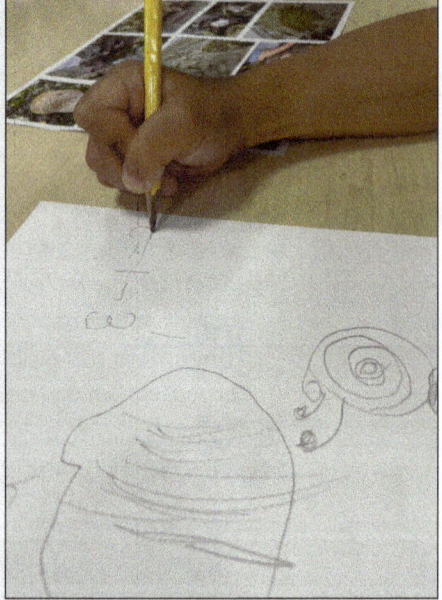

Ms. Turner: I'm thinking about whether we can make a math expression that matches your story. Ben was noticing something about the crabs. Let's draw two crabs (see Figure 6.10).

Ms. Turner's drawing skills grab the students' attention immediately!

Someone exclaims: Devil claws!

Students laugh as Ms. Turner repeats what they say, and she laughs along with them at her rendition of two crabs.

Ms. Turner: *(Reminding the students what Ben said)* So Ben said that a creature didn't want to eat them.

Annie: Why don't we make a question mark?

Ms. Turner: Okay and maybe we can imagine that a bird didn't want to eat them. Maybe they had eaten enough *(see Figure 6.11)*.

Ms. Turner adds a bird flying next to the crabs.

Ms. Turner: So how many crabs were left?

As students say "Two!" Ms. Turner writes the number 2 twice underneath the crabs to show that first there were 2 and there were still 2 when the bird decided not to eat them (see Figure 6.12).

Ms. Turner: I'm wondering what would go between these twos? What math symbols might go here between these twos to fit our story? Let's be sure to give everyone some time to think about that.

Ms. Turner is thinking that the context of Ben's problem can help them think about the use of zeros in equations as well as how to model the action in the problem with a subtraction sign. She pauses for some think time for the students.

Figure 6.10 Ms. Turner draws two crabs

Figure 6.11 Ms. Turner draws a bird next to the crabs

Figure 6.12 Ms. Turner adds numbers to the drawings

Ms. Turner: If you have an idea you'd like to share, you can put your thumb on your chest.

Ms. Turner scans the room, always having an eye out for new voices she can invite into the whole-group conversation as well as voices she wants to elevate. She notices Marco has something he'd like to share.

Ms. Turner: You think you know what we could do to finish it?
Marco: I think we should put a zero.
Ms. Turner: I'm seeing people agree with you. That seems like an important number. Where should that zero go? Let's see who can add to what you've shared with us.

Again Ms. Turner looks for new voices to bring in.

Danté: I think the zero should go in the middle.
Ms. Turner: I'm loving how we're adding to each other's ideas. Danté and Marco, why are you thinking a zero goes in between the two twos?
Marco: That means nobody ate the crabs.
Danté: Yeah, the bird didn't want to eat them.
Ms. Turner: So, we have 2 and then the bird doesn't want to eat them, and there are still 2. It kind of looks like it says 202. Are there signs we could add to this now? *(See Figure 6.13.)*

Students call out both "plus" and "minus."

Ms. Turner: This is fantastic. I'm hearing we need a plus. I'm hearing we need a minus. Let's hear that story that Ben told one more time and think about what those signs mean and whether one is better for Ben's story. Ben, will you remind us?

Figure 6.13 Ms. Turner asks students to discuss what symbols to add to create an equation that fits Ben's story.

Chapter 6 Targeted Discussion: Define and Clarify

Ben: There were 2 crabs and a creature did not eat those 2 crabs. There's still 2 crabs.

Ms. Turner: Thank you. So let's think about that, if a creature is eating food. Is he bringing more food or taking food away? Does that sound like a plus or a minus? What do those signs mean?

Giselle: It could be a plus or a minus. Because it's still 2.

Ms. Turner: You might be thinking it would be true either away. $2 + 0 = 2$ and $2 - 0 = 2$. Yeah if you add or take away zero, it's still 2. It still stays true. Is there one equation that matches what happens in Ben's story better and why?

Cecilia: I think it should be minus because the bird didn't take away any.

Ms. Turner: *(Revoicing what Cecilia says.)* So the bird was supposed to take something away but the bird wasn't hungry.

Cecilia: Yeah.

Ms. Turner: So let's think about that some more – what are you hearing Cecilia about why it makes sense for us to write $2 - 0 = 2$? Will you share with your partner? *(See Figure 6.13.)*

An idea like this takes some processing time, so slowing down the conversation is a good idea when we are trying to clarify. Ms. Turner is thinking on her feet about this discussion because she hadn't planned it ahead of time. It naturally emerged as part of the children's storytelling. This is a nice complex idea. She's happy that students have a good sense that 0 doesn't change the amount of crabs, and she feels good that they tied the action of eating, and in this case not eating, to a take away interpretation of subtraction. She knows that students will need multiple experiences understanding how story problems can be represented with equations and this conversation lays a foundation for that continued work.

Fourth Graders Ask, "Is Eight and Ten-tenths Written as 8.10 or 9?"

As the fourth-grade students in Ms. Allen's classroom are thinking about tenths, an important question arises: Is eight and ten-tenths written as 8.10 or 9? In order to support her students in clarifying the use of symbolic notations, specifically the correspondence between symbolic systems for fractions and decimals, Ms. Allen plans a *Define and Clarify* discussion (see Figure 6.14).

Figure 6.14 Ms. Allen's planning template for a *Define and Clarify* discussion on decimal notation

Define and Clarify

What new tool, representation, symbol, or vocabulary are we targeting in our discussion? Is this new to the students or are they using it in a new way?

How to write 8 10/10 as a decimal. Use the idea of 10/10 = 1 to make sense of why the number is not written 8.10 but instead is written 9.0.

What problem or task are we working on? How will I support meaning making? What partial understandings might arise?

Is 8 10/10 written like 8.10 or 9? (Question raised by students.)
Return to 10K representation and story context to support making meaning of how to write 10/10.

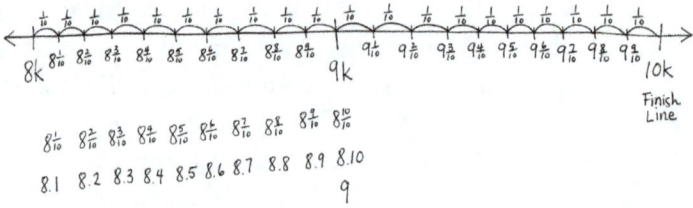

Ms. Allen: Okay, everybody, let's gather together to help each other make sense of a new way we are writing and recording fractions and decimals. Come on up to the carpet. Remember how we were talking about how I am becoming a runner and I have a goal of running in a 10K, or 10 kilometers? *(Smiling.)* I know some of you think that is funny! And remember how right now I can run about 8K, and my friends who are runners helped me learn that I can try running a little bit farther every day—a tenth of a kilometer longer each day—and you figured out that after going out for 20 more runs I will meet my goal! After our discussion, I was thinking more about

Chapter 6 Targeted Discussion: Define and Clarify

your ideas about fractions and decimals, and today I want to zoom in on a few ideas, a few questions actually, to make sure we all are feeling clear about how to write tenths as fractions and as decimals. To help us get started, I want to look again at the representation we made *(see Figure 6.15)*. Who can offer up some ideas to help us remember how this representation was helping us think about tenths? Saundra?

Figure 6.15 The class used this representation to count by tenths from 8 to 10 in a prior classroom discussion

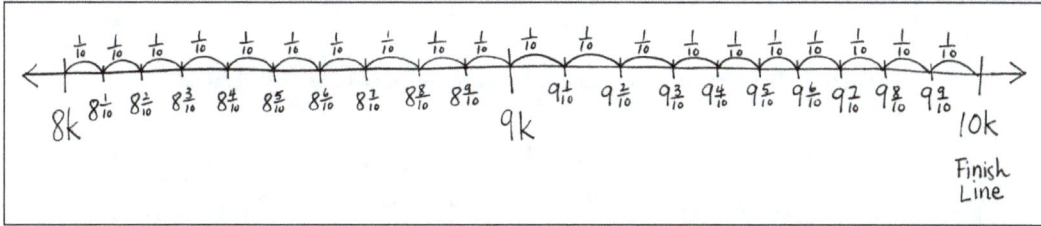

Saundra: You can run all the way to here right now *(pointing to the end of the 8K)*, but you want to be able to run to here *(pointing to the end of the 10K)*, and we were figuring out how much farther you need to go.

Ms. Allen: Saundra has gotten us started. Who can add on to what she is saying? Nicole?

Nicole: *(Pointing to the tenths.)* And each of these little parts is $\frac{1}{10}$ of a kilometer. It goes like $8\frac{1}{10}, 8\frac{2}{10}, 8\frac{3}{10}$.

Ms. Allen: So, each of these little parts *(pointing to $\frac{1}{10}$ of a kilometer)* represents $\frac{1}{10}$ of a kilometer, because we divided a kilometer into 10 lengths.

Meghan: And the lengths have to be the same size.

Ms. Allen: And the lengths have to be the same size. Yes. A tenth was one of 10 equal parts in each kilometer. Let's count them out loud together like Nicole started to do.

Students: Eight and $\frac{1}{10}, 8\frac{2}{10}, 8\frac{3}{10} \ldots 8\frac{9}{10}$, and $8\frac{10}{10}$.

Ms. Allen: It seems you're pretty comfortable counting by tenths and recording it this way—as fractions. Mathematicians write $\frac{10}{10}$ as a fraction *(pointing to $\frac{10}{10}$)*. Mathematicians also write $\frac{10}{10}$ as a decimal *(pointing to the row of decimals recorded beneath the representation)*, and here we can see how we also recorded this count in decimals. We agreed that $\frac{1}{10}$ written as a decimal looks like 0.1. This *(pointing to the decimal point)* is called the decimal point. Ten-tenths represents the same portion whether it is written as a fraction or a decimal.

The goal of this discussion is to make sure all students feel comfortable knowing how to write tenths as fractions and as decimals (see Figure 6.16). Defining and clarifying the correspondence between these symbolic systems is at the center of Ms. Allen's thinking as she facilitates this discussion. She is paying close attention to her language and is being explicit in how she talks about the ways mathematicians use symbols and words to represent tenths.

Figure 6.16 This representation compares fraction notation to decimal notation

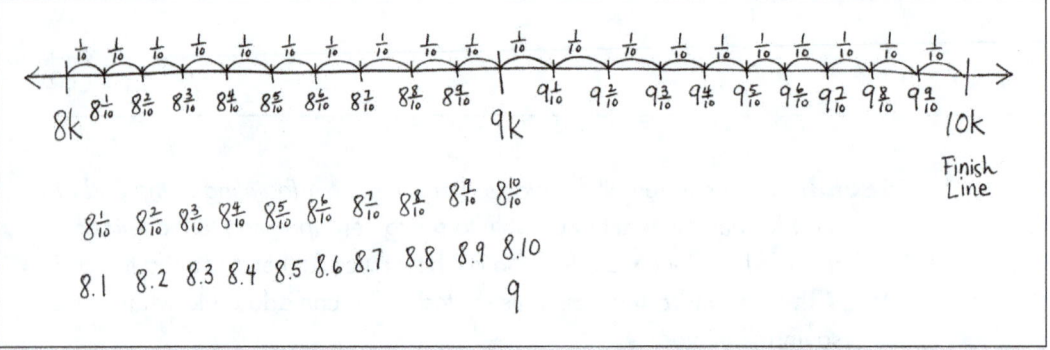

Ms. Allen: What really struck me during our conversation yesterday was a question that emerged. There was a lot of buzzing about how we should write $8\frac{10}{10}$ as a decimal. The two most common ideas were 8.10 and 9. Today I want us to talk together and reason about how we should write this. Our question is: Is $8\frac{10}{10}$ written like 8.10 or 9? And we need to get clear about this together. First, I would like for you to look at our representation and think to yourself about which number you would like to defend. *(After about 30 seconds of wait time.)* Terrance?

Terrance: Nine or 9.0.

Ms. Allen: Let's listen to why Terrance wants to defend 9.

Terrance: *(Walking up to the board.)* There could be a decimal point right here *(pointing to the space to the right of the 9)*, and then because the 9 would be in front of the decimal point, it means it is a whole, and if the 9 is behind the decimal point it means it is a tenth.

Ms. Allen: You are paying attention to the digit that is before and after the decimal. You are saying that the digit before the decimal is ones and after the decimal is tenths. I see people using our "me too" sign. Who else would like to defend 9? Thomasina?

Thomasina: I think it is 9 because it is not 8.10.

Ms. Allen: Say more about why you think it is not 8.10.

Thomasina: Because, um, 8.10 is going to be into the hundredths. Because the zero is in the hundredths spot.

Ms. Allen: *(Pauses with wait time before continuing.)* Anybody else want to add to that?

Ms. Allen can see her students are thinking and she wants more of them to jump into the discussion with their ideas. She is pulling back a bit here to give think time and airtime for students to join in. She chooses between repeating the ideas Terrance and Thomasina have offered or giving a prompt for more student voices. Because there is more to elaborate here she is leaving the door open for more student voices to weigh in.

Alisa: I'm confused. I was going to defend 8.10 but now I'm not sure. It seems like it should go 8 point 9 and then 8 point 10, because that sounds like $8\frac{10}{10}$.

Ms. Allen: Okay, it sounds like you're thinking about what you are hearing. Do you want to share what is confusing you or do you want more think time?

Alisa: More think time.

Ms. Allen: Okay. Who else has an idea to share? We have heard some support for 9. We have heard some people may be unsure or may be changing their thinking. Is there anyone who would like to defend 8.10? We are trying to clarify how to write $8\frac{10}{10}$ as a decimal. What do you think, Kurt?

Kurt: Well, I was just thinking that we learned that $\frac{10}{10}$ is equal to a whole. But 8 point 10 looks like 8 point 1.

Thomasina: Oh, oh. Yeah, I see what Kurt is saying. It's like $8\frac{10}{10}$ is like 8 and 1 whole. So doesn't that mean it's 9?

Ms. Allen: What do you think of what Thomasina and Kurt are saying, Alisa?

Ms. Allen's decision to go back to Alisa is intentional here. She regularly looks for opportunities for students to make their puzzlements more public, to show that wrestling with ideas is an important part of doing mathematics.

Alisa: I think I need to hear that again. It's starting to make sense.

Thomasina gets up to go to the board and gets an approving nod from Ms. Allen.

Thomasina: See, like if we write 8 and $\frac{10}{10}$ like a fraction, like this, $8\frac{10}{10}$, we can cross out the $\frac{10}{10}$ and make it a 1. Then we have 8 and 1, which is 9.

Alisa: Oohh! That makes sense.

Ms. Allen: Whenever we think we're on the verge of understanding something, it's always good to check with your neighbor and see if you have questions about what's happening.

Ms. Allen uses a turn and talk at this point to make sure she doesn't assume that everyone listening has developed the insight that Alisa has with Thomasina's explanation. She leans in on Alisa and her partner to check on what Alisa thinks she understands. Students can ask each other questions and spread ideas during a turn and talk. Ms. Allen listens in and sees that students are picking up on the idea of the equivalency between $\frac{10}{10}$ and 1.

Ms. Allen: So I think we've achieved a good point of clarification. Even though it's tempting to think that 8.10 says $8\frac{10}{10}$, we've convinced ourselves that $8\frac{10}{10}$ is equivalent to 9 and needs to be written 9.0 as a decimal. I want to go back to an idea that we heard earlier—that 8.1 and 8.10 seem to be the same thing. I'll let you chew on this a bit more. I'm interested in your thoughts on this, so I think I'll let you write about it in your math journals first before we talk about it together.

Fifth Graders Discuss Using an Open Array in a Different Way

Mr. Tavana can see that his fifth-grade students are using what they know about groups of ten to solve division problems with bigger numbers. When thinking about 240 divided by 12, students are using 10 groups of 12 and then 10 more groups of 12 to get to 240. He thinks an open array could support students in making meaning of this strategy and plans for a *Define and Clarify* discussion to

Figure 6.17 Mr. Tavana's planning template for a *Define and Clarify* discussion about using an array to solve a division problem

Define and Clarify

What new tool, representation, symbol, or vocabulary are we targeting in our discussion? Is this new to the students or are they using it in a new way?

Open array. Representation used for making meaning of multiplication—introducing new usage—to help make sense of division.

What problem or task are we working on? How will I support meaning making? What misconceptions might arise?

How to solve a division problem using what you know about multiplication, or groups. Support making meaning of groups of 10 strategy.

240 ÷ 12

12 × 10 = 120

12 × 10 = 120

120 + 120 = 240

How are we building up to the total of 240 with 10 groups of 12 and 10 more groups of 12?

Where is the 240? Where is the answer?

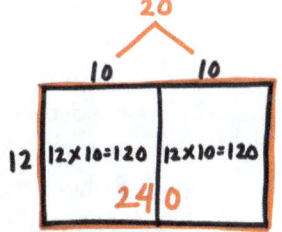

introduce using the open array as a tool for solving division problems and keeping track of a multiplying-up strategy (see Figure 6.17).

Mr. Tavana: *(Turning to his students, who are gathered on the carpet.)* The last few days, as we have been solving division problems, I have noticed that students in our class are using what they know about multiplication to think about division.

Pointing to the poster on an easel from yesterday's Open Strategy Sharing discussion, Mr. Tavana focuses on a particular strategy he saw students using for 240 divided by 12 (see Figure 6.18).

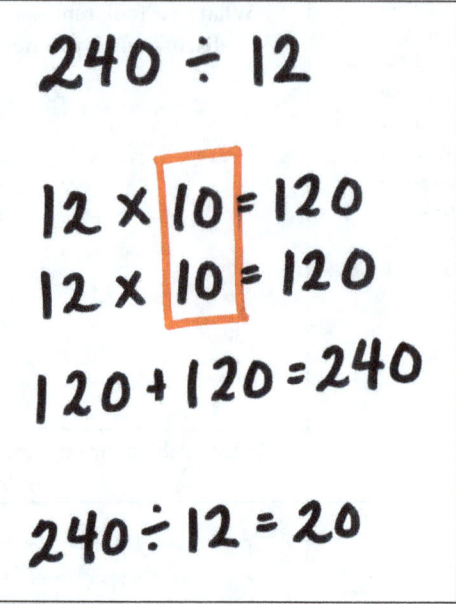

Figure 6.18 This portion of the poster shows a representation of multiplying up to solve 240 ÷ 12

Mr. Tavana: After we discussed this strategy of using 12 groups of 10, or 10 groups of 12, to build up to 240 yesterday, I wondered if building an open array could help us make sense of using multiplication, or groups, to think about division. Today I want to talk about how to use an open array, and I also want to clarify how we use this representation to help us think about division. Since people solved 240 divided by 12 in a few different ways, let's start by making sure we all understand the strategy we are focusing on today. Who was using this strategy and will explain it to us? Bethany?

Bethany: I like to use tens because they are easy for me. So I know that 10 groups of 12 is 120. I thought 12 times 10 equals 120, and then I needed to do that one more time to get to 240.

Mr. Tavana: Who else used this strategy and can add on to what Bethany has told us? Sam?

Sam: I thought about it the same as Bethany. It's like 12 ten times is 120. And 120 plus 120 gets me all the way to 240.

Mr. Tavana: Can someone who did not use this strategy repeat what Bethany and Sam are telling us? Laretha?

Laretha: They used what they know about groups of 10 to figure out how many 12s are in 240. They did a chunk of ten 12s and that is 120 and then another chunk of ten 12s and that got them to 240.

Mr. Tavana: It sounds like we are all grasping this solution. Just to make sure, can you turn to your neighbor and explain this strategy? If you notice it is challenging to explain, ask your partner or me for help.

Mr. Tavana wants to make sure every student understands this strategy, since it was not the way every child previously solved 240 divided by 12. He uses a turn and talk to offer students the chance to explain this strategy aloud and ask for help if needed. He also uses the turn and talk to listen in and quickly make sure there are not any lingering questions before moving on to more discussion about making sense of this solution through an open array. He kneels down next to a few students to check in and then decides it is okay to move on. Before calling the group back together, he moves the strategy poster from the easel to the whiteboard to make sure it is visible while they move into a discussion of the open array.

Mr. Tavana: We have used an open array before to help us think about multiplication. We can also use an open array to help us think about division. But, we use the open array in a different way when we are using it for division problems. Today I want to focus on using an open array to help us think about what is happening in this division strategy. *(Approaching the easel.)* Remember, an open array does not have all the marks drawn inside. It is a quick way for us to draw areas. I will think out loud as I get us started, and then I want to see what your ideas are about continuing our open array. Let's start with 12 down here *(drawing a line down)* since we know we are dividing by 12. And since students are using what they know about 10 groups of 12, let's show 10 groups of 12 by drawing 10 across here *(drawing a line across)*. Then we can make an open array that is 12 times 10 and label inside that 12 times 10 equals 120. *(See Figure 6.19.)* Let's check back with our strategy that is recorded on the poster. Which part of the solution have we shown in this open array?

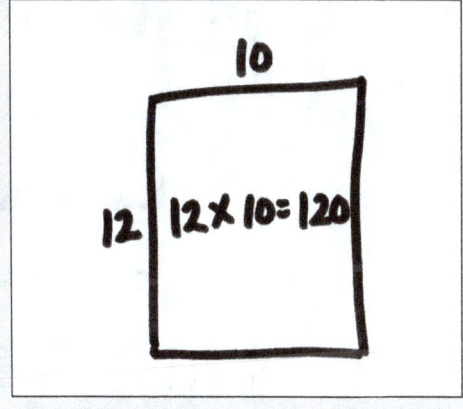

Figure 6.19 Mr. Tavana builds this array to keep track of the multiplying-up strategy for division

Clint: We have shown one of the 12 times 10s.

Mr. Tavana: Clint, can you point for us to the 12 times 10 on our strategy poster? *(Clint points to the first 12 × 10 in Figure 6.18.)* Okay, so this open array shows 12 times 10, which is the first step in this strategy. How could we add on to our array to show the entire strategy?

Munira: We could keep going and add on another 12 times 10.

Mr. Tavana: What would that look like, Munira?

Munira: You go 10 more over up here. *(Using her finger, she traces on the easel to show what it would look like to extend the line across. Mr. Tavana hands her the pen and she begins drawing—starting at the top and labeling it 10.)* And then go down and connect to the first array. That's another 12 times 10 equals 120, like from right here in the strategy *(pointing to the second recorded 12 × 10 = 120 in the solution on the strategy poster and then labeling the new 12 × 10 portion of the open array; see Figure 6.20).*

Figure 6.20 Munira has added on to the array to keep track of the multiplying-up strategy for division

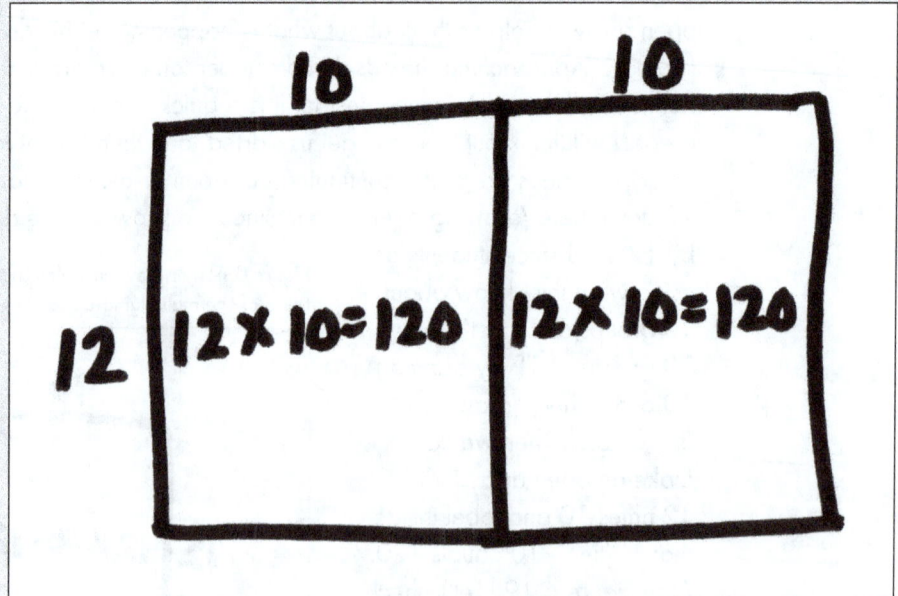

Mr. Tavana: Okay, Munira, thank you for helping us. Let's pause to think about what we are seeing in this open array. As you look at our open array, I want you to think about where we can see each part of the strategy. Where is the 12 times 10, 12 times 10, 120 plus 120 equals 240? *(Points to the poster and then gives wait time.)* Can you turn to your neighbor and take turns pointing to where each of these parts of the strategy can be seen in our open array? *(Students turn and talk and Mr. Tavana listens in to select a few students to share.)* I was listening in as you talked to your neighbor and I wanted to ask Jaddis to share what he was saying. Jaddis was pointing to the strategy poster and the open array poster. Jaddis, will you come up and point for us?

Jaddis: *(Standing between the strategy poster and the open array.)* Here is the first 12 times 10 *(pointing to the left-hand side of the open array drawing)*, and all of this in here, this chunk *(sliding his hand over the 12 × 10 area on the left side)* shows 120.

Mr. Tavana: Let's stop there for a moment, because Jaddis is telling us something important. In this open array on the left side, we see 12 down and 10 across, and together this whole area shows 120. This chunk, as Jaddis called it. In our problem we knew that we were dividing by 12, but we didn't know how many groups of 12 we would have in 240. We are seeing that we can build out in 10 groups of 12, something we all know, to try to get all the way to 240. Okay, keep going, Jaddis.

Jaddis: So then we did that same thing again. We made another 10 groups of 12 here, another chunk *(pointing to the open array on the right side of poster)*, and then *(moving his hand from left to right across the array)* all this area, a chunk of 120 and another chunk of 120, gets us out to 240.

Mr. Tavana: Did you just see the way Jaddis moved his hand all the way across the open array? Jaddis, do that again. *(Jaddis runs his hand across the first and second groups of 120.)* We knew we were making groups of 12, and we made 10 groups and then another 10 groups, and that built out our 240. This is an open array, so we don't draw all of the lines inside, but if we did, we could see that here is one group of 12, here is another group of 12 *(tracing his finger down in columns of 12)*, and in this first portion of the open array there would be 10 columns of 12 and in this second portion there would be another 10 columns of 12.

Mr. Tavana notices one student, Nicholas, has reached for Unifix cubes and is starting to build stacks of 12 cubes. He is keeping an eye on Nicholas, because if he is building 20 stacks of 12, it could illustrate all the parts of an array that would resemble more of a filled-in array. This visual may be handy in bridging to the idea of an open array.

Mr. Tavana: So, what would it look like to label the 240 in our open array? Faysal?

Faysal: This whole part here, all of this in here *(moving her hand around on the poster to cover the two sections of 12 × 10).*

Mr. Tavana: All of this in here. Let's show that. All together *(using a red pen, draws around the perimeter of the array and then labels the total)* we have 240. Now, where is our answer? What is 240 divided by 12? Noelia, I see you pointing to our poster. Where is our answer?

Noelia: *(Jumping up.)* It's right there. *(Points to the 10 and the 10 on top of the array.)*

Mr. Tavana: *(Turning to the class.)* Do you agree with Noelia's idea? And why?

Amara: I agree, because down here, this is the 12 *(pointing to the side of the array)*, and then inside, that's how much *(pointing to the 240)*, and so then up here *(pointing to the 10 and 10)*, this is the other number. And there is 10 and 10, so that is 20.

Mr. Tavana: Okay, let's label that 10 and 10 makes 20 at the top. *(He adds on to the drawing; see Figure 6.21.)* So we are saying that 10 groups of 12 *(tracing his hand across the left side of the open array)* and then 10 more groups of 12 *(tracing across both sides)*, or 20 groups of 12, is 240.

Mr. Tavana: What would a number sentence look like for 240 divided by 12?

Miski: Um, it would be like 240 divided by 12 is 20.

Mr. Tavana: Okay, Miski, will you label that for us? *(Miski writes the equation beneath the open array; see Figure 6.22.)*

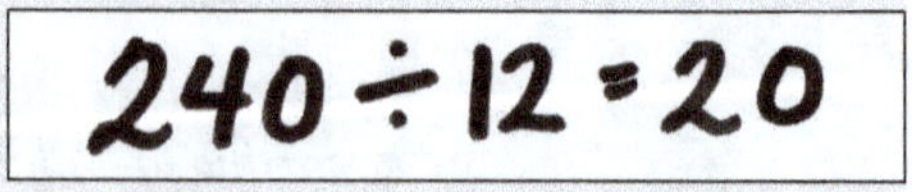

Mr. Tavana: Today we used a tool, an open array, to help us make sense of this division strategy. We have used an open array before, but today we are using the open array in a different way. When we use what we know about

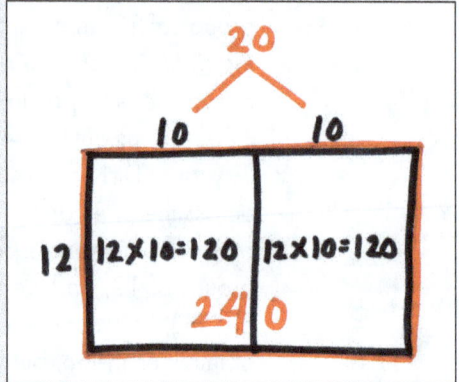

Figure 6.21 The array is annotated to show where the dividend and the quotient appear for the division problem 240 ÷ 12.

Figure 6.22 The array is labeled with this division equation

multiplication to divide, we are making chunks, like Jaddis said, to build up to our total, and an open array can help us see what those chunks look like. Making drawings of our thinking can help us really understand what we are doing when we use a strategy.

The lesson concludes, and Mr. Tavana is still keeping an eye on Nicholas, who is indeed building 20 stacks of 12 Unifix cubes. When Nicholas finishes, Mr. Tavana will check in with him to hear about his thinking and will likely use the array with cubes that Nicholas builds to connect the open array to a three-dimensional model.

Summary and Reflection Questions: When Do I Want to Have a *Define and Clarify* Discussion?

The vignettes in this chapter show how different mathematical objects can become the focus of a *Define and Clarify* discussion. Explicit conversations about how and when to use these tools and concepts accurately are important components of making mathematical work accessible and meaningful to students. Some of these discussions arose out of confusions or stumbling blocks that students faced, which we'll discuss further with the next chapter's *Troubleshoot and Revise* discussion structure.

Before you read on, reflect on the questions below, which are specific to tools and are inspired by questions that Victoria Jacobs and Julie Kusiak raise in their article "Got Tools? Exploring Children's Use of Mathematics Tools During Problem Solving" (2006):

- In your next unit, what are the key mathematical tools and concepts that students will be using: new terms, notations, representations, or tools? Which of these might be new to students? How might a *Define and Clarify* discussion support students to make the most out of the new tool or concept?
- Some students, especially upper-grade students, may be resistant to using concrete tools or objects, because they associate them with younger grades. What can you do to convince your students that using tools is not only acceptable but also an important mathematical strategy?

CHAPTER 7

TARGETED DISCUSSION: TROUBLESHOOT AND REVISE

Working through confusion and building on partial understanding plays an important role in learning mathematics. As the Common Core State Standards for Mathematical Practice remind us, mathematically proficient students "make sense of problems and persevere in solving them" (2012, 6). Engaging in discussions about puzzling mathematics allows a teacher and their students to take stock of what makes sense and work through stumbling blocks together. However, this is delicate work, because thinking through errors and revising your thinking publicly can be challenging—especially in mathematics, where there is a perception that "smart" students solve problems quickly and always get the right answer. The norms for learning from errors, which are nurtured in the classroom, are vital in making this type of discussion successful.

A *Troubleshoot and Revise* discussion can be initiated by the teacher or by one or more students. In either case, the teacher or student has noticed something is awry and seeks the collective engagement of the class to figure out what needs to be revised. The way Megan Staples and Melissa Colonis (2007) think about managing discussion of "wrong" answers is helpful. They find wrong answers to be a "catalyst" for discussions and point out that the discussion is more than an opportunity to just correct the wrong answer; it can "help the student and the class extend the idea that had been presented and continue to develop a viable solution collaboratively" (259). Therefore, a *Troubleshoot and Revise* discussion can be initiated for a variety of reasons. Students might recognize that they have partial understandings and are stuck. They might notice that a strategy they used, which seemed to make sense, resulted in an answer different from that of their classmates. The teacher might also notice a misunderstanding that is bubbling up and worthy of attention.

As we think about how teachers can use errors as opportunities for advancing mathematical thinking, we will also think carefully about how teachers can treat students as sense makers and find the logic in students' partial understandings as they facilitate mathematically productive and socially supportive discussions. We want students to know that thoughtful mathematicians voice their confusions; thinking collaboratively through errors can help everyone better understand the mathematics. We want to frame mistakes as "desirable contributions" (Staples 2008, 52).

The two vignettes in this chapter explore different ways of structuring a *Troubleshoot and Revise* discussion. In the first vignette, third-grade teacher Mr. Barber initiates a discussion about a misconception that arose when his students were finding fractions of a set. In the second vignette, one of Ms. Simpson's fourth graders requests a consultation from his peers when he becomes confused by a true/false number sentence.

Third Graders Troubleshoot Finding Fourths Versus Fours: "What's the Logic in This Thinking?" "What's Getting Mixed Up?"

Mr. Barber's third graders have been working with different ways of conceptualizing fractions. They are in the midst of finding fractions of a set: finding halves, fourths, and fifths. Mr. Barber ends many of his lessons with an exit ticket, asking students to show their understanding of the day's focal concept on a notecard that they leave with him. This allows him to get a quick read on how his students are using an idea.

When he reviewed the exit tickets after one lesson, he noticed that some students were confusing partitioning a set of objects into fourths with making groups of four. He uses the *Troubleshoot and Revise* planning template to plan a whole-class discussion about this issue (see Figure 7.1; a blank version of this planning template is provided in Appendix F).

Figure 7.1 Mr. Barber's planning template for a *Troubleshoot and Revise* discussion about finding fourths versus fours

Troubleshoot and Revise

What is the confusion or misunderstanding we will discuss and revise?

Finding fractions of a set—revise a strategy that confuses "how many in a group?" with "how many groups?" Students are making groups of 4 instead of seeing the whole group divided into four equal groups.

Use problem context of Mr. Barber's cookies from exit slip:
  Mr. Barber had 24 cookies. If he gave three-fourths of all the cookies to his friend, how many cookies did he give his friend?

What is the insight I'd like students to understand?

The set of 24 was divided into four equal groups, resulting in fourths. Mr. Barber gave three of those fourths to his friend.

Problem context, diagrams, or questions that might be useful to use during the discussion

- Show a solution in which 24 cookies were put into groups of 4, resulting in 6 groups:
  oooo oooo oooo oooo oooo oooo
- Why might someone think like this to solve the problem?
- How does it not match the problem situation?
- What would the problem say if it were asking you to make groups of 4? (Students might say: He gave 4 cookies to each friend.)
- What does the problem say to help you know that it's asking you to make 4 groups?
- What does "fourths" mean?

Exit ticket

What's the difference between putting something in groups of four and making fourths?

Mr. Barber: A few days ago we were talking about fractions of a set. After our discussion, you filled out an exit ticket to help me know how you were thinking about this idea. The problem on the exit ticket looked like this. *(Mr. Barber points to the board, where the exit ticket problem is displayed; see Figure 7.2.)*

Mr. Barber: Do you remember thinking about this problem? Let's read the problem again with partners to make sure we all remember. Partner 1, will you read the problem aloud? And partner 2, please repeat the problem. *(Students, who are all sitting on the carpet, turn to face their partners and read and repeat the problem.)*

Figure 7.2 The exit ticket problem

> Mr. Barber had 24 cookies. If he gave three-fourths of all the cookies to his friend, how many cookies did he give his friend?

Mr. Barber uses turn and talk here in a unique way. His students are assigned partners, and he often asks partner 1 or partner 2 to talk about certain things during turn and talks.

Mr. Barber: Okay, I can hear we have all read the problem. Today I want to have another discussion about this problem to help us understand what it means to find a fraction of a set. When I was looking at your thinking on the exit slips, I saw several students use a strategy that needs revision. In our class, we talk about our strategies, and when there is something we don't completely understand, we help each other think about how to revise our ideas. *(Pointing to the poster where he has already drawn the strategy of dividing 24 cookies into groups of 4; see Figure 7.3.)* Today, as we discuss the strategy I've drawn on this poster, I am going to ask us to think about two things. First, we are going

Figure 7.3 Mr. Barber prepared this poster to show the problem and the strategy that needs revision

> Mr. Barber had 24 cookies. If he gave 3 fourths to his friend, how much did he give to his friend?
>
> 0000 | 0000 | 0000 | 0000 |
> 0000 | 0000 |
>
> He gave 12 to his friend.

Chapter 7 Targeted Discussion: Troubleshoot and Revise

to talk about the logic in this solution. Or, why does it make sense that someone might try to solve this problem in this way? Second, we are going to talk about two ideas that are getting mixed up. Let's start by thinking about the logic in this thinking, or why someone would think about this problem in this way. Take a moment to look at the solution on this poster, and place a thumb on your chest when you have an idea about the logic in this thinking.

During the wait time, Mr. Barber is watching the students think, and he is also using the wait time to think for himself. He is thinking about how he is setting up this discussion. He is working hard to bring to life the idea that all children are sense makers and that their ideas are valued. This is especially delicate when the discussion focuses on a partial understanding. By starting with finding the logic in an approach, he is nurturing the idea that there are reasons why a solution contains a mistake.

Mr. Barber: I can see that many people have ideas. I think we should begin by chatting with our partners about this. Please turn and talk to your partner.

Mr. Barber listens in and overhears students talking about the picture on the poster, saying things like, "There are four cookies in each group," "This strategy shows four in a group," and "Yeah, there are four in a group, but we have to find four groups." He decides to invite some of these students to share their ideas.

Mr. Barber: I am going to invite Laloni and Rafi to share what they were noticing.

Laloni: Um, Rafi and I were saying that the problem says that you put the cookies into fourths, and we see fours in this picture.

Rafi: *(Standing up to point to the poster and circling the four cookies in each group with her finger; see Figure 7.4.)* These right here; here are the fours.

Figure 7.4 This portion of the poster shows four cookies in each group

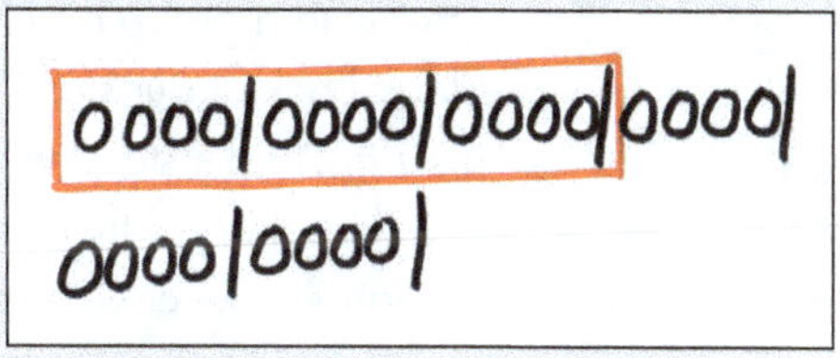

Mr. Barber: *(Turning to the class.)* Do you hear what Laloni and Rafi are noticing about what makes sense in this thinking? Did you hear the way Laloni remembered that this problem is about putting the cookies into fourths and how Rafi is seeing four cookies in each group? Can you add on to what they are noticing? Neeku? And let's stay focused on what makes sense about why someone would think this way.

Neeku: It makes sense that someone might want to put four in a group because we are finding fourths, but ... is it okay if we move to what someone using this solution might be confused about?

Mr. Barber: *(Glancing to their class to seek their approval before moving on, he nods.)* Yes, I think it is okay. What are you thinking about, Neeku?

Mr. Barber knows that beginning the discussion with a focus on the logic of the solution treats the students using this strategy as sense makers. Seeing that this solution puts four cookies in a group begins by honoring what children using this strategy understand about grouping and division. He now senses the logic is visible, and it is okay to move to make sense of what is confusing.

Neeku: It is kind of tricky, because you are supposed to put the cookies into four groups ... um ...

Mr. Barber: Here are some cubes to help you, or you can draw on the bottom of our poster to show your thinking.

Neeku: *(Taking the pen and approaching the poster.)* You see there are four in a group here? This mathematician put four in each group, four in a group. But what we really need is four groups.

Mr. Barber: Who can repeat what Neeku just said about the thinking of mathematicians who used this strategy? Rocio? Then, others, you can just jump in and repeat.

Rocio: There are four in each group, but we need four groups.

Ralph: The person who used this did not put them in four groups; he or she put four in a group.

Landen: There are four in a group, but we need four groups. It is, like, how many groups, not how many in a group.

Mr. Barber: We are hearing a difference between how many cookies to put in a group and how many groups of cookies to make. Let's look back at our story. "Mr. Barber had 24 cookies. He put them into fourths." Let's stop there and read that part again. "Mr. Barber had 24 cookies. He put them into fourths." What does it mean: he put them into fourths? How could we use the ideas that Neeku, Rocio, Ralph, and Landen shared to make sense of what it means to put the cookies into fourths? Jordan? You can use the cubes or the poster if that is helpful.

Jordan: *(Grabbing a handful of cubes and then quickly counting out 24.)* If these are your cookies, you have to put them into four groups.

Figure 7.5 Jordan makes four groups of cubes on the carpet

Mr. Barber: Four groups, or fourths. Can we watch you make those four groups?

Jordan: *(Doling out the cubes into four piles; see Figure 7.5)* 1, 2, 3, 4, 5, 6, 7, 8 ...

Mr. Barber: As you pass out those cookies into the four groups, Jordan, can you tell us why you are doing that for this problem?

Mr. Barber is asking Jordan to explain his thinking for two reasons. One is to hear the idea of making four groups again and underscore why that makes sense for this problem context. Another reason is to practice asking children questions when their solution is correct, not just incorrect. Mr. Barber frames ideas that are not fully mathematically correct as learning opportunities and also treats correct solutions as opportunities to ask students questions. Students can come to think a teacher's questions mean there is something wrong with their idea. The importance of a teacher pressing students to engage in this type of dialogue when the solution is correct will help children practice in sharing when their answer is correct as well as incorrect.

Jordan: I'm making four piles because the problem says the cookies were put into fourths. Once I make these four piles, the cookies will be in fourths. Like the whole group of cookies *(Mr. Barber inserts, "The 24 cookies")* will be in fourths, or four groups.

Eileen: Oh, wait! Wait, something is making sense to me now.

Mr. Barber: Eileen, what is happening for you?

Eileen: I was someone who used this strategy and I thought I needed to put four cookies in a group, but now I hear that I was really supposed to make four groups of cookies. Like this. *(Grabs the pen and draws on the poster.)* Here are four circles for groups and I'm putting a cookie in each group. *(See Figure 7.6.)*

Mr. Barber: Eileen, that is really exciting thinking you're doing! Smart mathematicians do just what you are doing—they continue thinking about problems and revise their thinking. In our classroom when you get more information and you want to change your thinking, you say, "I want to revise my thinking." Does anyone else want to revise their thinking like Eileen?

Figure 7.6 Here the poster shows four groups of cookies

Mr. Barber is supporting students in knowing that changing your idea when you have more information is a good thing to do, and he is explicitly telling children what you say when this happens.

Ruth: I do. I used this strategy too and I thought it was about making four in a group, but it is about making four groups like Jordan and Eileen did.

The class goes on to solve the rest of the story by figuring out how many cookies constitute three-fourths. Mr. Barber emphasizes the idea that everyone has a greater sense of fractions because of their opportunity to collectively think about this challenging concept together, and that without the investigation into this confusion, they would not all have the deeper understanding they now have about fractions of a set. The discussion ends with an affirmation of the way the class is able to make sense of this solution together and underscores the norms in this classroom for talking through misconceptions, the power of collaborative thinking, persisting through puzzling ideas, and revising ideas as new insights are developed. To check where each student is, Mr. Barber uses an exit ticket to collect students' ideas by asking them to answer the question, "What's the difference between putting something in groups of four versus finding fourths?"

"I Don't See Why This Statement Is False": Fourth Graders Troubleshoot and Revise Their Ideas About Relational Thinking

Ms. Simpson has noticed that her fourth graders are using ideas about the way multiplication behaves as they work on division strategies. In multiplication, students can break up either factor in order to create subproducts that can be combined to find the product. For example, when multiplying 75×14, students can break up the 75 or the 14 (or both).

$$75 \times 14 = (75 \times 10) + (75 \times 4)$$

or

$$75 \times 14 = (70 \times 14) + (5 \times 14)$$

This approach doesn't work in division, unless the divisor and dividend are both changed proportionally. When Ms. Simpson's class moves to a unit on division, she often uses true/false equations to challenge students to think relationally—to evaluate how the expressions are related on either side of the equal sign when determining whether a statement is true or false (Carpenter, Franke, and Levi 2003). When she sees one of her students, Jason, working hard to make sense of a particular true/false statement during morning work, Ms. Simpson asks him if he would like to troubleshoot his puzzlement with his class (see Figure 7.7).

Figure 7.7 Ms. Simpson has a consultation with Jason to see if he would like a troubleshooting discussion with his classmates

He thinks it would be a good idea. He has seen other classmates do this type of sharing and knows that all those minds working together can be really powerful. Since this situation has come up rather spontaneously, and it is in the midst of class, Ms. Simpson quickly sketches out her ideas on a planning template (see Figure 7.8).

Figure 7.8 Ms. Simpson's planning template for a *Troubleshoot and Revise* discussion about relational thinking

Troubleshoot and Revise

What is the confusion or misunderstanding we will discuss and revise?

Jason wants help explaining why this statement is false:

$$80 \div 4 = (80 \div 2) + (80 \div 2)$$

What is the insight I'd like students to understand?

The left side of the equation is about dividing 80 by 4.

The right side of the equation is about dividing 160 by 2, because 2 sets of 80 are each being divided by 2.

Problem context, diagrams, or questions that might be useful to use during the discussion

- Ask students to consider a problem context as a way of supporting Jason to think through the problem:
  Is 80 Skittles divided by 4 people the same as 80 Skittles divided by 2 people and another 80 Skittles divided by 2 people?
- Use turn-and-talk for students to first generate some ideas.
- Monitor turn-and-talk and select students who might be able to use the problem situation to determine whether the equation is true or false.
- Use a diagram to support visualizing what the equation is saying.
- Check in with Jason as explanations are provided to see if he is developing new insights. Ask him to state what his new insights are.

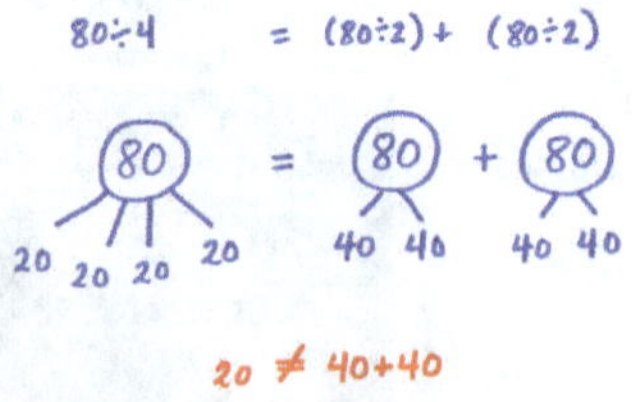

$80 \div 4 \quad = (80 \div 2) + (80 \div 2)$

(80) with 20 20 20 20 = (80) with 40 40 + (80) with 40 40

$20 \neq 40 + 40$

Exit ticket

Ask everyone to explain why the statement we focused on is false.

Chapter 7 Targeted Discussion: Troubleshoot and Revise

Ms. Simpson has to plan slightly differently for a troubleshooting discussion that begins with a student sharing. She has to prepare herself to slow down the conversation and really help the student who initiates the troubleshooting develop some new insights. But she also wants to be sure that the whole class benefits from the discussion.

Ms. Simpson: Okay, everyone, Jason would like our help with something he's finding quite perplexing. Remember, our job is to try to understand what Jason's questions are and then to help him think through the puzzle. We need to be generous with one another and be willing to look at this puzzle in more than one way. And you might find that you share Jason's puzzle, which is just great.

Ms. Simpson points to a poster she has made to remind students about ways of asking questions and stating ideas during a Troubleshoot and Revise discussion (see Figure 7.9). Ms. Simpson likes to remind her listeners how to think about the discussion that is about to take place.

Jason: So, I was working on this true/false problem that we got in our morning work and I thought it was true, but then Damien showed me that if you work out the numbers it can't be true. So now, I'm kind of confused.

Ms. Simpson: Let's put the true/false number sentence up so everyone can look at the one you're talking about. $80 ÷ 4 = (80 ÷ 2) + (80 ÷ 2)$

Figure 7.9 This poster provides sentence stems students can use during troubleshooting discussions

> **Troubleshooting**
>
> <u>For asking my classmates to help me think:</u>
> I am not sure about something and I want to ask for ideas.
> Can you help me understand why _____?
> I want to revise my thinking.
>
> <u>For helping my classmates think:</u>
> Can you tell us more about what is confusing you?
> What part feels the most confusing to you?
> What do you understand about _____?
> What do you know that can help you think about this?

Ms. Simpson: I'm wondering if someone can ask Jason a question.

Ms. Simpson prompts her students to ask Jason a question. She wants to help them learn how to ask questions of one another, so that she is not the only person asking questions.

Simon: Why did you think it was true?

Jason: I thought it was true because you're cutting 4 in half. It's 80 divided by 2, and then it's another 80 divided by 2. Because 2 plus 2 equals 4.

Preston: I thought it was true too. Because if you switch it around, it's 80 divided by 2 and 80 divided by 2 equals 80 divided 4. And 2 plus 2 equals 4. And the 80 stays the same.

Ms. Simpson sees a few other students nod in agreement. She often finds a Troubleshoot and Revise discussion supports more than just one student.

Ms. Simpson: Okay, so Jason, it's great that we are bringing this to the class for troubleshooting because it looks like some other people thought this was true as well. Let's be sure we understand the logic you were using to think through this. Who has another question for Jason?

Angela: *(Looking at the sentence stems on Ms. Simpson's poster.)* What do you understand about the 80?

Jason: I think the 80 is just what you're dividing.

Craig: What is the most confusing to you?

Jason: Well, I know that 2 plus 2 is 4, so I just don't understand why it's not true.

Ms. Simpson: So, can everyone turn to his or her partner and check in with one another? Do you understand what Jason is asking us?

Partners talk, pointing to the true/false equation as they talk. Ms. Simpson listens in on many of the conversations and hears that the class is focused on what Jason is saying.

Ms. Simpson: I think we're ready to give Jason some ideas to think about. What I heard Jason say is that he thought this statement had to be true because he saw that 4 was split up into 2 and 2 on the right side of the equal sign and the 80 stayed the same. Sometimes it helps us to think about a story problem as we think through a true/false statement. So, let me put a story problem around this. Is 80 Skittles divided by 4 children the same amount as 80 divided by 2 children and 80 divided by 2 children? Think about that.

Ms. Simpson decides to revoice Jason's question for the class herself. She also decides to offer a story problem context for the class to use, because contextualizing the quantities into a concrete situation can support relational thinking. She's not sure her students would necessarily think to generate a problem context themselves. Again, Ms. Simpson offers important thinking time for students to ponder the problem.

Min: What I think might help Jason is that if you have 80 Skittles and you do 80 divided by 2, then you already split up all the Skittles. You can't do it again, because all the Skittles are already gone. You can't change the divisor. You can only change the dividend.

Ms. Simpson: Jason, you look like you're not sure about what she said. Can you repeat what she said?

Jason: She said that you can't change the divisor, the 4.

Ms. Simpson: Right, that's part of what she said. Are you wondering why she said you can't change the divisor?

Jason: Yeah.

Ms. Simpson: Great. You can ask her to tell us again, and everyone, as you're listening, think about what Min is saying.

Ms. Simpson noticed that Jason picked up on the last part of what Min said; however, "You can't change the divisor" doesn't quite capture all of what is happening in this statement. She wants to slow this part of the conversation down and orient students to one another's ideas. She does this by asking Jason to hear from Min again.

Min: Because that's how many kids there are.

Ms. Simpson: And say again what were you saying about the 80 Skittles?

Min: If you split the 80 Skittles between the 2 people, then you already split all the Skittles and you can't split them again.

Ms. Simpson: So what do you think, Jason, about what she said? She said if you've split 80 Skittles between 2 people, you've used them up and you can't split them again. What do you think about that?

Jason: I'm beginning to think that it's false.

Ms. Simpson: So you're beginning to wonder. Akaya, what did you want to add?

Akaya: Can I come up? *(Ms. Simpson nods to her to come to the board.)* If you look at it, 80 divided by 4 is 20. Eighty divided by 2 is 40, and we can see that 20 is not the same as 40 + 40. *(She writes the inequality below the original one; see Figure 7.10.)*

Ms. Simpson: So Akaya is showing us that when we do the computation, we can see that the equation is not true. Let's try to connect that to the reasons Min is giving us too, about using up all the Skittles. Let's also add a picture of what this means. Let's draw a bag of Skittles. In this bag of Skittles, how many Skittles are there? Everyone?

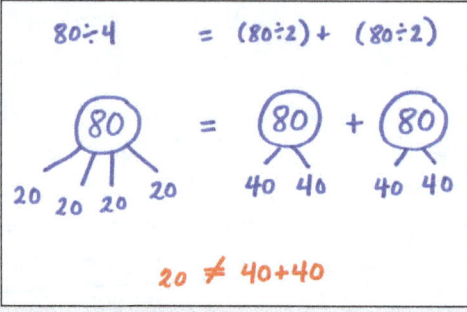

Figure 7.10 This class poster shows that 20 is not the same as 40 + 40

Everyone together: Eighty!

Ms. Simpson: And 80 divided by 4 tells us that we need 4 equal portions—so let me show that in the picture. *(Ms. Simpson adds to the poster by drawing a bag of Skittles divided up into 4 equal portions.)*

Now, with your partner, think about what the picture that goes on this side of the equation is going to look like *(pointing to the right-hand side of the poster)*. You can use your whiteboards to do this.

Ms. Simpson uses a turn and talk to again engage the whole class in making sense of the true/false statement. Because this Troubleshoot and Revise discussion was initiated by Jason, she moves to where he is talking with his partner to see the picture that he and his partner Addie are working on. She wants to support his choice of taking a risk in front of his classmates by bringing his confusion to the whole class. After seeing that he is making progress in figuring out what was confusing to him, she asks him to come up and finish the picture on the easel so that everyone can see a full representation of this equation.

Ms. Simpson: *(Signals the class to come back together.)* 5, 4, 3, 2, 1. Let me invite Jason to share the picture that goes with this side of the equation *(pointing to the open space on the right-hand side of the poster).*

Jason: Addie and I worked on this picture, and I think I see what Min is saying. On the other side, it has 80 divided by 2 and then another

Figure 7.11 The poster eventually shows the understanding reached by Jason and his classmates about why 80 ÷ 4 = (80 ÷ 2) + (80 ÷ 2) is false

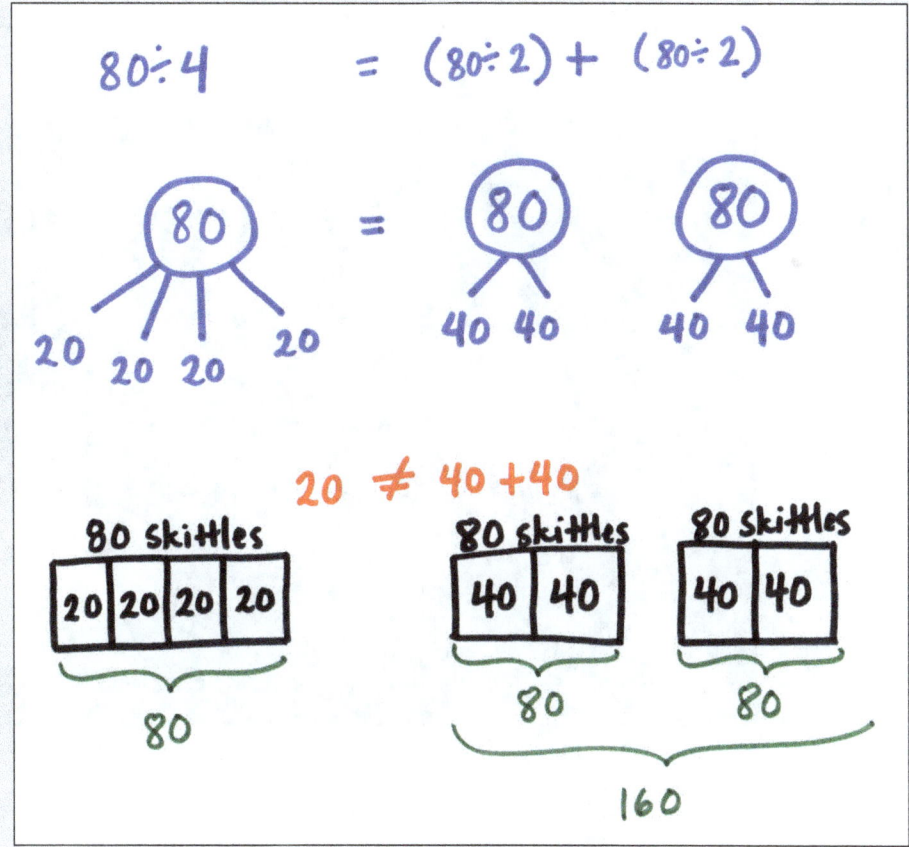

80 divided by 2. So I have to draw 2 bags of Skittles. What Min said makes sense. If I split up 80 for 2 people, like for me and Damien, then I don't really have any more Skittles left. But this side says I have 2 bags of 80 Skittles. So really, it's like I have 160 Skittles on this side, not 80. *(Jason finishes the picture; see Figure 7.11.)*

Ms. Simpson: This is a great time to check in with one another and see if we agree with the new thinking that Jason is sharing with us. Before we turn to talk, can you show Jason a thumbs-up if you are agreeing with his new thinking? *(See Figure 7.12.)*

After the pair share, Ms. Simpson asks everyone to write their thinking on an exit ticket. It's always helpful to get a read on the whole class. She has learned not to rely on just one discussion to solidify important ideas. She knows that individual time for reflection and trying to put

a new idea into one's own words is an important part of the learning process. She thinks the students have made progress today and sees the beginnings of many more explorations: When can you change the divisor in division? How might students explain why 80 ÷ 4 = (40 ÷ 2)?

Figure 7.12 Students show Jason they understand and agree with his new thinking

Summary and Reflection Questions: When Do I Want to Have a *Troubleshoot and Revise* Discussion?

We find the *Consultancy Protocol*, designed for use in Critical Friends Groups and developed by Gene Thompson-Grove and National School Reform Faculty, to be very helpful in thinking about how a teacher or student can initiate a discussion that works to *Troubleshoot and Revise* a mathematical idea or strategy. This protocol explains that:

> *a Consultancy is a structured process for helping an individual or a team think more expansively about a particular, concrete dilemma. Outside perspective is critical to this protocol working effectively; therefore, some of the participants in the group must be people who do not share the presenter's specific dilemma at that time* (n.d., 1).

Similarly, a *Troubleshoot and Revise* discussion is an opportunity for a student or group of students to think aloud together about mathematics that may be puzzling and, using the ideas of others, engage in collaborative sense making. Sometimes a confusion is minimal and may not warrant a group discussion. Other times, the confusion is greater, such as when students are mixing up important mathematical understandings or when an error is prevalent among the students in a class. A targeted discussion is useful in slowing down the conversation to uncover the confusion and bring new understanding. You may want to have a *Troubleshoot and Revise* discussion in these situations:

- You observe several students in your class grappling with an idea, and you think other students could help clarify the confusion.
- A student comes to you with an idea they are willing to put in front of the class, and you believe the class has the resources to support the student in thinking through the idea.
- You want to support norms for revising one's thinking.

Before you go on to the next chapter, reflect on these questions:

1. What worries me and excites me about facilitating *Troubleshoot and Revise* discussions with my students?
2. What do I think about the role of mistakes and confusion in learning mathematics with understanding?
3. How were mistakes and confusions framed when I was a learner of mathematics? How do I want to frame mistakes and confusions in my classroom?

CHAPTER 8

CONCLUSION: REFLECTING AND LEARNING

The vignettes in this book are not idealized portrayals of what students *might* be able to attain. They describe what students and teachers are capable of accomplishing together and are inspired by real discussions in elementary classrooms with our learning partners. We hope you've found them useful as you plan and consider how to foster joy for mathematics, navigate through your curricular resources, and support students to be successful mathematicians. We also hope the previous chapters have inspired you to try many new things in your classrooms and most importantly to learn from and with your students.

We know this work is hard and teachers face real pressures. At the same time, we don't want to give into the problems and pressures and put the work of finding space for discussions aside. Let's chew on some of the challenges together.

Do I Really Have Time for These Types of Discussions?

You may be wondering, "Do I really have time for these types of targeted discussions?" And you've probably already guessed our answer to this question! Most instructional materials in mathematics direct teachers to have discussions with their students but may not provide much explicit direction about what the goal of the discussion should be. For example, the text might say, "Have students compare their strategies" or "Discuss how to use an array." The next time you notice these directions, consider what the purpose is of students sharing or comparing solutions. Through discussion, we want students to make sense of each other's ideas, notice and analyze mathematical structure, model problem situations with mathematics, and develop viable mathematical arguments. These mathematical practices suggest different goals for discussion like the ones we have described such as comparing and connecting solutions to notice equivalencies, clarifying the meaning of mathematical representations and their use in problem solving, and revising strategies when they don't make sense. We think that when teachers take the time to facilitate sustained discussions, students will learn mathematics in ways that will stick.

My Students Don't Talk!

We regularly hear that it's hard for teachers to get students talking in mathematics class. You may be thinking that your students don't sound like the ones in our vignettes. When we shared our principles for engaging in talk and listening in Chapter 1, we stated that students need to be supported to learn how and what to share and listen in mathematics class. Sometimes, students don't talk as much because the question only has one right answer or the teacher asks all the follow-up questions and each exchange ends up being a dialogue only between one student and the teacher. Sometimes students don't talk because they really didn't follow what a classmate said, or they are not sure how to build on a classmate's idea.

One way to get all students talking is to ask certain follow-up questions to the whole group rather than just to the author of the solution. For example, you could ask your class to turn to a partner and say something about the strategy that was just shared: "How did Yara know where to stop counting?" "Why do you think the hundreds chart was helpful to Shaneé?" "Where do you see the answer in the steps that Sammy just described?" You could also prompt students to ask some of these questions themselves by saying something like "What can you ask Molly to better understand how she used the number line?" or "What do you wonder about how Keyvan kept track of the numbers he was adding?" Creating opportunities for student-to-student talk helps initiate interaction, encourage careful listening, and broaden participation. We have found the suggestions and minilessons in the book *Hands Down, Speak Out* to be useful in gauging how well your students are able to invite each other into conversation and learn how to guide conversations with quite minimal teacher facilitation (Omohundro Wedekind and Thompson 2020).

You know that your students are lively and talkative at lunch and during recess. So, what else can we do to encourage the free flow of ideas in mathematics class? You could practice having conversations about topics that students are really interested in and familiar with that are not necessarily mathematical. Conversation-worth prompts like "What was your favorite part of the field trip?" "Agree or disagree: Indoor recess is better than outdoor recess?" "How should we arrange our desks differently in class so that we can work with each other?" "What's your favorite thing to do with your family?" "The best superpower is …" "Which animal would you choose to be for a day?" can help students eagerly share their own ideas at the same time that they listen to their classmates' perspectives. During these more everyday conversations, you can explicitly model some of the moves that you want students to make like revising your thinking, sharing what your partner said, and asking questions. In the book *Classroom Discussions in Math* by Suzanne Chapin, Catherine O'Connor, and Nancy Anderson, the authors suggest introducing and working on one talk move at a time (2009). Slowing down is often a good way to broaden how many students feel comfortable trying on new ways of talking, listening, and using different strategies in the classroom.

The Same Students Talk! How do I Involve my Students More Intentionally in Orienting to Each Other?

It's very common for the same handful of students to do most of the talking during discussions. At some point, students get comfortable with letting certain students carry the conversation. You'll find the same voices eager to share their ideas and the same students more comfortable taking on listening roles. Although a lot of teachers are familiar with putting everyone's name on a popsicle stick and pulling a name at random, we encourage you to find other ways of working on equity of voice. We don't think randomized calling or cold calling supports students to decide how and when they can join conversations. We want to be intentional in how we create the conditions that invite a broad range of voices into discussions.

Being persistent in your framing about how and why everyone should contribute is important. We want to hear the wide variety of perspectives in our classroom. Honoring the different ways that students listen and talk also means that you pay attention to the hard work that listeners are doing. Providing good wait time and allowing students to share their initial thoughts in turn and talks helps students figure out what to contribute to whole-class discussions. Thinking time and turn and talks give each student a chance to try on or work through ideas. These participation structures also give you time to confer with students and select and invite new voices to bring into the conversation. We have seen teachers draw on a repertoire of strategies to help broaden whose ideas enter meaningfully into class discussions. Here's a list of those strategies we have highlighted in the vignettes in this book. What would you add to them?

- Invite students to listen to and share a partner's ideas.
- Invite students to ask a particular question that you might ask and open up space for students to ask questions.
- Ask a student to share how they got started in solving a problem and then pause. Invite students to talk in pairs about what they think the student might have done next. Then ask the student sharing to hear what some of her classmates think she might have done next.
- Use student work as a starting point for discussion (and be strategic about including work from students who may talk less in whole group discussions).
- Ask a student who shares less in whole group if it's okay for you to share their idea with the class.
- Facilitate a small-group discussion where each student takes a turn sharing to encourage listening and talking in a smaller learning environment.
- Use a video recording a student made to explain their work in their own voice to launch a discussion.
- Rotate who shares out from a partner conversation or small group work.
- Use exit cards and one-on-one conversations with students to understand what they thought was interesting, important, or confusing about a conversation and how they feel about sharing their ideas and listening.

Persistently working on each student in your class contributing to class discussions is also vital for changing the false narrative that only some people are good at math. If we pay attention to the language that circulates in schools about competence and ability–language like "low and high kids," "high flyers," "bubble kids," "IEP kids," "kids that don't have the language"—it's easy to see that we might be sending messages through our actions that there is a hierarchy of ability in mathematics. Stereotypes about gender and race in mathematics are still pervasive. It's very common to talk about the achievement gap in mathematics in racial terms, and these narratives of which students are successful or not in mathematics can influence the way we see our own students and therefore, the ways they see themselves (Aguirre, Mayfield Ingram and Martin 2024; Martin 2009).

Being attentive to how we think about our students and how we continue to invite students into the conversation through the discussion structures we share in this book is important for building broad participation among all the students in our class. The point of comparing and connecting strategies, for example, is not for students to see one strategy as better than another. As students learn to see the correspondences between one strategy and another, they make the mathematical structure underlying strategies explicit and visible to each other. Opening up conversations to understand the logic behind strategies, the processes of sense making and revision that students go through builds each students' confidence in their own ideas and connects them to the thinking of their classmates. Rachel Lambert writes about supporting students with disabilities in mathematics: "The opposite of deficit thinking is trusting in our students' thinking" (2024, 12). She goes on to say that teachers communicate this trust through the way they give students choices in how to solve problems, the intentional way they select tasks, and the fundamentally important decision to give students time to think.

I Don't See Myself as a Math Person

We know that many teachers had negative experiences with mathematics as students themselves and continue to find it hard to find teaching math enjoyable. For many teachers, opening up the classroom to see how students are approaching problems seems less efficient than just showing them how to solve problems and having them practice at their desks. If you're willing to try to understand the logic in students' ideas and are open to asking students to tell you what is and is not making sense to them, then you can start to put yourself in their shoes. Opening up conversations with your students can give you insights into what ideas students are grappling with, what connections are emerging for them, and why they chose to approach the problem in particular ways. If you are able to bring these noticings into your grade-level team meetings, your colleagues can help you think about the next opportunities that will help students build on their ideas. An important challenge in teaching is resisting the urge to just tell students how to think and instead create opportunities for them to develop their ideas together.

We want students to be successful, to get answers right in mathematics, but we don't serve students well if we always walk them through each problem. Problem solving is really a sense making process that requires a lot of trial and error. Our own ability to take risks in front of our students by trying out new pedagogical strategies and honing them over time through experimentation and conversation with colleagues is important for changing how we experience mathematics teaching and learning. Having a stance of curiosity about why things work and how children think about them will rub off on your students. Thinking about what's interesting and complex about the ideas that children are grappling with and the opportunity to work together with students and your colleagues can really shift what it means to be a math learner alongside your students. When you are conferring with students and small groups, take notes on what students are telling you about their work. Show that you are listening to their responses to your questions like "What makes this hard?" "Tell me about your drawing here?" "Why did you decide to do this first?" by writing their responses on their own work. Students appreciate that you're listening carefully and documenting what they tell you about their strategies on their paper. Your annotations have the added benefit of helping you remember what you learned while conferring with students. Our own growing identities as mathematicians shapes our students' identities.

Learning with Colleagues and with Students' Communities

We are firm believers that schools should be spaces where teachers learn with their colleagues and alongside their students. We know that schools continue to isolate teachers from one another, that grade-level team meetings and the ubiquitous professional learning communities (PLCs) can often feel like a chore rather than spaces that really inspire and invigorate our teaching. But time and again, we have seen the benefits of authentic teacher collaboration which includes making our practice public to one another so that we can puzzle through complex instructional decisions together. When we were working on the second edition of this book, we wanted to experiment with ways of connecting mathematical discussions to children's own interests and knowledge bases as well as what they were studying in other parts of their school day. We turned to our learning partners, and their experimentation inspired many of the new ideas within this book. We want to share a little window into the collaborative processes that took place as examples of how teachers can work together and with their instructional coaches to engage in learning together. The learning spaces and routines that we leveraged are described further in a book called *Learning Together* (Kazemi et al. 2024).

As we were thinking about new ideas in the second edition of this book, we reached out to Ms. Klein who is a mathematics coach and one of our learning partners. Because we wanted to explore ideas in both primary and upper grades, we joined her and the kindergarten and fourth-grade team during the regular PLC or grade-level team meetings she facilitates. During these meetings, the teachers think together about what they are learning from their students' participation and sense making in the prior lessons and how to build on the range of strategies they are noticing to plan for upcoming lessons. They also reflect on the ways the social and intellectual communities are developing in their classes. We joined their grade-level team meetings to consider how to adapt upcoming tasks by collaboratively revising and developing problem contexts that would activate students' everyday and community funds of knowledge (González, Moll, and Amanti 2005). We considered what events were happening in the school as well as topics that students were studying in other subjects and how they fit with the mathematical goals they were working on. We shared some examples we had been reading about in the literature and that our colleagues at Kamaliʻi Elementary School, who we write about in Chapter 2, had shown us. The teachers thought together, brainstorming possibilities and each had follow-up conversations with Ms. Klein (see Figure 8.1). We used a second PLC meeting to sketch out what each teacher might try and then debriefed and reflected what we learned from each lesson in a third PLC meeting. Three of the vignettes in

Figure 8.1 Ms. Klein meets with the fourth-grade team to brainstorm problem contexts

the book came from these conversations and collaborations: Ms. Root's lunch investigation in Chapter 4, Ms. Thomas's real life Mario Kart in Chapter 5, and Ms. Turner's beach field trip in Chapter 6. We wanted to share the other lessons that the broader team of teachers generated because they were joyful and authentic ways for children to have mathematical discussions within areas they were knowledgeable and invested in.

Kindergarten Lessons

1. Like Ms. Turner, Mr. Colasurdo invited his kindergarten class to share their experiences from a recent field trip to the beach (see Figure 8.2). Then he gave the children one particular photograph from the trip that could provoke many different mathematical stories and invited the children to share the stories they wrote.
2. Ms. Vinson wanted her kindergarten class's help in planning for their end-of-the-year class party. They needed to make lemonade for the party. So Ms. Vinson planned a hands-down conversation (Omohundro Wedekind and Thompson 2020) for students to comment on which pitcher to use to make the lemonade based on which they thought would hold the most lemonade and why (see Figure 8.3). Then they collected some data to compare their initial ideas and then filled each pitcher, comparing the actual number of cups each one took to fill.

Fourth-Grade Lessons

1. Ms. Todd had heard her fourth graders comment on places around the world that were meaningful to them either from their own travels or from their families' home places (see Figure 8.4). They used a world map to have a conversation about which places were important to them and why, marking the places with dots as they shared. After charting all the places, her students shared what they noticed about the distribution of the places and generated mathematical and non-mathematical questions they could ask about the distribution of the places around the world.
2. Ms. Simpson had taken many photographs and short videos from the school's field day, a favorite event among the students. One particularly joyful event was a foot race that teachers in the school participated in while wearing giant blow-up costumes. Ms. Simpson shared photographs and video clips from that particular race, and students reveled in the memories of that day and how funny it was to see their teachers try to run in these giant costumes. They asked important mathematical questions about the speed and distance involved in the race, leading to a question about how the mathematical concept of rate is determined (see Figure 8.5).

Chapter 8 Conclusion: Reflecting and Learning

Figure 8.2 Mr. Colasurdo listens to a student share his word problem based on their field trip

   We have seen so many examples of teachers adapting and experimenting with mathematical tasks that more richly connect students to one another and their communities. We share a few articles, books, and websites and invite you to collaborate with your colleagues and your students' families and communities to continue to imagine and create authentic communities for children to build their mathematical capabilities and identities together.

Figure 8.3 Ms. Vinson arranges pitchers of different sizes in the middle of the class circle. Which one will hold more lemonade?

We believe that school leaders—principals and coaches—play important roles in communicating that this work is valued and in creating space and time for collaboration. Our learning partners at Kamali'i Elementary have accomplished this collaboration through school-wide storybook read alouds like the one we described in Chapter 2. Claire Engelhard, a first-grade teacher working with a mathematics coach in her district, Bryan Street, and a team of colleagues

Figure 8.4 Ms. Todd listens to a student share his ideas about the data his class generated

Figure 8.5 Ms. Simpson invites students to mathematize a photograph from the school's field day

and teacher educators including Cathery Yeh, investigated how to bring Maria Zavala and Julia Aguirre's Culturally Responsive Mathematics Teaching Framework together with principles of universal design for learning (Zavala and Aguirre 2024; Yeh et al. 2024). As part of their collaboration, Ms. Engelhard was inspired to ask her students to interview family members about their jobs and the math they do in their everyday work. Her goal was to uplift and make visible the expertise in families' households and communities. These interviews helped build community and belonging within her classroom and were sources of pride as children were able to share the impressive ways that their family members used mathematics in their work. The interview provided openings for building rich and authentic contexts for mathematical investigations.

We know we have a long way to go before all students and all people feel a sense of belonging in mathematics class and in mathematics itself. For many students mathematics becomes a more and more difficult and inaccessible and uninviting subject as they progress through school. Many students see themselves more in the humanities than they do in mathematics. All of the classroom examples in this book have inspired us to think about how students can see mathematics as a way of expressing themselves and as an important and critical tool in understanding and asking questions of the world around them. Take a look at the resources in Appendix H for more sources of inspiration for supporting children to bring their whole selves to mathematics and for expressing themselves through mathematical problem solving.

How Can I Plan for Open and Targeted Discussions?

When you are making plans for a new unit, think about when you might use the discussion structures described in this book. Begin by listing the strategies that students are supposed to learn by the end of the unit. For example, in one second-grade unit on addition, students are expected to learn the following:

- Combining tens and ones (e.g., $67 + 34 = 60 + 30 + 7 + 4$)
- Incrementally adding on tens and then ones to a quantity (e.g., $67 + 34 = 67 + 30 + 4$)
- Regrouping tens when adding more than 10 ones

Once you have listed the focal strategies in the unit, you will have identified what strategies might emerge in *Open Strategy Sharing*. But this is just the beginning. We have to think more broadly about why we are learning these mathematical strategies so that the main learning is not just about arithmetic content. Thinking further about the concepts that are important and how the strategies are related to one another might lead you to consider when *Compare and Connect* discussions might be useful. For example, you might think about how analyzing the structure of numbers and understanding addition as joining quantities helps students make sense of why these strategies work and how they map on to each other.

You can plan to use other discussion structures in this book by noting the following:

1. What kinds of understandings, explanations, and justifications might students need to generate during this unit?
2. Are there times when one strategy might be more strategic than another?
3. What new mathematical objects (e.g., vocabulary, tools, representations, notation) will students be using?
4. What errors might students make and why? What's potentially confusing or challenging about the new strategies or tools that students will encounter?

5. How are social and community aspects of discussion developing in my class? What can I do to make sure that students are investing in each other's learning and feel connected to the content?
6. What community resources, student interests, family expertise, and other subject learning are connected to this unit? How might I encourage students' sense of belonging and connection to the community and to the mathematics we are studying?

Your responses to each of these questions and consideration of when they might be occurring in the unit will help you see openings for the discussion structures described in this book. Ask yourself what lessons in the unit lend themselves to one or more of the open or targeted discussions. You might not use all of the discussion structures in each unit. Thinking together with your colleagues and anticipating possibilities will help you be ready to recognize the possibilities as the unit unfolds. All of your planning and responding to students won't happen ahead of time. You'll be paying close attention to what's happening in the social and intellectual community in your class and adapt and improvise to emerging needs as the unit, and lessons, unfold.

Resources

In the appendices, you'll find blank planning templates for each of the discussion structures (Appendices A through F). Many of the lessons featured in this book are routine activities that can be used as warm-ups or lessons that you can seamlessly integrate into your math units at almost any grade level. In Appendices G and H you'll find more resources for imagining and using the discussion structures. Thank you for taking this journey with us. We know that your own experimentation with leading discussions will generate new ideas and support you and your students to experience mathematics as a rich and rewarding discipline.

APPENDIX

Appendix A: Planning Template for *Open Strategy Sharing* Discussion

Open Strategy Sharing		
Problem to pose		
Why I chose this problem	**Math Goal**	**Social or Community Goal**
Opening the lesson		
How might my students solve this problem?	**Who I saw solve it this way?**	**Share today?**
Notes to myself about what I'm trying to notice and listen for		
Other strategies that emerged during the lesson		
Closing the lesson		

Appendix B: Planning Template for *Compare and Connect* Discussion

Compare and Connect	
Strategy 1	**Strategy 2**
What are the connections that are important for students to notice?	
Supporting students' thinking	
What students might notice	**How I might respond to support their thinking**
What is the key mathematical idea I want to highlight?	

Appendix C: Planning Template for *Why? Let's Justify* Discussion

Why? Let's Justify

What mathematical strategy or idea are we targeting in our discussion?

What is the explanation I want the students to come up with?
(Include sketch of any representations that might be helpful for the explanation.)

Supporting student thinking
(If students say this... then I may ask them this to work toward stronger justification.)

What students might say	How I might respond

Appendix D: Planning Template for *What's Strategic and Why?* Discussion

What's Strategic and Why?
What are my mathematical and social goals? What are we trying to be strategic about?
What task/problems/prompt will help us discuss what is strategic and why?
What questions might I use? What would I like to hear from my students?

Intentional Talk and Listening: How to Structure and Lead Productive Mathematical Discussions by Elham Kazemi and Allison Hintz. Copyright © 2026. Taylor & Francis Group.

Appendix E: Planning Template for *Define and Clarify* Discussion

Define and Clarify

What new tool, representation, symbol, or vocabulary are we targeting in our discussion? Is this new to the students or are they using it in a new way?

What problem or task are we working on? How will I support meaning making? What partial understandings might arise?

Appendix F: Planning Template for *Troubleshoot & Revise* Discussion

Troubleshoot & Revise
What is the confusion or misunderstanding we will discuss and revise?
What is the insight I'd like the student to understand?
Problem context, diagrams, or questions that might be useful to use during the discussion
Exit ticket

Intentional Talk and Listening: How to Structure and Lead Productive Mathematical Discussions by Elham Kazemi and Allison Hintz. Copyright © 2026. Taylor & Francis Group.

Appendix G: *Open Strategy Sharing* Through Quick Images in a Fourth-Grade Classroom

In this appendix, we include an additional vignette to illustrate one way a teacher might use a familiar routine such as quick images within an *Open Strategy Share* discussion. In this discussion, Mr. William makes intentional moves to broaden who participates and how. He knows his students can share their thinking, but he wants to engage them as listeners to make sense of each other's ideas. Mr. William makes strategic use of turn and talks and the repeating talk move in order to broaden student participation in the discussion. Being mindful of using the talk moves in this way can keep students engaged in the conversation and build the class's ideas together.

Mr. William: Okay, here comes the image. Remember, your job is to figure out how many dots you see and remember how you saw them. Ready?

He displays the image (Figure G.1) with the document camera for three seconds, hides it for a few seconds, and then reveals it for another three seconds.

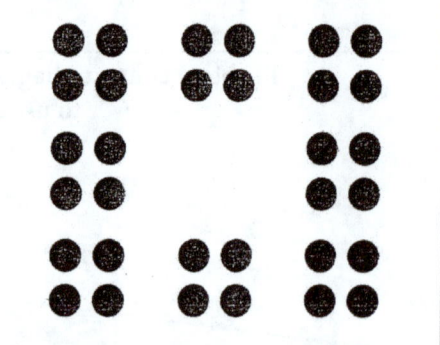

Figure G.1 Mr. William uses this as the second Quick Image for an *Open Strategy Sharing* session.

Mr. William: I want you to turn to your neighbor and share how many dots you saw and how you saw the dots. Make sure you both share. See if you have the same way or a different way.

By inviting the children to do a turn and talk about their solutions, Mr. William provides an opportunity for every student to share their strategy. He also has an opportunity to walk around the room and listen in to hear a range of ideas and to think about which ideas he wants to elicit.

Mr. William: I can hear a lot of interesting thinking. Let's come back together and share your solutions. I want to start with Divina. Divina, how did you think about this image? You explain, and I'll try to record what you saw.

Divina: *(Walking up to the screen and using her finger to point.)* I saw little groups of 4, and I saw 3 groups of 4 here *(pointing to the left-hand column)* and then 2 groups of 4 *(pointing to the middle column)* and then 3 more groups of 4 *(pointing to the right-hand column).*

Mr. William: Okay, let's stop there for a moment to make sure we all understand how you saw the groups of 4. Can someone repeat how Divina saw the groups of 4? Jose?

Mr. William will ask students to repeat their classmates' thinking at strategic and useful moments throughout the discussion. Repeating another person's idea helps students pay attention to each other's strategies to show they understand what their peers did. Putting their classmates' strategies in their own words allows students to practice and develop their academic language.

Jose: She said she saw them, like, in *(gesturing his hand up and down)* ... um ...

Mr. William: Columns? Are you showing columns with your hand? *(Jose nods.)* A column is a section that goes up and down. Okay, go on, Jose.

By the hand gestures Jose was using, Mr. William could see that he understood Divina's strategy for seeing the groups of four in columns. For Jose, an English language learner, and for many students, hand gestures are an important part of conveying what we mean. In this instance, Mr. William gave the student the mathematical word to use and supported him in showing his understanding.

Jose: And she saw them like a column of 3, then a column of 2, and then 1 more column of 3 groups. *(See Figure G.2.)*

Mr. William: Thank you, Jose. Divina, is that how you saw the dots? *(Divina nods, and Mr. William turns to the class.)* Do you think you could repeat to your neighbor what Jose just said about how Divina saw the dots in columns? *(Students turn and talk.)*

Figure G.2 Divina's strategy for counting dots

Mr. William now uses a turn and talk for a slightly different purpose. He wants to make sure everyone is on board with the strategy before moving on to a new one. It is another way his students are oriented to tracking and repeating others' strategies to show they understand what their peers did.

Mr. William: Let's come back together. Divina, how many dots did you see all together?

Divina: Thirty-two.

Mr. William: Who saw the dots the same way as Divina? *(Some students raise their hands.)* Who saw the dots in a different way? Ayoub?

Ayoub: I did. I saw groups of 4 also but when I had to figure out how many groups there were I filled in that hole in the middle. *(See Figure G.3.)*

Mr. William: What hole?

Ayoub: *(Pointing to the middle.)* Right there. Like, if there were 3 columns with 3 groups of 3 in each column.

Mr. William: *(To the class.)* Do you see the hole Ayoub is talking about? *(Students nod.)* Okay, go on.

Ayoub: So I knew if there were 9 groups of 4, that would be 36. But I had to take away that group of 4 in the middle that I had added.

Mr. William: How did you do that?

Ayoub: I went 36, 35, 34, 33.

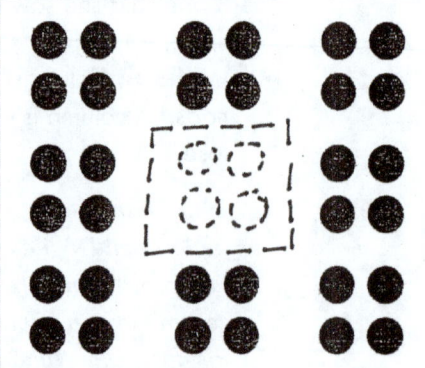

Figure G.3 Ayoub's strategy for counting dots

Mr. William: Okay. I hear you counting back to remove the 4. Can you use the number line to show us how you took those 4 away?

Ayoub: *(Pointing to 36 on the number line on the classroom wall and making jumps with his finger in the air.)* I start here and I jump back 1, 2, 3, 4. Wait, that's 32. I have to jump 4 times, so that's 32 I guess. I'm not sure why. I kind of think it should be 33.

Mr. William: Do you have another way to help you examine why that strategy isn't working?

Ayoub: Yeah, right, so if I didn't use the number line, I might just think 35, 34, 33, 32. Yeah, I see I should count the 36, but just go back from there. Yeah, I get it, it's 32. It's 32.

Mr. William: Okay, Ayoub, we hear the way you are revising your answer. You seem to be convinced now that your answer is 32. I want to be sure we're following what Ayoub said. It's important that you know you can ask Ayoub a question if you'd like to hear more about his choices. We may not always do a turn and talk, but you can jump in and ask.

Knowing Ayoub had made an error in his counting back, Mr. William is mindful of how to support him through this common misstep and position him as competent at the same time. Because Mr. William asks Ayoub if he has a different way, Ayoub finds a resolution to his error. Treating errors as important learning opportunities and a natural part of mathematical thinking maintains the norm that errors, even in intermediate grades, are not shameful. Mr. William is also shaping discussion expectations in his class by empowering students to be intent listeners and ask questions when they are not sure what a classmate did.

Savell: So, Ayoub said that he realized there were only 8 groups because if you count by threes, you'd have 9 groups of 4?

Ayoub: Yeah, I could see it sort of looked like a tic-tac-toe game, and there's 3, 3, and 3.

Mr. William: I really liked that you asked Ayoub to say more about his thinking. Let me see who used the same strategy as Ayoub. *(Five students raise their hand.)* Ayoub, you can see who was thinking like you on this problem. Well, we don't see everyone's hands, and we have time to hear one more way. Who has a different way than Divina and Ayoub? Olivia?

Olivia: I saw 8 groups of 4. And 8 times 4 is 32.

Mr. William: You saw 8 groups of 4. How many other people saw 8 groups of 4? Olivia, how did you know there were 8 groups?

Olivia: I started up here *(pointing to the upper left-hand group of dots)* and then I just continued around counting all the groups *(pointing in a clockwise circle around)*. (See Figure G.4.)

Mr. William: Let's see if we understand what Olivia did. Who can repeat what Olivia said? Hapsa?

Hapsa: She just went around. Like, 1, 2, 3, 4, 5, 6, 7, 8. Eight groups.

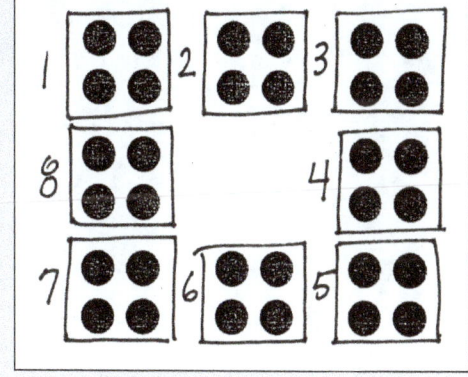

Figure G.4 Olivia's strategy for counting dots

Mr. William: Is that right, Olivia? *(Olivia nods.)* Okay, and how did you know that 8 groups of 4 is 32?

Olivia: I just know it. That's a fact for me.

Mr. William: You just know that one. Okay. *(Turning to the class.)* Do you agree with Olivia that 8 groups of 4, or 8 times 4 is 32? *(Students nod.)* Can we write a number sentence for what Olivia did? What would that look like? Emran?

Emran: It would be 8 times 4 equals 32. *(Mr. William records 8 × 4 = 32 on Olivia's image.)*

Mr. William: Nice. I want you to notice that we figured out three different ways to count out how many dots there were today.

Appendix H: Resources for Further Reading or Illustration

Video Resources for Developing Community and Leading Discussions

Watch examples of *Open Strategy Sharing* through Quick Images.	[QR code]
Watch a teacher lead *Open Strategy Sharing* followed by *Compare and Connect*.	[QR code]
Watch examples of *Why? Let's Justify* through true-false equations.	[QR code]
Watch how a teacher helps students come up with a set of social agreements for their mathematics class.	[QR code]
Watch an example of a *Why? Let's Justify* discussion in a second-grade classroom as students try to explain the commutative property of addition.	[QR code]

Watch an example of a discussion as second graders work to create a model for a separating situation.	[QR code]
Visit this site to access short student surveys that provide information about upper elementary school students' experiences with whole-class discussions.	[QR code]
Look at this book for many video clips of teachers supporting student reasoning and building equitable classroom communities.	Russell, Susan Jo, and Deborah Schifter. 2025. *Interweaving Equitable Participation and Deep Mathematics: Building Community in the Elementary Classroom*. Thousand Oaks, CA: Corwin.
Visit this site to access examples of routine mathematical activities that can build a productive classroom culture for discussions.	[QR code]
Visit this site to access resources and ideas for supporting teacher collaboration.	[QR code]

Books and Articles

- Aguirre, Julia, Karen Mayfield-Ingram, and Danny B. Martin. 2024. *The Impact of Identity in K–8 Mathematics: Rethinking Equity-Based Practice.* Reston, VA: National Council of Teachers of Mathematics.
  This book invites K-8 teachers to reflect on their own and their students' multiple identities to design and facilitate equity-based learning for all students, especially students who are marginalized by race, class, ethnicity, and/or gender.

- Carpenter, Thomas P., Elizabeth Fennema, Susan Empson, Megan L. Franke, and Linda Levi. 2014. *Children's Mathematics: Cognitively Guided Instruction.* Second edition. Portsmouth, NH: Heinemann.
  This book will develop your knowledge of the range of strategies that children use as they develop their conceptual and procedural knowledge of number and operations. It is full of video clips and examples that will help you focus your instructional decision making on children's thinking.

- Carpenter, Thomas P., Megan L. Franke, and Linda Levi. 2003. *Thinking Mathematically: Integrating Arithmetic and Algebra in Elementary School.* Portsmouth, NH: Heinemann.
  This book is an excellent source of true/false equations that can help you work on *Why? Let's Justify* targeted discussions.

- Carpenter, Thomas P., Megan L. Franke, Anita A. Wager, Angela C. Turrou, and Nicholas C. Johnson. 2016. *Young Children's Mathematics: Cognitively Guided Instruction in Early Childhood Education.* Portsmouth, NH: Heinemann.
  This book will give you lots of ideas about how children's early numeracy skills develop. It's full of video clips of children solving problems that will help you think about the mathematical goals of your lessons and the breadth of how children think.

- Chapin, Suzanne H., Catherine O'Connor, and Nancy C. Anderson. 2009. *Classroom Discussions: Using Math Talk to Help Students Learn.* Second edition. Sausalito, CA: Math Solutions.
  This book shows how to support students to learn the discussion expectations in your classroom, provides many vignettes to see the talk moves in action, and has practical lesson ideas for your classroom.

- Empson, Susan B., and Linda Levi. 2011. *Extending Children's Mathematics: Fractions and Decimals.* Portsmouth, NH: Heinemann.

This book will develop your knowledge of children's thinking in fractions and decimals.

- Featherstone, Helen, Sandra Crespo, Lisa M. Jilk, Joy A. Oslund, Amy N. Parks, and Marcy B. Wood. 2011. *Smarter Together! Collaboration and Equity in the Elementary Math Classroom.* Reston, VA: National Council of Teachers of Mathematics.
This book provides a vision for how to support students to work together and show all students that their ideas are valued.

- Franke, Megan, Elham Kazemi, and Angela Turrou. 2018. *Choral Counting and Counting Collections: Transforming the PreK-5 Classroom.* Portland, ME: Stenhouse.
This book focuses on two classroom routines—Choral Counting and Counting Collections—that support students' understanding of number and operations and reasoning through counting.

- Hintz, Allison, and Antony T. Smith. 2022. *Mathematizing Children's Literature: Sparking Connections, Joy, and Wonder Through Read-Alouds and Discussion.* Portsmouth, NH: Stenhouse.
This book invites teachers to think beyond counting and shapes books in mathematics classes to consider how to approach any story with a math lens. Through primary and intermediate vignettes, the book provides examples and ideas for interactive read-alouds that nurture students as mathematicians who ask their own questions and make connections to their lives and their world.

- Hintz, Allison, and Kersti Tyson. 2015. "Complex Listening: Supporting Students to Listen as Mathematical Sense Makers." *Mathematical Thinking and Learning* 17(4): 296–326.
This article brings attention to different types of complex listening entailed for students and teachers in classroom discussions.

- Hintz, Allison, Kersti Tyson, and Andrea English. 2018. "Actualizing the Rights of the Learner: The Role of Pedagogical Listening". *Democracy and Education* 26(2): 1–10.
This article helps illuminate the listening entailed for teachers to support young mathematicians in classroom discussions.

- Jansen, Amanda. 2020. *Rough Draft Math: Revising to Learn.* Portsmouth, NH: Stenhouse.
This book supports educators to facilitate classroom discussions where students share their evolving understandings and ongoing revision of their mathematical ideas.

Appendix

- Lambert, Rachel. 2024. *Rethinking Disability and Mathematics: A UDL Math Classroom Guide for Grades K-8*. Thousand Oaks, CA: Corwin.
  This book describes how to design math classrooms that empower disabled and neurodiverse students to engage in meaningful and joyful math learning.

- Omohundro Wedekind, Kassia, and Christy Hermann Thompson. 2020. *Hands Down, Speak Out: Listening and Talking across Literacy and Math*. Portsmouth, NH: Stenhouse.
  This book centers students' ideas and voices in classrooms where teachers focus on listening and helping students invite each other into conversation.

- Parrish, Sherry. 2010. *Number Talks: Whole Number Computation*. Sausalito, CA: Math Solutions.
  A source of sequenced computation problems to work on particular strategies. This book provides great fodder for *What's Strategic and Why?* discussions. Many video clips that accompany this book provide ideas for how to encourage students to participate and how to teach them to carefully use representations to make ideas clear to listeners.

- Rumsey, Chepina, and Jody Guarino. 2024. *Nurturing Math Curiosity with Learners in K-2*. Bloomington, IN: Solution Tree.
  This is a great resource for building students' argumentation skills through a variety of math routines that fit well with *Why? Let's Justify* discussions.

- Russell, Susan Jo, and Deborah Schifter. 2025. *Interweaving Equitable Participation and Deep Mathematics: Building Community in the Elementary Classroom*. Thousand Oaks, CA: Corwin.
  This book includes many case examples and video clips of teachers and students building community in a classroom to support student voice and agency.

- Russell, Susan Jo, Deborah Schifter, and Virginia Bastable. 2011. *Connecting Arithmetic to Algebra: Strategies for Building Algebraic Thinking in the Elementary Grades*. Portsmouth, NH: Heinemann.
  This book contains many examples of how to support students to generate strong justifications to develop their understanding of number and the behavior of the operations.

- Smith, Margaret S., and Mary Kay Stein, 2018. *5 Practices for Orchestrating Productive Mathematics Discussions*. Second edition. Thousand Oaks, CA: Corwin.
  The five practices for orchestrating discussions in this book are enormously helpful in planning for discussions in general.

- Shumway, Jessica. 2011. *Number Sense Routines: Building Numerical Literacy Every Day in Grades K–3.* Portland, ME: Stenhouse.
  In this book you will find lots of ideas for tasks that can build students' understanding of number, and routine activities to use regularly throughout the year.

- Storeygard, Judy, ed. 2009. *My Kids Can: Making Math Accessible to All Learners, K–5.* Portsmouth, NH: Heinemann.
  This book contains many examples of productive classroom discussions and describes how to engage a broad range of learners, particularly students with special needs. One of the many video clips that accompany this book provides a great example of a teacher asking students how they use the tens frame to help them count an arrangement of dots, which provides an example of *Define and Clarify*.

- Zager, Tracy J. 2017. *Becoming the Math Teacher You Wish You'd Had: Ideas and Strategies from Vibrant Classrooms.* Portland, ME: Stenhouse.
  This book inspires mathematics in schools to be more like mathematics as a discipline. Through student-centered problem solving, routines, and rich tasks, this book describes teaching that inspires collaboration, wonder, and joyful learning.

- Zavala, Maria, and Julia Aguirre. 2024. *Cultivating Mathematical Hearts: Culturally Responsive Mathematics Teaching in Elementary Classrooms.* Thousand Oaks, CA: Corwin Press.
  This book centers children and their humanity to create safe, inclusive spaces where all learners can develop a love for mathematics through engaged and meaningful learning that integrates their lived experiences and hearts.

REFERENCES

Aguirre, Julia, Karen Mayfield-Ingram, and Danny B. Martin. 2024. *The Impact of Identity in K–8 Mathematics: Rethinking Equity-Based Practice*. Reston, VA: National Council of Teachers of Mathematics.

Carpenter, Thomas P., Megan L. Franke, and Linda Levi. 2003. *Thinking Mathematically: Integrating Arithmetic and Algebra in Elementary School*. Portsmouth, NH: Heinemann.

Chapin, Suzanne H., Catherine O'Connor, and Nancy C. Anderson. 2009. *Classroom Discussions: Using Math Talk to Help Students Learn*. 2nd edition. Sausalito, CA: Math Solutions.

Common Core State Standards Initiative. 2012. "Standards for Mathematical Practice." http://www.corestandards.org/assets/CCSSI_Math%20Standards.pdf.

Featherstone, Helen, Sandra Crespo, Lisa M. Jilk, Joy A. Oslund, Amy N. Parks, and Marcy B. Wood. 2011. *Smarter Together! Collaboration and Equity in the Elementary Math Classroom*. Reston, VA: National Council of Teachers of Mathematics.

Franke, Megan, Elham Kazemi, and Angela Turrou. 2018. *Choral Counting and Counting Collections: Transforming the PreK-5 Classroom*. Portland, ME: Stenhouse.

Fosnot, Catherine T., and Maarten Dolk. 2001. *Constructing Number Sense, Addition, and Subtraction*. Portsmouth, NH: Heinemann.

González, Norma, Luis C. Moll, and Cathy Amanti. Eds. 2005. *Funds of Knowledge: Theorizing Practices in Households, Communities, and Classrooms*. Mahwah, NJ: Erlbaum.

Hiebert, James, Thomas P. Carpenter, Elizabeth Fennema, Karen C. Fuson, Diana Wearne, Hanlie Murray, Alwyn Olivier, and Piet Human. 1997. *Making Sense: Teaching and Learning Mathematics with Understanding*. Portsmouth, NH: Heinemann.

Humphreys, Cathy, and Ruth Parker. 2015. *Making Number Talks Matter*. Portland, ME: Stenhouse.

Jacobs, Victoria R., and Julie Kusiak. 2006. "Got Tools? Exploring Children's Use of Math Tools During Problem Solving." *Teaching Children Mathematics* 12(9): 470–7.

Jansen, Amanda. 2020. *Rough Draft Math: Revising to Learn*. New York: Routledge.

Kazemi, Elham, Calabrese, Jessica, Lind, Teresa, Lewis, Becca, Resnick, Alison, and Lynsey K. Gibbons. 2024. *Learning Together: Organizing Schools for Teacher and Student Learning.* Cambridge, MA: Harvard Education Press.

Kimmerer, Robin Wall. 2013. *Braiding Sweetgrass.* Minneapolis, MN: Milkweed Editions.

Lambert, Rachel. 2024. *Rethinking Disability and Mathematics: A UDL Math Classroom Guide for Grades K-8.* Thousand Oaks, CA: Corwin.

Lannin, John K., Amy B. Ellis, and Rebekah Elliott. 2011. *Developing Essential Understanding of Mathematical Reasoning for Teaching Mathematics in Prekindergarten–Grade 8.* Reston, VA: National Council of Teachers of Mathematics.

Loomis, Ilima. 2020. *'Ohana Means Family. Illustrated by Kenard Pak.* New York: Neal Porter Books.

Martin, Danny. 2009. "Does race matter?" *Teaching Children Mathematics* 16(3): 134–9.

Michaels, Sarah, Mary Catherine O'Connor, and Megan Williams Hall. 2010. *Accountable Talk Sourcebook: For Classroom Conversations That Work.* University of Pittsburgh: Institute for Learning. ifl.lrdc.pitt.edu/ifl/index.php/download/index/ats/.

Omohundro Wedekind, Kassia, and Christy Hermann Thompson. 2020. *Hands Down, Speak Out: Listening and Talking Across Literacy and Math K-5.* Portsmouth, NH: Stenhouse.

Paley, Vivian. G. 1986. "On Listening to What the Children Say." *Harvard Educational Review* 56(2): 122–31.

Parrish, Sherry. 2010. *Number Talks: Helping Children Build Mental Math and Computation Strategies.* Sausalito, CA: Math Solutions.

Russell, Susan Jo. 1999. "Mathematical Reasoning in the Elementary Grades." In *Developing Mathematical Reasoning in Grades K–12. 1999 NCTM Yearbook*, ed. L. Stiff. Reston, VA: National Council of Teachers of Mathematics.

Russell, Susan Jo, Deborah Schifter, and Virginia Bastable. 2011. *Connecting Arithmetic to Algebra: Strategies for Building Algebraic Thinking in the Elementary Grades.* Portsmouth, NH: Heinemann.

Russell, Susan Jo, Deborah Schifter, Reva Kasman, Virginia Bastable, and Traci Higgins. 2017. *But Why Does It Work?: Mathematical Argument in the Elementary Classroom.* Portsmouth, NH: Heinemann.

Shumway, Jessica F., 2011. *Number Sense Routines: Building Numerical Literacy Every Day in Grades K–3.* Portland, ME: Stenhouse.

Smith, Margaret S., and Mary Kay Stein, 2011. *5 Practices for Orchestrating Productive Mathematics Discussions.* Reston, VA: National Council of Teachers of Mathematics.

Staples, Megan. 2008. "Promoting Student Collaboration in a Detracked, Heterogeneous Secondary Mathematics Classroom." *Journal of Mathematics Teacher Education* 11(5): 349–71.

Staples, Megan, and Melissa Colonis. 2007. "Making the Most of Mathematical Discussions." *Mathematics Teacher* 101(4): 257–61.

Storeygard, Judy, ed. 2009. *My Kids Can: Making Math Accessible to All Learners, K–5.* Portsmouth, NH: Heinemann.

Thompson-Grove, Gene, and National School Reform Faculty. n.d. *Consultancy Protocol*. National School Reform Faculty. https://www.nsrfharmony.org/wp-content/uploads/2017/10/consultancy_0.pdf

Uttenbogaard, William, and Catherine Twomey Fosnot. 2008. *Minilessons for Extending Multiplication and Division: A Yearlong Resource*. Portsmouth, NH: Heinemann.

Yeh, Cathery, Rigby, Lauren, Huerta, Suzanne, and Claire Englehard. 2024. "Culturally Sustaining Universal Design for Mathematics Learning." *Mathematics Teacher Learning & Teaching* 117(11): 792–801.

Zavala, Maria, and Julia M. Aguirre. 2024. *Cultivating Mathematical Hearts: Culturally Responsive Mathematics Teaching in Elementary Classrooms*. Thousand Oaks, CA: Corwin.

INDEX

Note: For figure citations, page numbers appear in *italics*. For table citations, page numbers appear in **bold**.

A
accountable talk 3
active listening 25, 67, 73, 79, 88, 98
active participation 61, 63, 65, 67, 79
adding/addition: adding on **29**, 75; commutative property 205; even numbers 82; problems 96–7, 118, 190; strategies 63–72, *64*, **65**, *67*, *69*
agency 209; *see also* voice
agreement/disagreement with mathematics 26
Aguirre, Julia 4, 189, 207, 210
American Sign Language 9
Anderson, Nancy C. 26, 207
arrays 13–14, 20, 86–93, *89*; annotated *14*; Define and Clarify structure 152–9; open array *14*, 133, 134, 152–9; Troubleshoot and Revise strategy 15
asset-based approach 16

B
Bastable, Virginia 84, 109, 209
book resources 207–10 (App H)
brainstorming 185; sessions *185*
But Why Does It Work? Mathematical Argument in the Elementary Classroom (Russell, 2017) 82

C
Carpenter, Thomas P. 207
Chapin, Suzanne 26, 207
children's literature 33–52; *see also* '*Ohana Means Family*
Choral Counting 208
clarification **28**, 152
classroom communities 3–4, 6, 15, 26, 48, 54–5, 206
classroom discussion *see* targeted discussion
Classroom Discussions in Math (Chapin, O'Connor and Anderson, 2009) 26–7, 181, 207
collaboration 55, 206, 210
colleagues, learning with 184–90
Colonis, Melissa 162
Common Core State Standards for Mathematical Practice (2012) 13, 82, 123, 161–2
communication, importance of 2
community: goals 34; norms 61; resources 191
commutativity 83–4
Compare and Connect structure **6**, 20, 59–80, 190; adding strategies 63–72, *64*, **65**, *67*, *69*; discussion communities 60; hundreds chart *72*, *77*, *78*; mathematical discussions 60–1; number lines *64*, **65**, *67*, *69*, *72*, *74*; planning discussions 62–3; planning template *65*, 195 (App B); summary and reflection questions 79–80; video resources 205
compensation strategies 13, 19
competence 183

complex listening 208
computational number talks 55
Connecting Arithmetic to Algebra (Russell, Schifter, Bastable, 2011) 84, 209
consultancy, definition of 176
Consultancy Protocol 176
counting activities 54; 'Ohana Means Family 37–50; visual examples *38*, *43*, *49*
counting aloud 50
counting back *122*, *125*, 125–9; open number line *125*; planning template *122*; strategies 121–9, *125*
Counting Collections 208
counting cubes 73
counting dots *201*, *202*, *203* (App G)
counting on *122*, 125, 128–9; by bigger increments 63; by ones 63, 65–6, 70–1, 79; planning template *122*; by strategic increments 79; strategies 65, 121–9
counting out loud 89
counting up: by ones *67*, 130; by tens 130
Crespo, Sandra 208
Critical Friends Groups 176
cubes 133
Culturally Responsive Mathematics Teaching Framework 189
curiosity 2, 55, 112, 184

D

data analysis and discussion *188*
decimal notation: Define and Clarify 147–52, *148*, *150*; fraction notation compared *150*; planning template *148*; representation *148*, *149*, *150*
decimals 133–4, 147–51, 207–8
decomposing a factor in multiplication 94
Define and Clarify structure **6**, 21, 133–59, 210; counting past 100 134–8; decimal notation 147–52; division problems *158*; equations and story situations 138–47; field trips, photographs of *139*, *140*; hundred chart *136*; kindergartners 134–7; math story problems *143–6*; multiplying-up strategy *154*, *155*, *156*; notice and wonder activity *142*; noticing work *140*; open arrays 152–9; partners, listening and talking in *141*; planning template *135*, *148*, *153*, 198 (App E); summary and reflection questions 159; two-hundreds chart *136*
developing argumentation 13, 61
disability 25, 183, 209; *see also* neurodiversity
discussion expectations 27
division problems 82, 153, *158*, 169
Dolk, Maarten 121
doubles strategy 130

E

early numeracy skills 207
Empson, Susan 207
English, Andrea 3, 208
environment, classroom *see* classroom communities
equals sign 100, 169
equations 100; writing story situations 138–47; *see also* true/false equations
equity-based learning 207; classroom communities 206; participation 2; student voice 181–3
errors 190; *see also* mistakes
estimating/estimation 118–21
ethnicity 207
exit cards 164, 182
explanations 5

F

Featherstone, Helen 208
Fennema, Elizabeth 207
field trips 138–9, *139*, 186; word problems *187*
5 Practices for Orchestrating Productive Mathematics Discussions (Smith and Stein, 2011) 5
Fosnot, Catherine 121
fractions 83, 134, 147–52, 207–8; finding fractions of a set 162–8; notation *150*; Troubleshoot and Revise structure 162–8
Franke, Megan L. 207–8

G

gender 183, 207
gestures 25
gifts 2
'Got Tools? Exploring Children's Use of Mathematics Tools During Problem Solving' (Jacobs and Kusiak, 2006) 159
Guarino, Jody 209
Gutiérrez, Rochelle 3–4

H

Hands Down, Speak Out (Wedekind and Thompson, 2020) 112, 181, 209
Hiebert, James 134
Humphreys, Cathy 121
hundreds chart 20, 73, 76–9, 133; Compare and Connect structure *72, 77, 78*; Define and Clarify structure *136*

I

informal language 25
innovation 56
intelligence 24

J

Jacobs, Victoria 159
Jansen, Amanda 208
Jilk, Lisa M. 208
Johnson, Nicholas C. 207
journals 8–9; arrays 14
jumping forward *127*
justification 82, 98, 101, 103; appeal to authority 83; deductive argument 84; examples 83; generic examples 83–4; language of 106; *see also* Why? Let's Justify structure

K

Kimmerer, Robin Wall 2
Kusiak, Julie 159

L

Lambert, Rachel 183, 209
learning environments *see* classroom communities

Learning Together (Kazemi et al., 2024) 184
Levi, Linda 207
listening *see* active listening; complex listening; talk and listening moves
literature *see* children's literature
Loomis, Ilima 32

M

Making Number Talks Matter (Humphreys and Parker, 2015) 121
making sense of mathematics 25
Making Sense: Teaching and Learning Mathematics with Understanding (Hiebert et al., 1997) 134
making tens strategy 130
manipulatives 73
maps 115–16, *116*, 186
Mario Kart video game 112–18, 186; map and data discussion *116, 117*; YouTube video *113, 114*
Martin, Danny B. 207
mathematical discussions 5
mathematical goals 2, 5–6
mathematical objects 20–1, 133, 190; *see also* symbols; tools; vocabulary
mathematical quantities 13
mathematical reason 98
Mayfield-Ingram, Karen 207
mental math 8–12; benefits of 8; *see also* targeted sharing
meter/yard sticks 73
Michaels, Sarah 2, 24
Mini Lessons for Extending Multiplication and Division (Uttenbogaard and Fosnot, 2008) 84–5
mistakes 25, 61; *see also* errors
models 20–1
multilingual students 25
multiplication problems 8–12, 82, 91–3, 153, 169; decomposing factors *94*; 'Ohana Means Family 35–40
multiplying-up strategy 153, *154, 155, 156*

N

negative experiences 183–4
negative numbers 83

neurodiversity 209
non-verbal communication 25
norms for doing mathematics 25–6
notation 20–1, 190
notice and wonder 142
'noticings' in math 103–8, *104–7*, 115, 140–1, 183
number lines 20, 68–70, 133; Compare and Connect to hundreds chart *72*; counting back strategy *125*; jumping forward *127*; open 74–6, 78–9; visual examples *64*, **65**, *67*, *69*, *72*, *74*
number strings 121, *123*
number talk images 54, *54*
Number Talks (Parrish, 2014) 121, 209
number-and-operation sense 134, 207

O
O'Connor, Mary Catherine 2, 24, 26, 207
'Ohana Means Family' 32–52, 58; book cover *33*; circling activities *41*, *51*; counting activities *38*, *43*, *49*; counting strategies 37–50; multiplication strategies 35–40; story-time *45*; two-page spreads *34*, *37*, *46*
Omohundro Wedekind, Kassia 112, 209
one-on-one conversations 182
open discussions, planning for 190–1
Open Strategy Sharing 5, 8–12, 20, 23–58, 190, 200; in action 32–3; beginning 24–9; children's literature 33–52; circling activities *41*, *51*; Compare and Connect compared 63; counting activities *38*, *43*, *49*; Define and Clarify compared 154; definition of 24; discussion *36*; goals of 24; open-ended tasks 53–5; planning for 30–2; planning template *31*, *34–5*, *46–7*, 194 (App A); quick images 200–4 (App G), *200*, *201*, *202*, *203*; respectful communities 53–6; student discussion 55–6; student participation 56–7; summary and reflection questions 58; teachers, role of 52–3; video resources 205;
What's Strategic and Why? structure compared 130; wide participation 53–5
orientation, student 2, 7–8
Oslund, Joy A. 208

P
Pak, Kenard 32
Paley, Vivian 5
parallel lines 133
Parker, Ruth 121
Parks, Amy N. 208
Parrish, Sherry 121, 209
partners: learning 179, 184–5, 188; listening and talking in 141, *141*, 164–5, 172
persistence 25
photographs 186; field trip to the beach *139*, *140*; lunch containers 103–8, *104*; mathematizing *189*; school's field day *189*
place value 84, 94–5, 97–9, 102
planning templates: Compare and Connect structure *65*, 195 (App B); counting back and counting on *122*; decimal notation *148*; Define and Clarify structure *135*, *148*, *153*, 198 (App E); Open Strategy Sharing *31*, *34–5*, *46–7*, 194 (App A); Troubleshoot and Revise structure *163*, *170*, 199 (App F); What's Strategic and Why? structure *122*, *197* (App D); Why? Let's Justify structure *85*, *102*, 196 (App C)
problem-solving skills 134, 184, 210
problems, nature of 60–1
procedures 5
product 133
professional learning communities (PLCs) 184–5
protractors 133

Q
QR codes 113, 205–6
quantity: comparing 129; containers measuring *188*

questions, asking 26
Quick Images 55
quiet students 60, 180–1

R

race 183, 207; achievement gap in mathematics 183
rate, mathematical concept of 186
reasoning **28**, 82, 206, 208
recording discussions 55
reflecting and learning 179–91
relational thinking 169–76, *170*
repetition/repeating 11, 27, **28**, 75, 128
representations 5, 133, 190
resources 191; *see also* articles; book resources; video resources
revising **29**, 32, 52; one's thinking 27, 52
revoicing **28**, 98, 128
roller coaster examples 86–8
routines 54, 210; mathematical activities 206; maths tasks and *54*; world routine *54*
rulers 73
Rumsey, Chepina 209
Russell, Susan Jo 82, 84, 109, 209

S

'same as' 100
Schifter, Deborah 84, 109, 209
sense makers, students as 4–5
separating situations 206
Shumway, Jessica 210
sign language *see* American sign language
signing strategies 9, *10*
skip-counting tasks 84
small-group discussion **29**, 30, 35, 37, 39, 46, 61, 182, 184
'smartness' 4–5, 26, 162
Smith, Antony T. 208
Smith, Margaret S. 5, 209
social agreements 205
social goals 2, 5–6, 34, 78
Standards for Mathematical Practices, Common Core State Standards (2012) 25
Staples, Megan 162
Stein, Mary Kay 5, 209

Storeygard, Judy 210
strength-based approach 16
student communities, learning with 184–90
subtraction problems 73–6, 83, 121–9, 145–7
support for students 2, 6–7
surveys, student 206
symbolic notation 134, 147
symbols 133, *146*

T

talk and listening moves 26–9, **28**–**9**, *30*
targeted discussion 6, 12; planning for 190–1; structure **6**; time for 180
targeted sharing 13–19
tasks 54, *54*, 210; nature of 60–1
teachers, role of 52–3
tens frame 20
think time 29, *95*, 103, 116, 123–4, *124*, 145, 151
Thompson-Grove, Gene 176
Thompson, Christy Hermann 112, 209
tools 20–1, 73, 79–80, 133–4, 159, 190
toys 86–8
Troubleshoot and Revise structure **6**, 15–19, 21, 161–77; class posters *168*, *171*, *174*, *175*; classmate discussion *169*; exit ticket problem *164*; fractions 162–8; grouping cubes *167*; grouping strategies *167*, *168*; planning template *163*, *170*, 199 (App F); relational thinking 169–76, *170*; revision strategies *164*, *165*; sentence stems for discussion *171*; student agreement/feedback *176*; summary and reflection questions 176–7; teacher consultation *169*
true/false equations *95*, 94–7, 102, 169–73, 207
turn and talk 182, 200–3; Compare and Connect structure 73, 75; Define and Clarify structure 141, 155; Open Strategy Sharing 27, **29**, 52; Troubleshoot and Revise structure 164–5, 170, 174; What's Strategic and Why? structure 124, 128; Why? Let's Justify structure *99*

Turrou, Angela C. 207–8
two-hundreds chart 134–8, *136*
Tyson, Kersti 3, 7, 208

U

unifix cubes 84
universal design for learning 189

V

value: of experiences 4–5; of ideas 208
video recordings 182
video resources 205–7 (App H)
vocabulary 20–1, 133, 190
voice, student 181–3, 209; *see also* quiet students

W

Wager, Anita A. 207
wait time **29**, 75, 79
What's Strategic and Why? structure **6**, 20, 111–31, 209; counting back *vs* counting on 121–9, *122*; information organization 130; Mario Kart video and discussion *113*, *114*, *116*, *117*; mathematical ideas 131; planning template *122*, 197 (App D); strategically adding a set of numbers 112–21; summary and reflection questions 129–31; think time *124*; transitioning between strategies 130; useful strategies 130
whiteboards 86–7, 103, *105*, 155, 174
whole-class discussions 206
Why? Let's Justify structure **6**, 13–15, 20, 81–109, 207, 209; drawing pictures *101*; justification, forms of 83–4; kindergarteners 102–8; kneeling to listen 99; labelling and sorting activities *107*; lunch containers, photographs of *104*; planning template *85*, *102*, 196 (App C); sorting images *106*; summary and reflection questions 108–9; think time *95*; video resources 205; whiteboards, pointing to *105*; zeroes, appending 84–93, *85*, *91*
Williams Hall, Megan 2–3, 24
'wonderings', math 34–5, 45, *114*, 115, 142
Wood, Marcy B. 208
word problems 54, 55, 58, 143, *187*
'Would you rather?' question 130
wrong answers 15, 162

Y

Young Mathematicians at Work series (Fosnot and Dolk, 2001) 121
YouTube: Mario Kart video 113, *113*, *114*

Z

Zager, Tracy J. 210
Zavala, Maria 4, 189, 210
zeroes, appending 82, 84–93, *85*, *91*

For Product Safety Concerns and Information please contact our EU representative GPSR@taylorandfrancis.com
Taylor & Francis Verlag GmbH, Kaufingerstraße 24, 80331 München, Germany

www.ingramcontent.com/pod-product-compliance
Lightning Source LLC
Chambersburg PA
CBHW080803300426
44114CB00020B/2818